managing
TRANSPORT
OPERATIONS

3rd edition

managing
TRANSPORT
OPERATIONS

edmund j gubbins

The Institute of
Logistics and Transport

KOGAN
PAGE

First published in 1988
Reprinted 1991
Second edition 1996
Third edition 2003

Kogan Page Limited
120 Pentonville Road
London N1 9JN
United Kingdom
www.kogan-page.co.uk

© Edmund J Gubbins, 1988, 1996, 2003

British Library Cataloguing in Publication Data

A CIP record for this book is available from the British Library

ISBN 0 7494 3928 9

Typeset by Jean Cussons Typesetting, Diss, Norfolk
Printed and bound in Great Britain by Biddles Ltd, Guildford and King's Lynn
www.biddles.co.uk

Contents

List of Figures and Tables

1

Transport in a Modern Society

The development of modern society is very complex, the peace and stability of the world depending on the ease of social interaction and trade between nation states. Though the electronic communications system has developed to the stage where links between individuals and companies can be made in seconds worldwide, cohesion still depends to a large extent on the provision of an acceptable system of mechanized transport. This system must allow peoples to travel and meet as well as facilitating trade by enabling all kinds of goods to be exchanged and transported. People travel prodigious distances to fulfil their needs for business and leisure. Goods traverse the globe to satisfy the needs of the world's population for necessities and luxuries.

The importance of transport to society is obvious to anyone thinking about how people travel to fulfil their needs or how they are provided with their goods and services.[1]

In many countries, work place and living accommodation are no longer in close proximity to each other. People can now choose to live long distances from their place of work and travel every day using public passenger transport – bus, train, plane – or private car. They can live in places far removed from the city, factory or office, in suburban or rural areas and still work efficiently.

Vast crowds of people fly to distant countries for their holidays or to visit friends and relations who have emigrated. In many parts of the world, travellers speed along motorways across international boundaries, often towing caravans. Fans need no longer confine their interest to the local sports stadium or local entertainment centre but can now traverse the world to follow their team or see their favourite star.

Take a look around your home. Everything that you possess has at some time been transported: the raw materials to make the basic commodities like steel and plastic, the finished manufactures, and your food. Much of these goods will have been transported by ship, truck or train at some stage in their transformation from basic raw materials to the finished product. Without transport, the efficiency of the world economy would be severely curtailed.

Present-day society is dependent on cheap sources of energy to drive its manufacturing processes, to light and heat its homes and work places, and to power its transport. Some of the world's largest movable, self-propelled structures have been built and are operated to satisfy the world's needs for energy. Oil pumped out of the ground as crude is shipped aboard tankers, refined, and the products distributed by land and sea, in many cases by pipeline.

Modern society functions effectively because of the transport links that have been gradually built up over centuries. It is efficient because developments in science and technology have been introduced to transport, thus increasing the range and effectiveness of the various types of vehicle. Fast communications break down the barriers between nations and help all the component parts fit together.

Consideration of the foregoing reveals that there are a great number of organizations covering road, rail, air and sea that exist to ensure the maintenance of an adequate transport system. The organizations, ranging from operating companies in business to transport people and goods, to government agencies established to control transport activities, all have an interest in making transport safe and efficient.[2]

It is less easy to understand the important changes which have taken place in transport over the last 30 years and to anticipate the continuing process of change. In the UK, transport is now a major consumer of energy, employs a significant percentage of the work-force and uses a large part of the nation's resources.

Regardless of mode, transport has become more complex to operate and administer, both technologically and financially. It is widely recognized that the management and planning of the transport system of tomorrow requires highly qualified professionals, fully able to tackle and solve the problems presented by such complexities.

REASONS WHY TRANSPORT IS NEEDED[3]

Transport permeates the whole of civilized life, like the arteries and veins in the human body. Transport services take people to places where they want to go and deliver goods to places where people require them. Why is transport so important and vital to the functioning of modern society? There are many answers to this question and we can list some of the important ones in order to establish the role that transport plays in today's world.

Trade

The earth is a planet endowed with abundant natural resources but it is not homogeneous: that is, there are differences between localities. The climate, soil and fertility are non-uniform even within fairly small nations, and even more so on a world scale. Because of these variations in natural habitat, some areas are able to grow certain crops more efficiently and productively than others. The result of these differences is that one area can produce a surplus which can then be traded with another area. Often the trade is two-way, with a surplus crop from the second area flowing back to the first in exchange. Transport is essential to enable this trading process to take place, supplying the physical means to achieve the transfer of crops. With better transport methods – for example refrigeration and increased speed – greater varieties of food can be traded, allowing what was once only locally sold products to be marketed world-wide or at least over a wider area. The vast grain-growing prairies of the US and the coffee plantations of Brazil are just two examples of surplus crops which are marketed across the earth.

Climatic changes can have quite staggering and unforeseen effects on any nation's ability to feed its citizens, as the drought in many parts of Africa demonstrates. In emergencies, food and relief supplies can only be moved quickly, economically and efficiently by some form of organized transport. This may be difficult in emergency areas because of the state of the infrastructure, and the sight of food rotting on the quayside waiting for transport is very distressing to those people who give freely to help the people in need. These scenes only help to illustrate the vital need for adequate transport systems if any nation needs to move goods around within its borders.

Some areas of the world have the good fortune to have deposits of desirable raw materials like crude oil, iron ore and coal. Other places, like Japan, with almost no local sources of these commodities, have to import in large quantities to fuel their industrial development.

Transport is the means of balancing the source with the demand and use.

Because of the differences in natural resources, both human and physical, nations develop those industries with which they can product a surplus to use for trading. This specialization in itself creates the seeds of world trade, with nations becoming unable to meet the needs of its citizens from its own industries. So the two-way transfer of goods takes place between countries with surpluses in different commodities. To survive in a competitive world, nations need transport to bring in raw materials and carry out finished products. The distinction between countries is now blurred as more nations try to diversify and trade takes place in similar products.

The link with the market place

It is no longer necessary to have factories producing in every region. Industrial companies can now site their plants where production is most efficient and optimize on size to fit the cost/market equation. This is particularly true of large multi-national companies. With the effect of economies of scale, the production process can be less costly per unit to produce and more profitable for the producer. In reaping the benefits of local optimization and economies of scale, industry needs a system of efficient transport to connect the factory with the market place. The benefits of scale economies can only materialize, however, if the costs of transport are less than the savings made by increasing the size of the productive unit and decreasing the number of such units. Historians are always disputing the question of which came first, industrial development or improvements in transport. Whichever is true, the siting of large-scale enterprises well away from many of their markets to gain the advantages of economies of scale would be impossible without modern transport methods and infrastructure.

Social interaction

Man has from earliest times been a social animal, gathering in tribes and groups. Even today, people naturally congregate in communities, with very few people wishing to remain isolated. Even when transport and travel was very difficult, communities needed to contact other communities to establish social relationships and spread their thoughts and ideas. Transport is necessary for the spread of community relationships. Some groups would argue that the development of modern, fast transport links, together with the growing affluence and economic power of some people, is having a bad effect on the world's people, squashing local ideas and traditions, supplanting these with an alien Anglo-American culture. This may be so but it does not alter the fact that transport is required to enhance social interaction and social development. Of more importance to the argument about the submersion of local culture beneath the flood of cheap Anglo-American ideas is the subject of electronic communications, especially television – but that is beyond the scope of this book.

One recent trend is the mass gathering of large crowds at what are loosely termed cultural events in many locations. In some senses this is not new – one need only look back to the Greek Olympics. What is new is the mass participation of competitors and spectators, vast crowds of people gathered in one place from all parts of the earth, arriving within a very short time of their original departure. Modern transport methods enable these activities to be organized and to be enjoyed by more people. Without transport, sporting and cultural events would have to be staged locally or not at all. It was not very long ago that a cricket tour of Australia was a long drawn-out affair, involving a long sea voyage and a great deal of coach and train travel. Now, the team and spectators can leave home one day and, jet lag permitting, be playing and watching a couple of days later.

As people become more affluent, they move away from the old centres of activity into more isolated and better living conditions. From their homes, they demand access to work, shops and other social activities. The house in the country no longer means parochial submersion but an attractive life style with contacts over a very wide area enhanced by good transport links. Distances travelled increase, shopping opportunities move out of city centre locations and people demand access to a wider range of goods and services. Transport is the means of fulling the need to get to work, to the shops and to contact other people.

National cohesion

Finally, efficient transport links are vital for state security and identity. A nation is held together by the way in which separate communities are linked to a common purpose. The political process and national identity are enhanced by the ability of policy makers and leaders to travel to different parts of a country. All military rulers from earliest times have recognized the prime need for a system of internal transport whether to enable them to move men and equipment quickly to counter an invasion or to put down internal dissent. From the Roman roads spanning an empire to the railroads which helped to unify the United States, history demonstrates the necessity of good transport communications for the cohesion of any nation state. Sea links controlled and protected by the British Navy laid the foundations of another empire. Bad transport systems, lacking investment and expertise, are one of the causes of poor development in many African states.

Transport is required to enhance trade, hold nations together and enable people to improve the quality of their lives. It is instrumental in the spread of development and the mixing of cultures. It can have detrimental effects, such as pollution, but it is vital for a modern complex world society. Without such good transport systems, the world would be an altogether less exciting place.

THE FUNCTION OF TRANSPORT

The function of transport has been discussed and illustrated in the preceding paragraphs. In the case of passengers it is to enable them to travel from one place to another. For goods, it is to enable a person or company to send their goods from one place to another.

Why do people wish to travel and send goods to another place? Within the answer to this question lies both the reason and the need for transport. People travel to reach a place where they would rather be for reasons of business or pleasure. Goods are transported from one place to another to enable them to be sold for a higher price.

The function of transport can be defined as follows:

1. In the case of passenger transport, it is to move people from a place where they are to a place where they would rather be in the future.
2. In the case of freight transport, it is to move goods from a place where they are to a place where they will be of greater value to both the producer and the consumer.

It is the end statements of the two definitions that are significant: for passengers, a place where they would rather be in the future, for freight, a place where the goods will be of greater value to both the producer and consumer. Nowhere is it implied in these definitions that transport is used for its own sake. The definitions are quite explicit in saying that transport is not an end in itself but a means to an end. That is, enabling passengers to get to a place where they would rather be, enabling goods to get to a place where they will be of greater value.

To illustrate this point, let us borrow a thought from science fiction writers. In many of their books and films on space travel, the travellers can instantly transport themselves over quite long distances by stepping onto some electronic transfer apparatus. Given the choice of instant transfer to destination or making the time-consuming and often uncomfortable journey by any other form of transport, which would you choose?

If you could step into a box in the corner of your living room, punch a code into a computer and be instantly transported to your destination, you would be relieved. Contrast that with the necessity of a long drawn-out journey by public transport or driving your own car, and there would be no longer be any choice.

Think of the advantages for a large retail company with many large stores nationwide. There would no longer be a need to rely on a fleet of vehicles for the distribution of their merchandise, or a need for strategically placed warehouses. When the stocks in the stores needed replenishment, the manager could instantly order items and have them delivered immediately, with the added bonus of a reduction in the chances of damage and loss.

Few people really enjoy travelling but they have to do it because it is the only way to get from one place to another; it is to satisfy other desires and needs that people use transport.

(Alright, I can hear you thinking, what about cruise shipping, steam railways and aeroplane joyrides. I will conceded that people do flock to participate in these forms of transport, the main attraction being the travel. Within the context of this book, those activities are leisure pursuits, only peripheral to the main stream of commercial transport. They can be compared with people riding on fairground rides for the sensation, but their motive is enjoyment, not to get to another place.)

The purpose that transport fulfils is to change the location of people and goods. That is, to close the physical gap between a person's position now and his desired position in the near future.

Economists wrote of production as the growth of utilities, and the primary aim of transport is to add the utility of place. In other words, each stage of the process from production to consumption adds value to the product, adds to its utility.

As an example, a cabbage growing in a farmer's field has only limited value. When it has been picked, packaged and transported to a market, its value rises. Transport has added value by enabling the farmer to sell his product in a market where there are many potential consumers. Without the added utility of place that transport provides, the value of the cabbage would depend on the limited local market and the farmer's ability to get buyers to come to his farm.

As for people, a person sitting at home, has very little value. Transport that person to a place where his/her skills are in demand and that person's value will rise. Transport has added the utility of place to enable that person to add value to his/her life.

People use transport to satisfy desires and needs for other things. This is termed the *derived demand* for transport and will be a constant theme of this book. Transport enables people to satisfy desires for other things by taking them or their goods from one place to a place where they would rather be. It is a means of fulfilling other wishes, not the wish fulfilment in itself.

OPERATING OBJECTIVES

If the function of transport is to move people or goods from one place to another, the accomplishment of this task must be the main operating objective. This is the purpose for which transport exists and for which transport managers work.

There are other objectives linked to this over-riding concern. Moving goods or people from place to place must be undertaken safely, economically and to the proposed timetable. This does not mean at the fastest possible speed but consistent with the price and quality of service on offer.

Equally, all businesses, not merely transport ones, must have the objective of survival in a competitive market place. This implies generating enough surplus income over expenditure to invest in new plant and equipment to meet the ever-changing operating circumstances. The surplus can be generated by the rates charged to consumers or by a combination of rates and various forms of 'subsidy' for undertaking social and unprofitable work or to preserve some service in the face of uneconomic competition. The subject of subsidies will be dealt with at length in Chapters 7 and 9.

THE TRANSPORT PRODUCT

All business involves the selling of a 'product', whether they are manufacturing concerns or service companies like transport. It is the product which consumers buy.

It is very difficult to define the 'product' of a service industry like transport. Like doctors, solicitors and accountants, transport companies charge for their services. The doctor is paid to use his professional skill to diagnose and treat illness, the solicitor to give expert advice on legal questions, and the accountant to help people and companies keep control of their financial affairs. They do not sell their customers a physical product like a pair of shoes or a car, but something that is far more intangible.

The question usually asked by transport managers when looking at the product is, 'What are we trying to sell?'. The answer seems obvious: a seat or a cabin for passengers, or space on a goods vehicle for freight. This approach is very production-oriented, by which I mean it is looking at transport from the operator's perspective. It leads to the situation, all too prevalent in the past, of transport operators setting up a service which suits their professional experience and then going out into the market place to sell what they have produced. This attitude may prevail because it is easy to identify the product as a seat, a cabin or some space, and the service thus produced is easier to manage. It can also lead to a resistance to change, the idea that transport has always been undertaken in this manner.

I would much rather phrase the same question in another way and ask, 'What does the consumer wish to buy?' The answer once more can be the same – a seat, a cabin or some freight space. For a transport terminal the answer will be a safe place to unload/load the vehicle and storage/waiting space for cargo/passengers waiting for the journey to commence. Again, we are back to the production view of transport.

It is no longer accepted practice for manufacturers of consumer goods to produce products and then go out into the market place. It has long been realized that although a car is a means of getting a person from place A to place B, there are all sorts of motives which make people buy a particular car. A coat is a means of keeping warm, but coats are sold not only to keep people warm but because of other considerations. Cars and coats give people a feeling of status, make them feel good, attract the opposite sex, and so on. Advertising producers have realized this, as shown by the way products are presented to us in television commercials.

What in reality is the passenger or the freight shipper wanting from transport? It has been established that if the transport user could find some way of instantly transferring himself/herself or his/her goods from one place to another, he/she would avail himself/herself of that opportunity. People use transport because they have no other choice, other than not travelling at all, to fulfil some other objective in their lives.

It must be borne in mind that the passenger in particular, and to some extent the freight shipper, not only has to pay the price asked for the journey but has to sacrifice time that could be put to other uses. There is also the possibility that the passenger will have to put up with some discomfort during the journey, or that cargo may become damaged.

Many people, some consciously, some unconsciously, place values on their time, as many research studies have shown.[4] There is no easy method of measuring the value of time. Different people have varying perceptions of the worth of their time and these perceptions can change with their life style, the task that they are pursuing and the importance they place on material rewards.

To simplify a very complex theory, if the value of any individual's time is high, that individual will pay a high price for a quick journey. This is not to say that all travel time is wasted. A person travelling by train can work and many prefer this to driving, even though driving may be quicker.

Going back to the product of transport: from the production point of view people buy a seat, cabin or freight space and the price they are willing to pay must be a factor of the speed and comfort of travel. However, as we have been discussing, all consumers of transport have one over-riding objective and that it is to be in some other place than their origin. Overwhelmingly, what they want from transport is to arrive at their destination so that they can satisfy their desire for business, leisure or selling their product. To a great extent, therefore, it is the *arrival* that the transport operator is selling, all else being subsumed into this.

The arrival is the product of transport though this is not enough in itself. The arrival must be accomplished safely so that the passengers arrive uninjured, freight undamaged. Linked to the safe arrival must be that the service arrives to some predetermined timetable. I am not saying that all transport is scheduled, which is what some people infer from the use of the word 'timetable', but even one-off charters have some form of time-scale written into their governing contracts.

The service mix of speed, reliability, comfort and frequency depends to a large extent on the quality of service for which the consumer is willing to pay to achieve the objectives.

By putting the safe arrival at the starting point when discussing the transport product, the consumer's needs then become paramount when designing services. The time of arrival dictates the type of service and changes in consumer needs can be foreshadowed by the changes in what different places have to offer the traveller.

TRANSPORT OBJECTIVES

Transport is a political subject, with a small p. It is something that is discussed at length in the homes, pubs and meeting places of any nation. It is often said that everybody is convinced that they cold run the railway/bus company far better than those professionals currently struggling to manage these companies. Transport is a high profile profession because everybody is affected by transport – whether by the lack of provision, the lateness of arrival, the poor service or the road congestion caused by an overloaded system. It is easier to sit back and advocate what must be done from the comfort of your own home than to actually manage a transport system.

The way in which we choose to do things is shaped by the political decision-making process in the country in which we live. These political decisions often involve choosing a course of action from among a number of alternatives which affects the how and where of transport provision. If it is true that the provision of transport services is one necessity of a complex society, then it is also true that political decisions on subjects far removed from transport will have far-reaching effects on transport policy.

To illustrate the political nature of transport, some of the questions that have to be addressed are briefly listed and can only be answered by political decision:

1. To what extent must railway services be provided in a nation for both passengers and freight traffic? The importance of the railways to the nation's economy has to be established in terms of substitute services (like bus or air for passengers, and lorry, coastal shipping or pipeline for freight). The perceived importance can then be measured against the level of public financial support that would be needed to maintain the required level of service to meet national need. Of course, people with different political ideas will answer the question about the vitalness of the railway in different ways but the level of support for the railways will affect the provision of other modes of transport services. Unless a railway is profit-making, and free from all political interference except as regards safety standards, there is bound to be some debate about what level of provision can be supported out of the public purse.

2. How much infrastructure must be made available for cars and trucks in town centres and on routes between towns? This question touches on the effects of congestion, pollution, both visual and physical, and the efficiencies of the nation's distribution system. It is again easy to advocate that more freight should be carried by rail, more passengers taken out of their cars and onto buses and trains, but very difficult to decide how this should be brought about. Mixed in with this is the question of how the infrastructure is to be financed and whether this is fair to the railways. This will be expanded upon in Chapter 2.

3. What levels of public transport services are necessary in urban and in rural areas? Necessary provision of bus and suburban rail services is coloured by political ideology and differs quite markedly between regions. This adds the dimension of fairness to the political debate and what is perceived as fair at one end of the

political spectrum is look on as unfair by those at the other end. In other words, is it fair that old-age pensioners in some parts of Britain can claim free travel on a town's bus service while in other parts they have to pay the full fare?

4. At what price should public transport services be provided? The level of public financial support will often dictate the level of fares or freight rates. Subsidies are granted to all forms of transport and the reasons for them will be discussed in Chapter 9.

5. What is the relationship between land use and transport activities and how should this relationship be used to help with transport policy-making?

When formulating transport policy objectives, questions like these must be answered, although in some cases the answers may conflict and make policy agreement difficult.

The goal of transport policy must be to ensure the maintenance and development of the transport system necessary for the social and commercial interactions internal and external to a country. This must be accomplished within the framework of the available resources and the political consequences of the resulting resource allocation.

There are three major methods of allocating resources to transport, all of which have been tried in a number of countries:

1. Allowing market forces to dictate where, when, for what price and in what quantity transport will be provided. In effect this means leaving the decision as far as possible to those who are willing to risk their money in the hope of making an adequate return on their investment by their management skills. The likely result of this policy is that transport services will be provided only where they will be profitable, and the fragmentation of the market. The fragmentation into sub-sectors will result from operators trying to satisfy consumer demands for varying quality of service and price levels. Most of the deregulation arguments covered in Chapter 7 will be concerned with the proposition to let market forces dictate levels of service and investment decisions.

2. The government of a country can legislate for organizations to administer transport, keeping the day-to-day running away from influence by the political process. An attempt was made to do this in Britain in 1947 by the creation of the British Transport Commission. The results of having administrative bodies making decisions about transport investment and the allocation of resources can be very bureaucratic processes and systems. They do have the claimed advantage of allocating resources to meet people's needs rather than being guided only by the profit motive.

3. Transport resources can be explicitly allocated by political decision either through the relevant government minister or a local authority. Allocation in this way is according to the whim of a particularly political ideology but can in certain circumstances lead to stability. Such circumstances are where one political party has permanent control of the government, whether national or local. In this situation where the political complexion of the party in power changes at each election, violent shifts in policy can result in misallocation of resources, delays in decisions and sudden changes in direction.

GOVERNMENT EXPENDITURE ON TRANSPORT

Given the political nature of many aspects of transport, we must now address the question of why governments interfere in the provision of transport services and spend large amounts of tax payers' money pursuing their policies.

There are four easily identified areas of government concern open to the political persuasion of the controlling party:

1. To address any perceived misallocation of resources within the transport industry.
2. To help the provision of common facilities which the free market mechanism is unlikely to provide.
3. To move towards equalling the costs of different modes of transport and providing socially necessary services.
4. To give a lead on the placing and building of large infrastructure projects.

In 1979 a Conservative government took power in the UK that was determined to stem the rise in inflation, which they believed was caused by too high levels of government expenditure. To control the level of government spending, the government imposed publicly stated monetary targets on public spending. In addition, the Conservative government put in place policies designed to get value for money from all the services supported via the public purse and to reduce the number of services supplied by the state. During the term of the Conservative government this led to the rationalization of services, the privatization of state owned (nationalized) corporations, the organization of local government owned and operated transport services under the Companies Act and the deregulation of the transport industry. Many publicly owned corporations were sold to the public or employees forming publicly owned businesses, many being quoted on the stock exchange. In addition to the privatization process, the government opened the markets to competition.

Before outlining the arguments in favour of privatization, there is a need to define what is generally taken to be the difference between privatization and commercialization.

Privatization is the transfer, usually by selling the assets, by the government of publicly owned enterprises to private investors and, in many cases, creating companies where the shares of those companies are traded on the stock exchange.

Commercialization is the introduction of commercial objectives into publicly owned enterprises with the aim of getting better utilization of assets, maximizing revenue, reducing costs and making the enterprises more customer focused in their business strategies and operations. In many instances, commercialization precedes privatization. The main thrust of the arguments for privatizing state owned transport enterprises are that privatization enhances economic freedom for the corporation and increases efficiency. There are, in addition, the fiscal and political arguments. Public borrowing will be reduced because the newly privatized companies will finance their investment programmes through the capital markets rather than use tax payers money supplied by the government. There will be less political interference in the day-to-day operations of these companies because they are no longer the responsibility of the government.

However, as has been shown by the history of privatization, there is a need for some regulation to protect consumers. This regulation has to accomplish two things: promote competition within the transport market and prevent the abuse of monopoly power where competition is not feasible.

In the transport industries, the government policy resulted in the privatization of British Airways, National Freight Corporation, British Transport Docks Board, British Airports Authority, National Bus Company and British Rail.

In 1997, a Labour government was elected, replacing the Conservatives. Although they pledged to improve public services, the new government has abided by the previous government's public expenditure targets while continuing the privatization and deregulation process.

The Department For Transport[5] is the ministry responsible for overseeing transport in the UK in conjunction with the Scottish and Welsh Assemblies.

The department supervises a number of semi-autonomous agencies as illustrated in Figure 1.1.

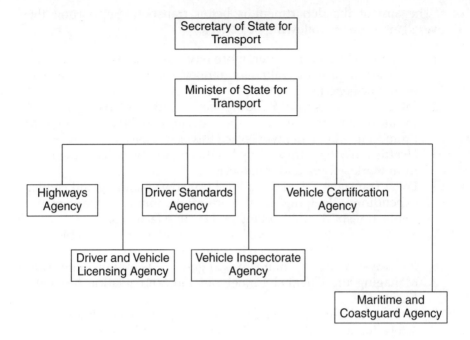

Figure 1.1 *Department for Transport*

In its duties to the transport sector, the main functions of the department are:

1. To regulate private and public transport both with regard to safety (see Chapter 6 Safety Regulation) and within the sphere of competition policy (see Chapter 7 Economic Regulation).
2. To allocate funds from government expenditure both by direct action in the form of subsidies or grants and through the allocation of funds to local authorities and other organizations.
3. To oversee the design, costing, building and maintenance of major road trunk routes including the nations motorway system through the Highways Agency.
4. To give guidance on policy issues to the Secretary of State for Transport.
5. To fund research through various outside organizations.

It is important to note that the department uses public funds to augment areas where transport services cannot be provided profitably but are deemed socially necessary.

The aim of the department is better transport. Supporting the overall aims are the following objectives:

1. Aviation: Developing safer, more environmentally friendly civil aviation to provide value for money services and social and economic benefits.
2. Integrated Transport: Building better links between different forms of transport to give the travelling public more choice. Promoting school and workplace travel schemes.
3. Health and Safety: Improving health and safety by reducing risks from work activity and transport.
4. Local Transport: Overseeing local transport planning and capital expenditure. Helping local authorities improve local roads, public transport, and walking and cycling facilities.
5. Mobility and Inclusion: Making transport more accessible and affordable to promote social inclusion.
6. Railways: Winning more passengers and freight onto rail. Managing the Channel tunnel rail link and relationship with Eurotunnel.
7. Roads, Vehicles and Safety: Improving road conditions and safety for users. Reducing the impact of roads on the environment. Ensuring efficient regulation.
8. Shipping: Promoting sustainable development of shipping, ports and inland distribution systems.
9. Transport Statistics: Providing data on all aspects of transport.
10. Transport Research: Developing and commissioning prog-rammes of transport and transport related research.

To emphasize the role of transport and the government's current thinking on transport issues, in 2000 the government issued a policy document entitled *Transport 2010, the Ten Year Plan*.

The plan lays out the government's vision of what type of transport system the UK will have by the year 2010 and what that transport system will provide for the country.

The main ideas in the plan are:

■ Modern high quality public transport, both locally and nationally. People will have more choice about how they travel and more people will use public transport.
■ More light rail systems and attractive bus services that are fully accessible and integrated with other types of transport.
■ High quality park and ride schemes so that people do not have to drive into congested town centres.
■ Easier access to jobs and services through improved transport links to regeneration areas and better land use planning.

■ A modern train fleet with reliable and more frequent services and faster trains cutting inter-city journey times.
■ A well-maintained road network with real time driver information for strategic routes and reduced congestion.
■ Fully integrated public transport information, booking and ticketing systems with a single ticket or card covering the whole system.
■ A transport system that has less impact on the environment.
■ Safer and more secure transport accessible to all.

To achieve the objectives laid out in the plan, a £180 billion 10-year investment process was included. The plan sets out the investment and spending targets:

■ £60 billion to improve the national rail network with new track, signalling, stations and rolling stock.
■ £21 billion for national roads to tackle congestion hotspots, safety through road widening schemes, bypasses and junction improvements.
■ £59 billion to improve local transport, including up to 25 new light rail schemes in our major cities, guided bus schemes, park and ride, priority routes and funding rural transport.
■ £25 billion for London.
■ £15 billion in reserve against the need for new schemes.

It is apparent, when studying the aims and objectives of the department and the 10-year plan, that the emphasis within transport policy has changed since the present government came to power in 1997. Previously there was an emphasis on roads that was reflected in the number of department staff that were engaged in road policy. Now many of these roles are provide by semi-autonomous organizations like The Highways Agency. The emphasis is now on better public transport, which is hoped will relieve road congestion and improve the environment.

The public expenditure on transport for the years 1995 to 2001 is listed in Table 1.1. This table shows a decline in real terms in the money spent on transport in line with the government's policy of controlling public expenditure.

Table 1.1 *Public expenditure on transport, Great Britain, 1995/96 to 2000/01*

1995/96	1996/97	1997/98	1998/99	1999/00	2000/01
8842	8670	8686	8142	8297	9043

It is also apparent when studying the full range of expenditure figures for transport (see *Transport Statistics Great Britain* and the *Government Expenditure Plans*, HMSO, for the appropriate year) that the availability of funds from the government to support the activities of transporting people and goods is decreasing while fund for regulation and control are rising. This is in line with the 1987 Conservative government's policy for the economy as a whole, of which transport is only a part. Publicly owned and funded companies are made profitable by various methods and then sold either to the general public, as with British Airways, or to their own employees, as with the National Freight Company. This results in these companies obtaining finance through the private sector rather than the Treasury and in the risks of enterprise being borne by their shareholders rather than being subjected to political interference. In the government's view of economic realities, this cuts out the 'wasting' of public money and increases the efficiency of operations as the company has to compete for its share of the market. In order for the consumer to get a better or fair service, the government are having to pass regulations on competition policy and set up some organizations to supervise this aspect, which in turn is reflected in the risk in this aspect of government expenditure on transport.

Using the present government's policies and actions as an example, I have outlined how political thinking and the political process has a significant effect on the production of transport services. Legislation by different governments has changed the structure of the transport industry from, on the one hand, periods of state ownership of major companies to, on the other, the emphasis on private enterprise.[6] The provision of passenger services and the pattern of support changes with alterations in the organization of local government and the subsidy policy of the governing party. Changes in the regulating framework can have profound consequences on transport management. All of this serves to spotlight the political nature of transport provision.[7]

THE EUROPEAN UNION[8]

In the UK, much transport provision and operation is subject to legislation and regulation emanating from the European Union.

The EU is constructed on an institutional system that is the only one of its kind in the world. The member states delegate sovereignty for certain matters to independent institutions that represent the interests of the EU as a whole, its member countries and its citizens. The European Commission traditionally upholds the interests of the

European Union as a whole, while each government is represented within the Council of Ministers, and the European Parliament is directly elected.

Transport matters are dealt with via the European Council, the EU's main decision making body. The Council, when deliberating on transport matters, is made up of the transport ministers of each member state. It is through the Council that all transport policies and initiatives are adopted.

The European Commission is composed of commissioners appointed by the member states, each commissioner taking responsibility for one area of policy and headed by a president. The Commission has the right to propose European Union legislation and is responsible for implementing legislation adopted by the Council. The Commission acts as the guardian of the treaties that govern the conduct of the Union.

The European Parliament shares with the Council the power to legislate, influences EU spending and has the right to censure the Commission.

The Court of Justice and the Court of Auditors provide the legal and financial checks on the system.

European legislation is promulgated through four administrative procedures:

■ Regulations – are generally binding on all member states and prevail over national law. They apply directly to member states and do not have to be confirmed by national parliaments.
■ Directives – require member states to achieve a result by a certain date. Directives do not have legal force in the member state until the relevant national legislation is passed. Some directives can become legally binding if time limits imposed for their implementation run out before national legislation is passed.
■ Decisions – are specific and binding on those states to which they are addressed.
■ Recommendations and Opinions – are the way the Commission state their view on certain issues and are a way for the Commission to suggest the direction of future policy and to test the reaction of the member states.

The concept of a single market has changed the common transport policy with the liberalization of transport services, the slackening of cabotage regulations, the harmonization of social conditions, the harmonization of national rules governing the provision of transport services and the recognition of qualifications. These measures have been adopted and applied taking into account the specific nature of each mode of transport.

MODAL CHANGES

Political thinking and government action can change people's perception of transport but as a service industry, transport is also conditioned by events which, although peripheral to itself, can still cause
large changes. As has already been discussed in this chapter, transport
is used by people to fulfil other desires – the 'derived demand' nature
of transport – and changes will occur when people's needs and
desires themselves changes.

The following three examples of changes in transport illustrate this
point.

Changing railways

As a result of changing and improving technologies in motor transport during the First World War, the railways came under severe
competition from road transport in the 1920s. In addition, the railways were in financial difficulties caused by the heavy working and
minimum maintenance during the war years. They also had great
difficulty responding to the changed economic circumstances after
the war. Before the war, the railways had a virtual monopoly over
long-distance travel for both freight and passengers, as witnessed by
the legislation which was more concerned with protecting the
consumer from the abuses of monopoly power than with helping the
railways to overcome their difficulties.

It can be argued that the full import of what was happening took a
long time to become obvious to both politicians and railway managements. It wasn't until the 1950s that a true modernization scheme was
planned, but this plan failed to improved the railway's financial
performance. Many writers and commentators at the time felt that the
plan had come too late to halt the downward drift and, in any case,
was ill thought through as a means of making the railways viable. In
1963, the 'Beeching Report' drew attention to the concentration of
traffic on the network, with almost 50 per cent of the network carrying
only 5 per cent of the freight traffic and 4 per cent of the passengers.
The report concluded that the revenue being generated could only
cover the operation of a much smaller network and resulted in the
decision to close about one quarter of the route miles. To add a political dimension, even this plan met with sometimes illogical opposition from politicians and the general public.

In some areas the railways do enjoy technical advantages over
other modes (see Chapter 2) but since the 1920s they have had to face
the problem of adapting a network designed to carry virtually all
traffic to all places into a network for specific traffics. The slow decline

of the railway traffic has left the railways without sufficient finances to change their services to meet present needs.

The Railways Act of 1993 changes once again the way in which the railways are structured. The government's objective is to introduce into the railways the involvement of the private sector which ensures continuity of services, assured safety and value for money. The government sees privatization as the means of stopping the decline of the railways and providing better services for the customer.

This example serves to highlight the problems of the changing nature of demand which can be met by other modes using different operating methods and newer techniques. Whether the railways could ever have met the challenge of road transport, even with unlimited access to finance and the will to change, is beyond the scope of this book, but failure of both politicians and management to perceive the rising competition from other forms of transport and the changing needs of the consumer surely played a large part in the decline of railway services.

Passenger shipping

The past 30 years have seen major changes in passenger shipping, with the virtual elimination of scheduled services. During the years from 1945 to 1956 passenger shipping was at its height, with over 1 million passengers crossing the North Atlantic from Europe in 1956. After this peak, the total number of passengers using these services started to decline rapidly. At the same time, the number of passengers crossing the North Atlantic by air increased and passenger ships were unable to compete with scheduled air transport.

The passenger shipping industry is very labour-intensive and very vulnerable to changes in the labour cost element in the running costs. A further factor in the competitive position of passenger shipping with regard to air transport competition is the capital requirements needed to finance the building of new ships and the ability of the air transport industry to introduce new technology fairly quickly.

The sheer time span of most ocean passages is inconvenient for business passengers who require a fast service so that their time is used productively. The ability to board a plane in Europe and arrive in the USA a few hours later ready for a business meeting contrasts starkly with the four or five days needed at sea. The fixed costs involved in providing a luxury service on a passenger line also meant that fares had to increase to such an extent that sea voyages became priced out of the reach of ordinary people. This is directly the opposite of air transport where technological developments have led to reductions in costs and therefore prices bringing air travel within the reach of a large proportion of the population. By the mid-1960s, a great proportion of long-haul passenger journeys were being made by plane.

Passenger liner operators switched many of their now redundant ships, designed for scheduled services, into the cruise market where the growing affluence of the population in the USA provided a ready market. It soon became obvious to shipping people that the cruise market demanded a different type of management, a new company strategy and purpose-built cruise ships. The market was really for people's leisure time, not their transport needs, and the ships had to have the same facilities as any modern hotel catering for tourists.

This example serves to emphasize that for a transport company it is not only important to provide a service that is competitive within the mode, but also to be aware of what developments are taking place in potential competing modes. Those people who are restricted in their view and see transport in purely modal terms can miss changes in other modes which serve as a lesson from which they can tackle problems in their own working environment or which may even threaten their own existence as a viable operation.

Urban transport

Developments in transport have partly been instrumental in encouraging the outward dispersal of populations from many city centres by making the amenities offered there more accessible from peripheral areas. By the early 1990s, most British towns and cities had extended urban railway networks and/or expanding tramway systems. The Tramways Act of 1870 enabled local authorities to take this opportunity to improve their networks both by technological developments and integration. In the 1920s the motor bus proved more flexible and more efficient, and these began to replace trams first on extended routes and then throughout the network until the tram virtually disappeared as a means of mass urban movement in the late 1950s.

These changes in pubic transport provision helped to create the intensive suburban housing developments of the inter-war years adjacent to main roads radiating outwards from the city centre served by bus or tram services. Where they extended, suburban railways served densely populated corridors along the route of their lines with stations as mode points. Thus in the period up to the 1940s, cities and towns expanded outwards along transport served corridors, almost forming the classic star-shaped cities.

The coming of the motor age further expanded the suburbs but the corridors widened because it was no longer necessary to live within walking distance of public transport so the land between the old corridors was developed, and people were able to live still further from the city centres. The car offered the user a level of mobility previously unheard of – personal door-to-door transport on demand, with greater flexibility, comfort and reliability than public transport.

Obviously, the demand for cars as a means of transport is fuelled by rising affluence within society bringing the possibility of car ownership within the reach of most people. This increasing affluence is also a factor in the demand for lower density suburban housing. The ownership of cars by a large proportion of the population is the major cause of what has become known as the 'urban transport problem'. Increases in car ownership and, more importantly, usage, result in a decrease in the use of public transport by the population. The classic demand cycle is most evident where decreases in public transport patronage result in higher fares and service cut-backs, resulting in more people taking advantage of car ownership leading to higher fares and further service cut-backs. Those people (the young, the elderly and the disabled) unfortunately left reliant on public transport for their mobility have to put up with a very inferior service.

Another problem for public transport with its main objective of mass travel is the unsuitability of low density housing for efficient operations. The layout and locations away from the main public transport-served corridors render these estates unsuitable for direct public transport links with city centres.

The obvious and most easily observed effect of increasing car ownership is congestion on busy routes into the main towns which hinders all road users, including public transport modes sharing the same way as the car. Buses are made unreliable due to the delays caused by traffic jams. Even so, there is still significant peak demand for public transport services in most major towns and cities. Unfortunately, the morning and evening peaks with a slack period in between mean high operating costs for transport operators. These costs are necessarily borne due to the large number of vehicles and staff needed at peak times but under-employed during the rest of the day.

This pattern of development has to be accepted but further problems for public transport are now evident in the dispersal of activities around the city and away from the city centre.

CONCLUSIONS

Transport is important to modern society because the level of provision of services affects the way in which people live. Because of this, transport is a political subject, part of the government's overall policy deliberations, and taking a significant proportion of scarce resources. As F.F. Socconcano[9] points out: 'Large investments in transport have complex and far-reaching consequences because of the relationship between transport and the various components of the urban system. Therefore, decisions future transport systems are very difficult to make. At the root of this process lies a cost accounting exercise based on welfare economics: costs are estimated, intangibles where applicable are valued and benefits and disbenefits are assigned.'

H.P. White and M.L. Senior[10] state: 'The essential importance and function of transport was admirably summarised by Marshall (Mike & Laight, 1965): "The transport industries which undertake nothing more than the mere movement of persons from one place to another, have constructed one of the most important activities of man in every stage of advanced civilisation. It is not only a basic human activity but is also a movement in space." '

References

1. Thomson, J.M. *Modern Transport Economics* Penguin Books Ltd, London 1974
2. Faulks, R.W. *The Principles of Transport* Ian Allan, London 1982
3. Bell, G.A. Blackledge, D.A. and Bowen, P. *The Economics and Planning of Transport*, Heinemann, London 1983
4. Forsyth, P.J. 'The value of time in an economy with taxation' *Journal of Transport Economics and Policy* Vol. 14, 1980
5. DTLR, www.dtlr.gov.uk
6. Aldcroft, D.H. *British Transport Since 1914* David and Charles, London 1975
7. Button, K. and Gillingwater, D. *Future Transport Policy* Croom Helm, London 1986
8. www.europa.en.int
9. Socconcano, F.F. 'Transport policy analysis through site value transfer' *Journal of Transport Economics and Policy* Vol 1, 1980
10. White, H.P. and Senior, M.L. *Transport Geography* Longman, London 1983

2

Modal Characteristics

The way along or through which a transport mode travels has effects upon that mode's operating characteristics and its operating efficiency. The form of one transport mode's way differs from another mainly due to the technological differences between the modes.[1] It is often said that there are two types of ways, built ways and natural ways. The railway, the road, the canal and the pipeline are examples of transport ways which have been constructed by man to serve the prevailing technologies of those modes. On the other hand, the sea and the air can be used without man-made structures by any person having the right equipment and expertise.

This is not entirely true, as will be made apparent later in the chapter. Even though the sea and the air are provided by nature, commercial shipping and air transport have to rely on man-made infrastructure in order to operate safely and efficiently. In both modes, terminals are required at each end of the route, for the loading and unloading of ships and aeroplanes. Along the route, guidance systems like radio beacons, buoys and lighthouses, and air traffic control must be provided by some organization so that the vehicles can be safely and efficiently navigated. These systems have to be paid for by the users in the form of light dues or airport landing charges.

In this chapter we will use the theoretical classification of transport ways, built and natural, to study the modal characteristics. First, we will look at each mode separately, emphasizing the factors which give one mode advantages over others, or which put that mode at a disadvantage. By this method, a clear picture will emerge which will help to take account of the trends in transport usage shown by some of the published statistics. It will help to put into perspective some of the arguments about why one mode prospers while another mode declines, especially in terms of the technological developments in both the mode and society in general.

RAILWAYS

In order to operate, the rail mode needs a completely uninterrupted right of way and, because of this factor, the way is exclusive to rail operations.

Where other modes impact on the railway, grade separation is necessary in the form of tunnels, bridges or controlled level crossing points giving rail the right of way. This entails an elaborate infrastructure and in most countries, the railways are under unified control. In Britain, the railway ownership is split between a number of companies and organizations. The infrastructure is owned, planned, built and maintained by Railtrack. There are 25 train operating companies operating trains on the system. Rolling stock leasing companies who leases the trains to the train operating companies owns the rolling stock. Providing strategic direction for the system is the Strategic Rail Authority that is tasked with carrying out government policy towards the railways and with the responsibility for consumer protection. Railway freight services are operated by a separate company but use the same tracks as passenger services.

The modern railway is constructed of continuously welded steel rails connected to concrete sleepers embedded in loose ballast. The continuous welded construction provides a much smoother ride for passengers and freight, needs less maintenance and allows faster running speeds than the old system of short lengths of rail joined by fish plates. The sleepers serve to maintain the correct spacing between the rails and to transmit the loads imposed by the heavy rolling stock through to the ballast. The ballast acts as a drainage medium and to spread the forces through to the road bed.

The railway functions by the action of smooth steel wheels on smooth steel rails which reduces resistance to rolling and reduces the power needed to pull really heavy loads. The nature of the rail wheel contact does, however, cause problems with the starting and stopping of trains. It also causes problems when attempting to haul heavily laden trains up steep inclines. To be able to function efficiently, the railway must be constructed with relatively shallow gradients and large radius curves. The sharper the curve, the slower the speed at which the vehicle can negotiate that part of the system with safety. The faster the speed and the tighter the curve, the more wear there is on the rails, leading to greater maintenance costs.

The particular characteristics of the railway mean that when the way is constructed the civil engineer cannot ignore the contours of the topography in the same manner as the road builder can. Railway construction entails large engineering works with cuttings through hills, tunnels under mountains, embankments across small valleys or viaducts across deep valleys. The need to separate the railway from other transport networks entails the construction of bridges, tunnels or, where these are not possible, level crossings.

These level crossings are basically of two types. The first type is automatic, where the barrier and road lights are operated automatically when the train is a certain distance from the crossing point giving enough time for the road vehicles to stop before the train arrives. The second type is controlled manually, where the gates are shut by a crossing keeper when the train is due. No matter which system is used, on busy roads severe road congestion can result from the interruption of the traffic flow and so in most urban areas where congestion is liable to occur, grade separation is accomplished by tunnels or bridges.

Rail vehicles are guided by the rail on which they run and not by the driver so there is no way in which one train can avoid another on the same stretch of track by steering clear of any obstruction. As already noted, steel wheels on steel rails give excellent reduced friction but this means that trains need long stopping distances, especially as speeds approaching 100 miles per hour. On most rail networks it is impossible for the driver to see far enough ahead to have time to stop his train in time to avoid any obstructions on the line.

Regulation of the traffic on the railway is achieved by some form of signalling, the complexities of which are beyond the scope of this book. In very simple terms, the aim of signalling systems is to prevent two trains occupying the same section of track at the same time. The network is split into blocks which are controlled by signals at either end. Only when a block is unoccupied by another train will the signal controlling the entrance to that block allow another train to enter. In this way, trains are allowed to proceed along the track, separated by specified minimum distances from other trains. Of course, on two-way single line working the system has to be more complex to make sure that trains travelling in opposite directions do not meet on the same section of track.

There are two standard definitions that are important to an understanding of rail operations. The gauge is the distance between the rails and has a direct bearing on the radius of curvature of the track and the loads which can be carried. The standard gauge used by the majority of railways is four feet eight and one half inches, but some railways have five feet six inches, and even three feet six inches, is used in some parts of the world. Broader gauges can carry heavier vehicles but they demand greater curves and take up more land space. The use of different gauges by neighbouring countries causes problems at frontier points with discontinuity of the track and the need for the transfer of passengers and freight or the use of more expensive dual gauge vehicles.

Of more importance to railway managements is the loading gauge. This is the maximum permitted height and width of the rolling stock which determines the internal capacity of each unit making up a train. The loading gauge is a function of the height of overhead obstructions like bridges and tunnels, the distance between parallel tracks, and the siting of signal gantries, station platforms and other constructions. The greater the loading gauge, the greater the throughput of the system within the limits of safe practice.

This last point notwithstanding, the maximum throughput of any section of railway is achieved if all trains, no matter what particular market they are serving, run at the fastest possible speed. In addition, the longer the train, the greater the productivity of any given section of line.

The greatest problem facing all rail managements is when the same stretch of line has to be used by trains running at widely different speeds.

Since privatization in the UK, this problem has become acute because trains serving different functions and owned by different companies have to use the same running lines on most of the system. As we have seen, the British railway system has been split into its various functions causing major headaches when trying to organize the railways as a coherent whole. Fast inter-city passenger trains, slower stopping trains, cross-country trains and freight trains have to be given paths on the system. The services operated by different companies often serve different market sectors and have speed profiles that stem from the different tasks they are trying to perform. All clamour to Railtrack to give their trains priority.

A balance must somehow be struck between the utilization of the track by all the various functions. It is technically possible to design, build and run all trains on the network at the same speed but to make sure that the fastest passenger trains are not delayed, this speed would have to be the highest that the line is capable of supporting. A policy of this nature would be highly uneconomical because the cost of providing the high power-to-weight ratios necessary to integrate freight trains into the system and fast stopping passenger trains would make freight rates and fares uncompetitive.

The situation leaves the railway with a number of choices if profitable inter-city trains are to run uninterrupted along paths used by other slower trains:

1. Complete specialisation of the track between different types of train which would entail great capital expenditure. The French railways have gone some way towards this by building a completely separate track for their high speed passenger trains.
2. Providing some pattern of non-stop paths for all trains. The longer the two track system, the greater the speed difference and the greater frequency of high speed trains, the fewer paths there will be for slower trains. This solution to the problem makes scheduling of train route patterns complex but it is the solution most favoured by Railtrack.
3. Abandoning all attempts to provide non-stop paths for all but the highest speed services and using passing loops and sidings for slower trains. This means that slower services will be delayed and increase the costs of operation.

Strengths and weaknesses

An examination of the operational strengths and weaknesses of the railway in relation to the tasks that it is trying to perform will help towards an understanding of how the modal characteristics of the system affect the operating environment.

Strengths

1. High average speeds for journeys in the range of 50 to 300 miles, which is especially important for passengers.
2. Rail in the majority of cases runs city centre to city centre which can cut the overall journey time to a minimum.
3. The railway effectively utilizes land space. Over any strip of land of a given width, the railway can carry more passengers and freight than any other land-based system.
4. The general public perceive railways as being less environmentally adverse, both visually and as regards physical pollution, than other forms of transport.
5. The bulk handling capacity of the railway means that they are very cost effective when handling bulk materials in coupled train

loads thus relieving the road system of large numbers of heavy lorries.

6. The railways are energy flexible and energy efficient. The use of electric traction relieves the railway of reliance on oil for energy which is the case with most other modes.
7. The safety record of the railways is excellent with both passengers and freight. This is especially true with the carriage of hazardous cargoes.
8. There is great scope for automation on the railway, with even the possibility of driverless trains.
9. It is possible to provide an extensive range of services for passengers during transit including catering, on board telephones and secretarial assistance.
10. Of all the land-based modes, the railways are least affected by bad weather.

Weaknesses

1. The railways are extremely vulnerable to the level of industrial activity especially with regard to the major primary products such as coal, iron ore and petroleum products. When there is an economic recession, traffic on the railway falls but because of the nature of the fixed cost element, ie track, signalling and infrastructure, it is very difficult for the railway management to shed these costs quickly. Much of the railway infrastructure is shared jointly by different types of service and the allocation of these joint costs between different services causes problems when accounting for the true costs of operating each service and service reliability. This problem is compounded during a recession when falling traffic levels mean that the allocation of joint costs between services has to change, making once viable services marginal.
2. One of the major weaknesses of the railway is the inherent inflexibility of operation. The route network was laid down in an era when economic business and social activities were dominated by railway working as the only means of large-scale mobility. The railway is tied to this fixed pattern of operation, although, as we have seen in Chapter 1, activities are much more widespread. It is almost impossible for the railways to adapt their infrastructure to meet the challenges of the changing patterns of economic and social activities. The result is that the railways have to concentrate on seeking to satisfy needs that can be fitted into their pattern of operation rather than redesigning the network to meet changing customer needs.
3. The railways suffer in the freight field especially, but also to a lesser extent in the passenger field, from the need to tranship from

rail to other modes or from other modes to rail at some part of the journey. The result is that rail is efficient over longer journeys when the costs of transhipment can more easily be absorbed and the time element is not so significant.

4. For nearly half a century, the railways in Britain have been been the subject of political interference, indeed some writers believe that this has been the case since railways were first built. Since nationalization in 1947, this problem has become acute (see Chapter 3) and even since privatization the problem does not seem to have improved.

5. For many years, despite the best efforts of British Rail management before privatization and Railtrack and the train operating companies since privatization, the image of the British railways has been one of inefficiency and unreliability. This factor puts questions into the minds of customers and potential customers, both passengers and freight, about whether to use the railways or to find alternative ways to travel or ship freight. This hampers the railways in attempting to fulfil their objectives.

6. As a labour intensive and heavily unionised industry, the railways are very vulnerable to industrial action. Stoppages during industrial disputes, often with little warning, make potential customers wary of relying on the railways for their journeys.

7. The general public perceive that the railway is more expensive than other modes. This applies to car users who fail to take into account the time costs of running a car.

8. Despite trains running half empty, at peak times some trains are very overcrowded leading to complaints about the level of service and the quality of the rolling stock.

ROADS

The road is a specifically designed and surfaced highway for the passage of wheeled vehicles, each vehicle being controlled and guided independently by a driver. In Great Britain the road network is extensive, with over 200,000 miles of pathed roadway. The network is almost universal in that virtually every house, farm, factory, shop and place of entertainment has access to a road.

The Department for Transport has put forward the following aims with regard to the roads network:

1. To divert long-distance road traffic and particularly heavy goods vehicles from large numbers of town and villages so that they are relieved of the dirt, noise and danger which are associated with through-traffic.

2. To create and maintain a comprehensive strategic trunk route network to promote economic growth, linking remote and less prosperous areas of the country to the national network.
3. To make sure that all major airports and seaports are connected to the major trunk network to promote the growth of the export trade.

For administrative and financial reasons, the road network of Great Britain is divided into two categories, namely trunk roads and other roads. The trunk network is financed directly by central government and includes all motorways and the non-motorway strategic network. Motorways account for about 0.07 per cent of the roads network but carry a large proportion of the traffic. The non-motorway strategic network comprises another 4 per cent but carries about 20 per cent of the traffic volume.

Other roads are financed by local government though there is an element of central government funding in this local finance. There are six categories of road in this classification.

1. Primary distributor roads in urban areas connecting major activities or land use areas within cities.
2. District distributor roads in urban areas which connect local areas to the primary distributor roads.
3. Local distributors confined within local areas.
4. Access roads providing access to houses, shops and industrial plant.
5. Other main rural roads.
6. Other rural roads.

Road finance

Road finance in the UK, as in many other countries, is a very contentious subject. In many countries, motorways are paid for by tolls but the distances between exits and entrances are great and alternative routes are slow and circuitous. In Britain tolls would be expensive to administer with the relatively short distances between entrances and exits and alternative routes being plentiful. The only part that tolls play is on certain well-defined sections of the infrastructure like bridges and tunnels.

A road fund was instituted in 1909, automatically receiving the bulk of the money from vehicle licence duty. Out of this fund, the Road Board paid grants for major road works. In 1919 the functions of the Road Board were taken over by the Department of Transport.

In 1926, Winston Churchill, then Chancellor of the Exchequer, appropriated £7m from the road fund into the general taxation account and provided that one-third of all monies from car and motorcycle taxation be diverted to the general taxation account in the future. In 1927 a larger sum of £12m was transferred from the road fund to the general taxation account. In 1936 a new system of road finance was instituted by which all monies collected through the fund were paid directly to the Exchequer while the road fund made annual estimates of its requirements for finance and the monies were voted to it by Parliament. In 1956 the road fund was abolished and road expenditure became part of the normal Department of Transport budget. From this time, the public expenditure on roads infrastructure had no direct link or relationship to the amount of money collected in taxation from road users. This fact has a direct bearing on the continuing discussions between the advocates of more road building and the champions of the railways. The central disagreement between these two lobbies is whether the road user pays the full cost of the provided infrastructure or whether there is a hidden subsidy in favour of the road user.

To sum up, trunk roads are paid for by central government out of general taxation receipts and as part of the general government expenditure. Non-trunk roads are partly paid for by local taxation, ie through the local rate system, and partly by government grants through rate support systems.

As can be readily seen from the foregoing brief outline of the development of road finances in the UK, road users do not directly build or maintain the infrastructure on which they rely for operation of their vehicles – which is in direct contrast to the railways. The cost of building and upkeep is shared by all users through the different forms of taxation which the user pays. There is no direct correlation between road user and payment, though heavier vehicles do pay a higher rate of road fund duty. In addition, property owners contribute to the maintenance of the roads bordering their homes through the local taxation system, whether they use the road or not.

Though the total tax amount collected from road users appears to be very large (see Table 2.1), individual contributions are small and can only be tenuously connected with wear and tear by the user.

At this point, it is as well to advise the reader to be very cautious when discussing the question of whether the railway is at a disadvantage in matters of infrastructure costs with respect to the road user. The rail operator builds and maintains the infrastructure, the whole cost of the civil and mechanical engineering having to be recovered through the charges made for services or the Public Service obligation grants. Railwaymen often claim that the roads are paid for out of taxation and the user is thus subsidized, which constitutes unfair competition.

Table 2.1 *Motoring taxes and road costs 1993/94 (£m)*

Vehicle	Fuel duty	Excise duty	Total	Costs	Taxes less costs	Ratio
Cars	10200	3115	13315	3805	9510	3.5:1
Buses	305	25	330	225	75	1.3:1
Goods vehicles	280	20	300	150	145	2.0:1
All vehicles	12655	3695	16350	6170	10180	2.7:1

Source: BRF

On the other hand, it is claimed by the road user that the amount taken in taxation far exceeds the amount spent on road building and maintenance. The figures (Table 2.1) shows that it is very difficult to refute this argument when looking at the global figures but caution must be exercised when viewing the data. It can be argued that only the amounts paid by road users in road fund licence taxes should be taken into account when assessing the contribution of the road user to infrastructure costs because the other forms of payment are in reality only general taxes which happen to fall on the road user. These are exactly the same as excise duties levelled on other citizens. I have heard the argument put forward strongly that if all taxes paid by the road user should be used to build roads, then taxes on tobacco should be used to build cigarette factories! This, of course, is seen by most people as absurd. A better way of addressing this question is to relate categories of road user to their tax payments and road expenditure, as in Table 2.1. In this way, it can be seen that even using the road fund element on its own, most road users pay for the infrastructure with the heaviest trucks being the marked exception.

The last characteristic that must be emphasized about the road is that all categories of road user share the same way and this common use can lead to congestion and delays on busy sections of the network. Because the way is shared and each vehicle is individually controlled by the driver, accident rates are higher than for other forms of travel. The question asked by many people is whether the costs of these accidents to the individual and society are adequately related to the accounting costs of road transport.

Taking each category of road user, the advantages and disadvantages of these categories can now be assessed in terms of their usefulness as a means of transport.

Bus and coach

Strengths

1. In relation to forms of transport other than the car, buses and coaches have a relatively modest capital cost, meaning that the capital element in the overall operating cost is low.
2. In terms of road space usage per passenger seat provided on any journey, the bus or coach is a relatively high capacity vehicle. This is a very important strength in conjunction with road provision and congestion.
3. Because of the comprehensive nature of the road system and the ease with which buses of different sizes can be interchanged, buses are a very flexible form of passenger transport.
4. Long-distance coach travel using the most advanced equipment benefits greatly from the motorway network and improvements in other trunk routes.
5. Unlike the train and the aeroplane which are 'fixed' to the exclusive infrastructure, the railway and the airport, buses can give an comprehensive coverage of an area. With no physical need for large terminal infrastructure (a bus or coach can put down or pick up passengers at any place on its route), the bus or coach can change its operation to meet other developments in rural or urban form.
6. To most people, buses and coaches are more environmentally 'acceptable' than the private car.
7. The capacity potential of buses makes them a major element in any highway traffic control programme whether to ease congestion or to relieve city centre parking problems. 'Park and ride' schemes are an example of this strength.
8. Any transfer of users from cars to buses benefits society in terms of energy saving, noise reductions, better safety and reductions in air pollution.

Weaknesses

1. Buses share the way with other road users and have to contend with any resulting congestions. Congestion, especially at peak times, can make schedule keeping very difficult and result in unsatisfactory service.
2. Buses, except in the case of dial-a-ride and other demand responsive or unconventional services, are tailored to fixed routes and times, the customers having to fit their journey times and patterns to the bus timetable and the route network. In many cases, this means users having to walk to and from the boarding/alighting point even in bad weather.

3. Services are very susceptible to usage, inflation and labour related problems because the industry – even in an era of one person operation, is relatively labour intensive. It is also true to argue that the industry can find labour difficult to attract because of the unsocial nature of working hours, ie early morning starts and late finishes on some shifts.
4. The general public have a perception, which is very difficult to alter, that the bus is more expensive to use than the car. This is because the car driver only considers the marginal cost of his petrol when making comparisons between bus fares and motoring costs, choosing to ignore the sunk costs like capital and maintenance.
5. Bus operations in urban areas suffer from peak cost problems caused by the nature of the demand for bus services. High morning and evening demand for vehicles and staff when spread throughout the working day result in high average costs of operation.
6. Comfort for the passenger is often poor in urban areas and the service is seen as 'second class' by many non-users.
7. Buses are not easily used by the physically handicapped, mothers with very young children and passengers with baggage. This weakness has been compounded by the adoption of one person operation without a conductor to help people onto and off the platform.

Cars

Strengths

1. The major strength of the motor car stems from the factor of personal transport use being controlled by the user. The car provides the user with 'door-to-door' transport and is available on demand at times convenient to the user.
2. Speed is generally higher in a car for most journeys than by other forms of transport.
3. The carrying capacity for luggage and shopping is very high and when coupled with the 'door-to-door' nature makes the car a very convenient form of transport in the context of the present pattern of social integration.
4. The comfort for the passenger is very high and to a large extent can be tailored to the user's personal requirements.
5. Cars are relatively reliable and relatively cheap to maintain.
6. Cars are the only satisfactory form of transport for many people living in sparsely population rural areas.

Weaknesses

1. The reliance on oil-based products for energy makes the cost of running a car susceptible to oil price fluctuations and conditioned by any interruption in supply.
2. Mass use of cars is incompatible with satisfactory public transport provision.
3. The environmental impact of cars is severe, especially in densely populated urban areas. Cars are noisy, they cause air pollution, the accident toll is heavy and roads are visually intrusive.
4. High usage of cars requires heavy expenditure on highway construction and maintenance.
5. For passenger transport, cars have a low capacity in terms of road space used per passenger and take up large amounts of land space for parking, often in valuable city centre sites.
6. The driver is not able to undertake any other task while driving and has to stop for refreshment and other breaks.

Trucks

Strengths

1. The comprehensive nature of the road network means that the truck is the most flexible form of freight transport, giving a 'door-to-door' service without, in many cases, any need for costly transhipment. For any one journey, there are many alternative routes available allowing the driver to choose the best route using his experience and the information available to all road users.
2. With the management of the vehicle in the control of the driver, the security of the load and the vehicle can be more easily monitored, making delivery on time more certain and performance easier to measure.
3. Payment for the infrastructure is spread over many users limiting the amount each user has to pay. Road haulage companies are able to concentrate their whole management effort on organizing their main business effort, leaving the design, building and maintenance of the highway to other organizations.
4. Costs of each operation are far easier to calculate in road haulage than on the railways, giving the haulier a better insight into which contracts are likely to be profitable and which will make a loss.
5. Trucks are very visible and can be used as mobile advertising hoardings.

Weaknesses

1. Trucks are perceived by most of the population as being environmentally suspect as they produce noise, air pollution, structural damage and visual intrusion.
2. It is commonly held by people that heavy trucks pose a bigger safety hazard on the roads than other road users and that the truck can be intimidating.
3. The capacity of the truck is low compared to the train and the barge/coastal ship, which is especially relevant to the carriage of bulk commodities.
4. Like the car, trucks rely on oil for fuel and their operation is reliant on the oil price and availability of supplies.
5. The use of trucks to carry hazardous cargoes results in the danger inherent in carrying these commodities being spread to other road users. There is, therefore, the potential for horrendous accidents.

Taxis

As Beesely[2] states: 'In recent years the growth in both the number and patronage of both taxis and private hire cars has been in remarkable contrast to other modes of local passenger transport, although little is known about their operation, characteristics and the types of trips for which they are needed.'

Taxis have never been considered of any great importance in the long-range transportation studies in the UK although they have been analysed more closely in the USA. The Leicester Traffic Plan of 1963 recommended an integrated transport system and recognized that taxis should be considered part of a unified transport system. This is because taxis offer many of the advantages of both public and private transport. Although these advantages had been identified, nothing was subsequently done to incorporate taxis into the public transport system of the city (see Chapter 9).

Strengths

1. Taxis offer many of the advantages of both mass public transport and private car ownership.
2. There is no need to own a car for short journeys and, in theory, taxis can cater for the needs of the disadvantages and the elderly.
3. The user has no requirement for driving skill, in sharp contrast to the private car.
4. Taxis provide 'door-to-door' transport, virtually on demand, ie a fully personalized service, unlike the shared facilities of public transport.

5. The mass use of taxis could reduce the need for extensive parking facilities, especially in town centres, releasing valuable land for more productive purposes.
6. The customer is able to travel by taxi at any time, including late at night, and to any place that is accessible by car.
7. Taxis are responsive to much lower levels of demand in that it takes only one person to initiate a journey. Public transport facilities, on the other hand, need high levels of demand at set times to be successful. This is especially relevant late at night, early in the morning and at other slack times during the day.
8. The taxi user does not require an extensive knowledge of the physical layout of an area to which they wish to travel. As long as the destination address is known, the taxi driver will select the most appropriate route and deliver the passenger to the required destination.
9. Taxis have extensive space for luggage and other packages.
10. There is less stress associated with using taxis because the customer feels that the service is reliable.

Weaknesses

1. The occupancy factor is very low, similar in many ways to a private car, and taxis add to congestion especially when putting down or picking up passengers in busy streets.
2. Taxis take patronage away from other forms of public transport and extensive use could result in deterioration of other public transport services.
3. Taxis are a relatively high cost system of transport and the exact fare for any journey is rarely known before the journey commences.
4. As with private cars, taxis add to pollution in city centres.

Conclusions

As can be seen, road transport does have a number of advantages over other forms of transport.

Any dwelling or work place in the country can be serviced by road and the selected route can be changed at very short notice because of the nature and comprehensiveness of the road network. There is less need for expensive terminal facilities and management effort can be concentrated on scheduling without the need to supervise the construction, maintenance and planning of track.

A fleet of road vehicles is easier to control than the railway fleet because each individual vehicle is managed by one person who can react quickly to the changing circumstances of the journey.

There are, however, a number of disadvantages:

■ The size of the load is restricted by legislation with limits on vehicle size and weights, not by the prevailing technology and economies as with other modes.
■ The distance travelled in one day is a function of drivers' working hours limitations which are also controlled by legislation. Increased crew costs are incurred by operating outside these limits. Speed of journey is also circumscribed by the law regarding maximum permitted road speeds rather than physical capacities.
■ Roads are not used exclusively by one form of transport and congestion can occur which interferes with schedule planning and time keeping. In addition, restrictions are placed on the operation of road vehicles, especially heavy trucks, in certain localities. These restrictions include banning vehicles at certain times or completely, parking restrictions, pedestrian only areas and control over loading and unloading times.

INLAND WATERWAYS

An inland waterway suitable for the transport of passengers and goods can take the form of a natural river, an upgraded river with dredging and widening or an artificial man-made canal. Flat land and sufficient water supplies are the main topographical requirements: differences in elevation must be overcome by the use of lock systems or water elevators. The use of locks or elevators inevitably entails the loss of water from the higher to the lower levels of the system and of time by the transport operator.

On the European mainland and in the USA, canals are used extensively to feed into the great river system. Long strings of barges are pushed/towed many miles and industrial complexes have been sited along the canal and river banks to take advantage from this form of transport. Barge-carrying ships have been built to overcome the need for transhipment between the inland waterway barge and the deep sea ship for the sea passage.

In Britain canals have largely been neglected since the coming of the railway age except for short stretches of esturial rivers and canal systems like the South Yorkshire navigation.

There are three types of inland waterway in Britain: wide navigations used by vessels with a capacity of about 400 tonnes, narrow commercial canals used by 'narrow boats' with a capacity of about 25 to 30 tonnes, and recreational canals used by pleasure craft. On the European mainland, canals are classified according to the size of vessel able to use them.

The use of the way is shared by all users, with the canal authority responsible for the upkeep. The expense of maintaining the system is met by the payment of tolls usually on the tonne/mile or tonne/kilometre.

Canal transport is cheaper per unit carried than other modes of inland transport and gives good access to the sea. It suffers the disadvantage of being relatively slow, needing transhipment if the goods are not required at a site on the inland waterway, and being inflexible.

Ship canals like the Suez, Panama, Kiel and Manchester have sufficient depth of water to accommodate large ocean going ships. They are built and maintained for one of the following reasons:

1. To maintain deep water access to the sea for old ports such as the Noord Sea Canal to Amsterdam. Only by building such a waterway could Amsterdam remain a port for ocean-going ships.
2. To connect inland industrial towns to the open sea and turn them into ports, which was the main aim of the Manchester Ship Canal.
3. To shorten the sea journey between ports by cutting across a narrow strip of land as, for example, the Panama and Suez Canals. Building canals of this sort can completely alter the world-wide pattern of trade routes and have profound effects on the design and size of ship. There are many bulk carriers in the world fleet specifically designed to carry the maximum deadweight possible within the limitations on size imposed by the dimensions of the Panama Canal. There are clear indications that container ships have now reached a size where similar considerations will play a large part in future design criteria.

PIPELINES

The pipeline is unique as a form of transport: the way or infrastructure is also the carrying unit. Pipelines are well established for trunk hauls especially for crude oil and petroleum products. There are pipelines connecting the Arabian Gulf oil fields with the Mediterranean sea ports and, in Britain, networks of pipelines from oil refineries on the coast serving oil distribution depots inland. Pipelines have been used for decades in the grid distribution of water and gas and about 3 per cent of freight traffic in the UK is carried by this method.

The usual system employed for trunk haul purposes is to lay a welded steel pipe coated with bitumen and using cathodic protection in a trench deep enough to avoid damage by other activities such as ploughing but near enough to the surface to make repairs relatively straightforward. In some parts of the world, for example in the Arctic, the pipeline is laid above the surface with attention being paid to environmental disturbances.

Pipelines are in the main environmentally sound as they can easily be buried, can traverse difficult topography and be laid under water. They do not give off fumes or make a lot of noise, and can be disguised against visual intrusion. Only if they are damaged will there be pollution by spillage and detection techniques are so advanced that there have been no cases of serious pollution from pipelines for a number of years.

Pipelines are at their operating optimum when being used to full capacity on a continuous process. Costs of transport rise rapidly per unit handled as actual usage falls from the optimum because of the high proportion of fixed cost in the total cost of operation. They are inflexible geographically in that they are designed to serve fixed locations and there is a finite capacity which cannot be altered to accommodate sudden surges in demand. One advantage is that they are largely automated with very few personnel needed to control the pumps and valves or to undertake maintenance.

Fluids are the main products utilizing pipeline technology (mainly oil products and natural gas) for commercial purposes and they are used extensively for both trunk hauls and local delivery of water and gas.

The greatest utilization can often be accomplished by using the same pipeline for different products at separate times. Excessive mixing of these products is avoided either by maintaining a turbulent flow or by the use of physical separators.

The importance of solids transport by pipeline is increasing year by year as experimentation and research overcome the problems. Solid particles can be transported by pipeline in one of two ways – slurry or capsules. Slurrying involves mixing or entrapping the granules of solid material within a liquid and pumping the mixture at such a rate that the movement of the solids takes place. As with a river, the faster the flow, the larger the granules that can be transported by this method. Some form of drying or de-liquifying plant is required at the delivery end of the pipeline. This process has advanced to the point where even some ships are loaded and discharged using slurrying techniques to handle bulk commodities through pipelines. Slurried material requires about 50 per cent more pumping power for the same volume when compared to pure liquids and, of course, vast amounts of the liquid transporter.

With the capsule process, packages of cargo are formed into stable slugs and pushed along by the liquid under pressure. The main advantage of this method is that there is no need for drying facilities at the reception end of the pipeline. Pneumatic capsule systems are used to move freight over short distances.

NATURAL WAYS

The sea and the air both have buoyancy properties that can be utilized without the need to design, build and maintain a way. In theory, for the operator they are free. Users do, however, need systems of navigation to enable vehicles to journey from one place to another and these are increasing, based on the products of the electronic industry. The equipment has to be supplied and can be paid for by the rental charges for the apparatus or by dues or charges levied on the aeroplane landing at an airport or a ship arriving in port.

The air and the sea can be used for commercial transport purposes by anybody who has the right equipment, subject to restrictions laid down by national and international organizations. These regulations concerning safety and use will be discussed in Chapters 6 and 7.

Airways

During the flight, the crew of an aircraft have to communicate with stations on the ground to give details of the position, receive information and instructions as to the position of other aircraft, the weather conditions en route and at the destination airport. Many other ground facilities are needed for the safe and efficient operation of the aircraft. These include air traffic control services, radio aids to navigation and radio and visual aids to take off and landing.

From the foregoing, it becomes obvious that aircraft are not as free to use the air space as seems possible at first sight. All flights must inevitably begin and end at an airport, whether this is a sophisticated complex like Heathrow or a small grass strip in a farmer's field. All commercial flights are guided during flight by ground located radio aids and radio beacons.

Because of the need to operate from airports which form node points in the flow of air routes, there is a danger of too many planes approaching these points at the same time. A system of air routes controlled from the ground has been developed world wide, based on the main routes between major airports.

Each nation state has control over the airspace above its territory by agreement at international conferences in Paris in 1919 and Chicago in 1944. These agreements result in government interference in air transport (see Chapter 7). This sovereignty means that no plane can fly over a country without first obtaining permission. For all commercial air transport this means governments negotiating bi-lateral air agreements with all other nations with which they wish to be connected by air services.

Air transport is international and to operate efficiently must be operated to laid-down standards. These standards are agreed through the work of the International Civil Aviation Organization (ICAO), as explained in Chapter 6.

The conduct of a commercial airline pilot during the flight is closely controlled by a system of air rules which established basic principles for the protection of aircraft, persons and property. These include minimum flying altitudes over built-up areas, rules for avoiding collisions and the provision of flight information.

The collision rules are split into two categories. Visual flight rules lay down the action to be taken when confronted with a collision situation. They lay down rules concerning lights that have to be carried during the hours of darkness. The other category is instrument flight rules, the principles of which are:

1. The pilot must file a flight plan before departure and adhere to this plan unless cleared to change by air traffic control.
2. Within controlled airspace, the aeroplane should be on a track and at an altitude at which the aircraft has been cleared by air traffic control.
3. The position of the aircraft must be reported at designated points or at other times with such other information that may be required by air traffic control.

There are three aspects to air traffic control:

1. To prevent collisions between aircraft and between aircraft and ground-based obstructions.
2. To provide aircraft with information and advice for the safe and efficient conduct of the flight.
3. To initiate search and rescue operations when they are needed by an aircraft under their control.

To make sure that aircraft in controlled airspace are kept separated, the air traffic controller surrounds each aircraft with a slab of empty airspace which other aircraft are not allowed to enter. The dimensions of the slab of airspace are called separation criteria and they are expressed in terms of lateral, vertical, and longitudinal distances.

As can be seen, aircraft are not free to use the airways when and how they like. They have to use designated routes and for much of the time their movements are controlled by ground staff. The navigation aids are provided by either government agencies or international bodies and are paid for by airport taxes or landing fees.

Strengths

1. The major strength of air transport over all other modes of transport is the speed of travel. The longer the distance of the flight, the greater the time saving of the customer.
2. Air transport has a good safety record and employs highly trained professionals at all levels of the industry.
3. Air transport has a good public image and is perceived to be very glamorous.

Weaknesses

1. Inflexible in that an aeroplane has to land and take off at an airport, which in the main is sited well away from the city centres. This means that for both passengers and freight there is a need to change mode before reaching the final destination.
2. Aeroplanes are noisy, subjecting houses under the approaches to airports to almost unacceptable noise levels.
3. For freight, in comparison to sea transport, air transport is expensive for the shipper and the cargo carrying capacity is small.

Seat routes[3]

Like airways, the popular concept of the sea as a transport way is one where if anybody has the right equipment, they can sail anywhere without obstruction. In practice, the sea is a highway which is in the main free but has some restrictions placed upon movement. Shipping movements are influenced by the following factors.

The physical environment of the oceans places restrictions on the free movement of most ships at some time in their working lives. Wind forces generated by the ocean weather systems can build up very large wave and swell patterns resulting at best in slowing the ship's speed, at worst in damage to the ship, passengers, cargo or crew, and in some cases in total loss of the vessel. Modern electronic navigation systems using space satellites can be used to fix the position of the ship with extreme accuracy and, coupled with weather routeing advice schemes, can help the sailor avoid the worst of the weather. On the other hand, advances in design techniques and the types of materials used in construction have resulted in ever bigger ships with deep drafts: such ships are no longer able to use some of the long-established ports or pass through shallow straits like the Dover Strait.

Political events can cause problems that are both trade related and operationally significant. For example, the closure of the Suez Canal led to mammoth tankers being routed around Southern Africa to serve North West Europe.

Shipping has become highly specialized over the last 30 years, each specialist type of ship being designed to marginally improve productivity over the ship it is intended to replace. The employment of these ships in a narrow segment of the market calls for a completely different management style from the system prevalent in the traditional, widely dispersed expertise in shipping companies of a few decades ago. Specialization has also resulted in ships becoming part of the overall transport of goods, designed to be complementary to the other parts of the transport chain. As such, they are often designed for a specific trade route and commodity type with no prospect of employment on other trade routes.

Navigation of a ship is by a mixed system of buoys and lighthouses on the coast, and manual and electronic navigation techniques deep sea. The lighthouses and buoys are built and maintained by various authorities and paid for by charging each ship a fee when it enters a port in that country, the fee being calculated to recover the costs of providing the navigation marks.

Shipowners, therefore, are free to trade their ships wherever they can find employment as long as there is sufficient depth of water in proposed ports of call and *en route*, there is no overt political restriction on their trading in certain areas, and the weather is suitable. In addition, shipowners do not have to design, build or maintain the way but, like road users, pay for this in the form of charges.

The main operating strength of the shipping industry lies in the capability of moving vast quantities of cargo in one ship on one voyage. For the users, this is the cheapest method of moving goods world wide.

The main drawback is the speed of the ship which, at 360 nautical miles per day on average, is very slow especially when it is realized that the ship operates continuously without a break. Although ships are relatively safe, accidents can involve severe pollution and sometimes loss of life.

TERMINALS

The terminal is the beginning and the end of a transport way, though to widen this definition we should say that the terminal can be described as a place where interchange facilities are provided for the transfer of passengers or freight from one mode to another mode or between vehicles of the same mode.

The function of the terminal is to provide the necessary equipment and infrastructure for the transfer of passengers and/or goods to take place as economically, quickly and safely as possible within prudent practice. This function will be carried out in differing ways according to the extent of use, the average and maximum size of vehicle being accommodated, the number of vehicles unloading, loading or waiting at any given time, the length of the journey which the goods or passengers are undertaking, the complexity of the unloading and loading arrangements and the effect of the weather on the services being offered.

Passenger terminals

The airport is dependent on air transport for its custom and is not a production entity in itself. The services it provides for its customers and users vary according to whether it is an airline, the travelling public, concessionary firms trading on the airport, or visitors. The main ones catered for are:

1. The marshalling, parking, handling, taking off and landing of aircraft.
2. The refuelling and supplying of, and dealing with, aircraft.
3. The repair and maintenance of aircraft.
4. Security in the form of a fire service and the police.
5. Embarkation and disembarkation facilities for passengers.
6. Legal formalities such as customs and immigration.
7. Reception, information and check-in facilities.
8. Shelter, food and accommodation for waiting passengers.
9. Services for the handling of passengers' luggage and air cargo.

Bus stations are either owned and operated by one bus company for that company's exclusive use, or provided for all bus services in a locality by the local council. Bus stations in town centres provide a means of removing stationary vehicles from the side of the road, thus helping to relieve one source of city congestion, provide rest facilities for the crew, accommodate the office space for the operational organization and provide a focus for the public on local bus services.

Railway stations in this country are owned and operated by Railtrack and are fully integrated into the railway operations. The size and the function obviously depends on whether the station is a main-line terminal or a small rural halt. One function all railway stations perform, except for the obvious one of transfer of passengers, is the dissemination of information about railway services. The mainline terminal has to cater for the movement of large numbers of passengers in short time periods. It also, like the airport and bus station, provides office accommodation for operating staff, crew rest rooms and facilities for waiting passengers.

Goods terminals

The freight terminal is the place where goods are handled between vehicles. It can be between vehicles in the same mode, as at a warehouse where loads are broken down from trunk haul to local delivery, or between different modes as at a seaport.

The focal point of the goods terminal must be the point at which the actual transfer takes places. This is where the efficiency of the terminal will be spotlighted and where most delays occur. The work involved at the transfer interface varies in complexity according to the size and type of vehicle and the nature of the goods being handled. Bulk commodities need different handling techniques to, for example, rolls of newsprint. The task of transferring the goods can be mechanized, the extent of mechanization and the complexity of the mechanical handling aids varying again according to the size and type of vehicle and the nature of the goods being handled.

The following factors are important when studying the organization of a freight terminal.

Planning the terminal must involve the overall cost of the operation especially bearing in mind that handling increases the cost without adding to the value. Movement should be continuous and in as horizontal a direction as possible. Storage should be utilized so that the vertical height is used and that it takes a minimum amount of effort to get the goods moving again.

The *layout* should ensure that the handling takes place efficiently and safely, with loads kept as one unit for a long as possible. Using the force of gravity is the cheapest way to handle freight but mechanical is more efficient than manual. All mechanical equipment must be placed under a planned maintenance scheme to avoid the loss of performance through the breakdown of mechanical handling aids at critical times during the operation of the system.

It is almost invariably true that no one piece of *equipment* is adequate for all handling operations in a freight terminal and the whole system should be researched to arrive at the optimum use of the available equipment. It is good practice to standardize the equipment as much as possible so that the costs of maintenance and spare parts can be minimized.

The overall cost of running a freight terminal is relatively straight-forward to calculate but it is good management practice to establish the cost of each freight movement. It is the small, often overlooked, movements that add considerably to the costs of running a terminal.

Warehouses

The internal layout of the average warehouse is fairly simple with storage areas divided by equipment access corridors. The method employed for moving goods in the warehouse depends on the type of packaging, the type of commodity and the physical size of the unit to be handled.

The dimensions of the access corridors is crucial to the total storage capacity available from any given size of warehouse and the dimensions of the corridors are a product of the equipment turning circle (or manoeuvrability) and the storage method. The larger the unit size, the greater the space required to handle the unit and, because the corridor space is largely unproductive, this space should be kept to a minimum.

Seaports

The major problem facing seaports around the world is congestion especially in the general cargo handling area. Port congestion adds to the cost of trade. The reasons for congestion and delays in seaports are many but the major ones are as follows:

1. Poor planning of port facilities by port authorities resulting in low productivity and lack of adequate berths to meet the demand.
2. Poor labour relations and docker training which lead to strikes and low productivity work.
3. Lack of co-ordination between port authorities and port users in designing new facilities and in organizing loading/unloading arrangements.
4. Slow processing of documentation by government agencies which can go against time saved by careful planning on the part of the port authority.

MODAL CHOICE

Our study of the major modal characteristics leads us finally to consider the question of why people choose one mode rather than another to transport their goods or themselves as passengers.

The transport decision on modal choice is a very complex matter and the relative effect of costs should not be underestimated. However, surveys have highlighted the crucial and sometimes overwhelming importance of factors which can be grouped under the general heading of 'quality of service'. These are known as 'the non-cost factors' though this term is somewhat misleading; orders lost through non-delivery of freight or unreliable service to passengers can be regarded as costs to the transport user.

The principal quality of service factors include:

1. *Speed of delivery*
   (a) When a product is perishable, greater speed ensures delivery with minimum loss through deterioration of the product. The need for speed may far outweigh any consideration of relative costs of different forms of transport.
   (b) When the customer's demand is urgent as in the case of a spare part for a machine which has to remain idle unless the part is fitted. The loss of revenue due to the failure to produce will far outweigh the costs of transport, making speed, not costs, the dominant factor.
   (c) Speed of delivery can be used to lower the amount of stockholding necessary to service a given market. Speedy delivery reduces the need for stockholding and lowers the warehousing and storage costs. If the reduced costs are more than any increased costs of transport, it will pay the shipper to send his goods by a more expensive but faster service.
   (d) The perceived value of time by travellers can have direct effects on modal choice decisions, with the high speed service being used in preference to a cheaper, slower speed service. It is perceived that any time saved in transit is more valuable to the passenger than any increase in costs that may be necessary.
2. *Certainty of timing*. Where a productive or distributive process requires a constant flow of inputs, certainty of timing of delivery eliminates the need to build up buffer stocks of components against the chance of interruption of supply. The same argument applies to the dispatch of finished products and to passenger transport decisions.
3. *Freedom from interruption*. The requirement of uninterrupted supply leads many companies to either use several modes of transport for their freight even though the short run cost of such a policy may be higher than is necessary, or to undertake the transport on their own account, which includes providing company cars to their senior managers.

4. *Avoidance of damage.* Damage is most likely to occur at transhipment points and fragile traffic therefore tends to be allocated to
   those modes offering the most uninterrupted through-carriage.
   From this viewpoint one can see the seeds of specialization, with
   vehicles being specifically designed to cater for a particular type of
   product or commodity.
5. *Avoidance of loss through pilferage.* Traditionally theft has been a
   serious problem for transhipment facility operators and security of
   transit is an important determinant in modal choice decisions.
6. *Ancillary services.* Some shippers prefer own account transport
   because it allows the transport to be combined with other services
   such as advertising on vehicle, sales by drivers and prompt return
   of empty units.

The notion of the time sensitivity of merchandise is a useful concept
because it includes three modal choice parameters: speed of delivery,
certainty of timing and freedom from interruption. Some products
must not remain in transit for more than a strictly limited period
because of the danger of deterioration. This sensitivity can be mitigated by the use of specifically designed vehicles, transfer and
handling equipment. In the case of many bulk commodities such as
coal, it may be sufficient to complete a shipment by a given date or to
maintain stipulated levels of delivery over a given time period. There
may, on the other hand, be pressure to reduce distribution costs by a
reduction in stockholding by maintaining regular shipments. Some
goods form part of the production chain and there is little tolerance in
delivery dates if the production process is not to be interrupted by
lack of supplies (unless stockholding is kept on uneconomic levels).

The degree of control that a consignor can exert over the whole
transport operation is very important to many companies. It tends to
be a function of the size of the transport economy and is an area in
which road haulage, by hire and reward or own account, is considerably superior to rail.

Distance is a further parameter of modal choice and studies have
found that hauls less than 50 miles are dominated by road vehicles.
Most studies, however, conclude that length of haul has only limited
influence compared with some of the other factors already
mentioned.

Thus, the choice of mode is governed by the characteristics of the
mode and the weight that the user attaches to the various factors
which make the mode attractive in any given situation. Many users
are prepared to pay more than the minimum possible cost for a
service which guarantees them a performance which is in line with
their own standards and objectives.

References

1. White, H.P. and Senior, M.L. *Transport Geography* Longman, England 1983
2. Beesely, M.E. 'Competition and supply in London taxi cabs' *Journal of Transport Economics and Policy* January 1979
3. Gubbins, E.J. *The Shipping Industry* Gordon and Breach, Switzerland 1986

3

Ownership and Organization

The form of ownership of the operating companies in the transport industry varies from the owner/driver of the road haulage industry to the very large state owned corporation such as British Rail (before privatization of the railways). The suitability of any form of ownership can only be determined by a study of the needs for organization in the sector of the industry concerned. The factors which most closely relate to organizational form are the nature of the business, the type and extent of international and national regulation regarding entry to the industry, the technology of the particular transport mode, the capital requirements to service the company, and the extent of the government or political control.

This chapter will address the question of what type of ownership by describing the main forms of ownership, the various theoretical philosophies about organization and the types of transport organizations that have evolved in practice to meet the particular needs of some transport companies.

THE SOLE TRADER

The sole trader, as the name implies, is both the owner and the manager of the business. The company is traded under the owner's name or any other name which the owner cares to adopt as long as the chosen name is not intended to mislead the public.

When one person provides the capital to start the business, ie all the money to buy or lease premises and equipment and to employ staff, that person is known as the sole proprietor. He alone takes all the risks of failure and is responsible for any losses incurred by the business. It is only fair that he alone distributes any profits the business may generate in a way that he sees fit.

The sole trader is completely responsible for the management of the business. He can employ other people to carry out the necessary tasks or manage the business on his own. Because he puts up all the capital and takes all the risks, the funds of a sole trader are limited to his personal wealth and the business usually stays small in scale. It is difficult for one person to organize and operate a business of any size given the complexities of management that sheer scale imposes on day-to-day management.

The direct personal interest that the sole trader imparts to his business affairs can make this form of enterprise very profitable and it can lead to personal service to the customer not found in larger scale organizations. In a service industry like transport, this can be very advantageous.

On big disadvantage of the sole trader is the difficulty of ascertaining true costs of operation. In road haulage, many sole traders employ members of their family at rates of pay which are not a true reflection of market conditions. This makes the allocation of cost and the calculation of rates very suspect, meaning that the proper costs of operation may not be allocated.

THE PARTNERSHIP

Whenever two or more people join together in a venture, the objective of which is gain, a partnership exists. The individual partners are rewarded by a share of the profits of the enterprise proportional to their involvement in the enterprise.

Legal arrangement are made through the partnership agreement which allocates the remuneration each partner is entitled to and lays out each partner's liability for any debts of the partnership.

With partnerships, the true costs of operation are more likely to be accounted for because of the need to split up profits among the partners or to allocate the liability for any debts.

Partnerships tend to give good personal service to the customer and usually have a good working relationship with their staff. They are not used a great deal in transport as a form of ownership but are extensive in other service industries like accountancy and the legal profession.

THE LIMITED COMPANY

If the capital to start a business is provided by shareholders whose liability for the debts of the business is limited to the amounts paid for their shares, the business is known as a limited liability company. The finance gained through the share issue is used to buy the assets needed to operate the company. The continuing growth in the size and complexity of operation has led to a similar growth in the amount of finance needed to establish many transport businesses. As liability is restricted to the amount an individual has paid for the shares, the removal of the risk for the investor of losing his whole fortune results in far greater investment funds being made available. In theory, protection of other creditors is assured by the amount of information that has to be published by the company under statutory provisions or divulged through the Registrar of Companies.

There are two forms of limited liability company, the private limited liability company and the public limited liability company.

The private limited liability company is by far the most widespread form of business ownership. There must be at least 2 shareholders but not more than 50. Each company must have at least one director and a company secretary who must be a separate person from the director. The company is not allowed to invite the public to buy shares; in other words, private limited liability companies are not listed on the stock exchange. The liability of a shareholder to the company is limited to the nominal value of the shares held by that individual.

Public limited liability companies may be formed by any seven people and the number of shareholders is unrestricted. Each company must have at least two directors and a company secretary; it is able to sell shares to the public at large through the stock exchange.

All limited liability companies have to have a constitution consisting of the Memorandum of Association and the Articles of Association.

The Memorandum includes the name of the company, the registered office, the objectives of the company and the amount of authorized share capital. The company is not allowed to exceed the provisions laid down in the objectives clause.

The Articles contain the internal organization, the structure and the method of management of the company. It also contains details of how shares can be transferred, when shareholders' meetings will be held, and how voting will take place.

Each company is required by law to keep a register showing the information as detailed in the Companies Acts. This includes the name, address, and occupation of, and the date at which shares were acquired by any shareholder, the number and identification of the shares and record book of share transfers. Included in these requirements are the nature and form of the published accounts of the company.

The day-to-day management of the business is the responsibility of directors who are voted into office at the annual general meeting by the shareholders. Directors are responsible, therefore, to the shareholders for the good conduct and efficient management of the company. They engage managers on a salary basis to organize the work of the company, the number depending on the size of the company.

The theory behind limited liability companies is that because the board of directors is elected by the votes of all the shareholders, the ordinary shareholder has control over the actions of the company. In practice, individual small shareholders have little opportunity to affect the day-to-day running of the company, the voting at annual general meetings being dominated by the large, block shareholders. Indeed, small shareholders can vote on issues without being present at the annual general meeting by passing their voting rights to somebody else in the form of what is known as a proxy.

When a company ceases trading for whatever reason, it has to be 'wound up'. This is the process whereby the legal existence of the company comes to an end and its property value is realized for the benefit of the creditors and the shareholders. This is called 'liquidation'. Voluntary liquidation occurs when the company agrees at a general meeting to cease trading. Compulsory liquidation occurs when the company is insolvent and cannot financially continue trading. 'Winding up under supervision' takes place under the supervision of the courts. Winding up involves the appointment of a liquidator who will realize the financial value of the company's assets, pay all the creditors and distribute any balance left to the shareholders.

CO-OPERATIVES

A co-operative, in company organization terms, is a voluntary association of economic units which enables the members to improve their economic situation through joint ventures while maintaining and protecting the independence of the individual in a competitive environment.

Given the additional dimension with some co-operatives of a political ideology which regards the co-operative venture as a path to equality and the ending of capitalism, a co-operative is a voluntary association of workers or businesses based on equality of treatment and the carrying through of joint objectives.

The main principles of co-operative enterprise are open membership, democratic control, and agreement on how the benefits are to be distributed.

Co-operatives should be owned as permanent business ventures by their members, not as temporary arrangements to overcome particular problems. Involvement in a co-operative venture rarely entails undue risks because excessive risk is unattractive to many potential members who do not like speculation. Co-operatives are self-help organizations, not cartels. What this means is that the members are relatively weak and small within the market in which they operate.

PUBLIC AUTHORITIES

Public authorities are statutory organizations set up as autonomous bodies by the state. They are free from day-to-day control by the state and their purpose is to provide a service to the public. The capital is in the form of fixed interest loan stock, the interest paid according to the Act of Parliament setting up the authority. The government appoint trustees who choose the board of control which then exercises management subject to the powers laid out in the Act of Parliament.

DEPARTMENT OF STATE

The overall responsibility for the running of the business is vested in a government minister and all the employees are civil servants. The great disadvantage of this form of organization is that decisions tend to reflect the ministerial responsibility to Parliament and not any real commercial criteria.

THE MUNICIPALITY

Management of a municipal undertaking is controlled by the local authority through the appropriate committee. This results in the organization being run for the benefit of those people living in the local authority area and in political direction by local authority councillors. The capital is supplied by loans, profits going to pay off the loans and any surplus going into the general revenue account of the local authority. Any losses are paid for by subventions from the general revenue account.

THE PUBLIC CORPORATION

The public corporation is an organization set up by an Act of Parliament, the Act setting out the responsibilities and the rights of the management. All the shares in the corporation are held by the government.

We have to look back to 1947 and the large-scale nationalization programme of the Labour government to understand the rationale behind the creation of public corporations. The arguments concerning nationalization were fierce but there was a fair measure of agreement across the country about the need for government support for certain industries.

For example, it was felt that to further integration of transport services, central control of the transport industry would result in larger units. The large-scale enterprises would be able to take advantage of economies of scale especially in an era of scarcity of resources following the war. This in itself, it was hoped, would lead to greater use of technology, allowing the mode most suited to the task to undertake that transport service.

It was further argued that there were areas of the transport industry where fixed costs formed a high proportion of total costs. Competition, it was believed, would lead to a wasteful allocation of scarce resources, both financial and physical. Common ownership would ensure that there was a large measure of the correct allocation of traffic between the modes.

Through common ownership, benefits would accrue to many parts of the community that had suffered from poor transport provision. This implies that the costs of the system could be spread between high cost areas and low cost areas, resulting in more equitable treatment for the whole community. Underlying this trend of argument is the belief that transport is a public utility to be enjoyed equally by the whole of the population, like the postal service. At the same time, there were severe doubts in many people's minds about the ability of certain modes of transport to attract enough finance from the financial community to be able to invest in adequate facilities. The returns on capital investment were bound to be low, and thus the only adequate source of finance was through the government.

The reasons for creating public corporations, rather than having the Department of Transport manage the businesses, were twofold:

1. Public corporations have the same flexibility in day-to-day management as any private company.
2. Because of the state ownership, a public corporation is still accountable in performance to Parliament through the relevant minister.

What has to be asked, and answered, is the question of just how private are public corporations. Are they in fact, though not in law, only another branch of the government?

Public corporations are granted a separate legal personality. In other words, they can sue other companies or individuals in their own name. They have limited liability, as with private or public limited liability companies. The employees are not civil servants though there is a tendency for them to take on some of the public service functions of civil servants.

The directors or board members are appointed by the minister and the board has to comply with directives from the government through the minister responsible. The idea of a public corporation is to allow the management freedom to manage, without political interference, within the broad policy guidelines laid down by the government. This, in theory, is exactly the same position as that enjoyed by any other limited liability company where the shareholders appoint the directors to run the business within the collectively agreed broad guidelines and bring them to account for their actions periodically at an annual general meeting. It is because of this theory, that public corporations can never really be separated from other state institutions, the state being the sole shareholder.

Since the setting up of the public corporations in transport (the Railways Board, the British Transport Docks Board, the National Bus Company, etc) there has been an increasing level of central direction and control which has been one of the main reasons put forward for privatization. Ministers hold frequent informal talks with board members which result in a fair measure of interference with the day-to-day management decision-making. According to Hanson[1], the public corporation has become a special ministerial agency whose corporate status is only a convenient legal and administrative function.

Theoretically, the corporation's employees are responsible for the day-to-day management, and the minister for overall policy direction. This fine division of responsibility tends to get confused. Whenever a public corporation gets criticized in Parliament, the minister feels that it is his responsibility to defend the corporation's record whether the criticism is directed at his sphere of responsibility or not. Ministers tend to identify with the success or failure of the corporations sponsored by their departments and thus to identify very closely with that particular corporation's record. This fact of identification can induce a minister to exercise control over aspects of the corporation activities which should really be left to the management.

Reviewing these arguments about public corporations, it is easy to see why any government suspicious of state ownership should question the need for this type of organization. They will argue that, though the intentions of the founding fathers may have been honourable, the public corporation because of its nature and organization becomes no more than an organ of state policy-making. The separate legal status and personality cannot be equated with independent management. The main reason for granting legal status and personality is to limit the company's legal liability to the assets of the corporation. It is further argued that although the employees are not civil servants, they often act as if they are. It is no wonder that many people feel that the public corporation is an old-fashioned idea and that these organizations should be privatized or some other forms of state control found.

THE STRUCTURE OF THE TRANSPORT INDUSTRIES

Before looking at the types of company found in each mode of transport, it is as well to remind ourselves of the way in which government legislation has moulded the structure and organization of the industry.[2] Since 1945, the structure and ownership patterns of British transport have changed considerably according to which political party has formed the government. These changes have resulted from the legislation passed by Parliament, setting out the main structural framework for the transport industry.

It must be noted that for the railways and civil aviation some form of state assistance would have been necessary no matter which party had assumed power in 1945. The railways had been over-worked and starved of investment during the war years and were in need of a drastic overhaul and modernization to meet the requirements of the system during peacetime. The civil aviation industry had to start peacetime operation almost from scratch after a complete dominance by the military during the war. In addition, there was a widespread fear that without government backing civil aviation would become a monopoly of the USA.

The effects of legislation

The Transport Act of 1947 set up the British Transport Commission as the authority for inland transport. The commission was charged with the duty to provide an efficient, adequate, economical and properly integrated system of inland transport and port facilities. The British Transport Commission was the policy and directing body whose main objective was to promote integration of transport facilities. Management functions were carried out by executives, of which there were five: railway, docks and inland waterways, road transport (split into road passenger and road freight in 1949), London Transport, and ancillary services. Each executive was responsible for the general management and for carrying out the functions designated by the British Transport Commission.

The underlying philosophy for the British Transport Commission was that transport was so important to the national economy that central ownership and direction, guaranteeing efficient operation, was essential. The British Transport Commission, however, never attained a complete monopoly of transport services. The railways and London Transport were nationalized entirely along with those waterways, ports and road passenger undertakings which belonged to the railways. In road haulage, the British Transport Commission had to start from scratch by taking over those companies with fleets operating more than 40 miles from base. This resulted in the 400 largest firms being nationalized and forming British Road Services. Even by 1951, the British Transport Commission was some way short of a monopoly because there was still a sizeable private sector in road haulage, especially own account, in the bus and coach sector, and a number of trust and local authority owned ports.

The Civil Aviation Act of 1946 created three separate state owned airlines, BOAC, BSAA, and BEA. These three state corporations were given exclusive rights to fly services from the UK to countries within their particular sphere of influence. The Act enhanced the prevalent feeling that national ownership was the best guarantee to the travelling public of disinterested expansion of the nation's air services with economy and efficiency. The Act also made provisions for deficiency grants to be paid to the corporations while they were regaining their international competitive edge. In 1949 BOAC and BSAA were merged under the banner of the BOAC.

The major aim of the Transport Act 1953 was to denationalize the road haulage part of the British Transport Commission. A board was established to supervize the sale of BRS assets to the private sector but even by 1956 BRS was still by far the largest road haulage company with a number of big long-term contracts.

The 1962 Act abolished the British Transport Commission, recognizing the political reality that without complete state ownership and control, integration of transport was not really feasible. In place of the BTC five public corporations were created: the British Railways Board, British Waterways Board, British Transport Docks Board, London Transport Board and the Transport Holding Company. The idea of achieving an integration of transport that had underlined the 1947 Act had finally been abandoned.

The 1968 Act had as the control theme 'putting the railways into a stable financial situation' but it also affected the structure of the industry. The Transport Holding Company was wound up and replaced by the National Freight Corporation, the National Bus Company and the Scottish Transport Group. Within the provisions of the Act were powers to create passenger transport authorities to run transport in the major conurbations of the UK. In 1969 an Act gave similar powers to the London region.

The Local Government Act of 1972 created the Metropolitan Counties to take over the powers of the PTAs and to establish passenger transport executives in their areas to integrate public passenger transport. The county councils were given powers to co-ordinate public transport within the county boundaries.

Since 1979, the main emphasis of legislation has changed. The new Conservative government pledged to 'privatize' as much of state owned industry as was possible or made commercial since. In 1980 came a management and worker buy out of the National Freight Corporation and, with this action, the end of the state involvement in the management of the road haulage industry. In 1981, the British Transport Docks Board was privatized and now trades as a private company under the name of Associated British Ports. The 1985 Transport Act, though mainly about the 'deregulation' of the bus industry, included provisions for the sale of the National Bus Company and the creation of 'private' companies to replace the municipal bus operators. ('Private' because the net result has been to replace the municipal bus operators controlled by committees of the local authority with 'private' companies wholly owned by the local authority.)

The Civil Aviation Act 1971 created the Civil Aviation Authority to oversee air transport, legislated that at least one scheduled international British carrier must be privately owned, laid the foundations for the British Airport Authority and merged BOAC and BEA to form British Airways. In 1987 British Airways was privatized and the Airports Act 1986 laid out the basis for privatization of BAA. The same Act created similar 'private' companies to run the municipally owned airports as were created in the bus industry. The Railways Act

1993 privatized British Rail by setting up Railtrack to own and maintain the infrastructure and 25 Train Operating Companies to operate train services.

A good deal can be learnt from this review of the way in which legislation has altered the ownership and structure of the transport industry. At the time of writing, the UK is in a privatization-of-state-assets phase of development with the added dimension of 'deregulation'. This is leading to more competition in transport services, both intra- and inter-modal. It is also resulting in more attention to commercial management with the subsequent down-grading of social obligations.

It is important to realize that a review of what has happened in the past is not wasted even in today's political climate. Before the last election, the British Labour Party published policy documents advocating more social ownership (nationalization by another name) and a British Transport Authority to oversee the integration of the transport sector, though since taking power in 1997 the Labour government has not pursued this policy option. What is vital in this situation is to learn the lesson that the ownership, structure and policy objectives of transport undertakings are affected fundamentally by political processes and government legislation.

ORGANIZATION

The word organization has two distinct meanings, which are often confused. The first refers to an entity – for example the transport company. The second refers to organization as a process.

There are three characteristics of organizations as entities: they are composed of people; they have a distinct purpose; and they have some degree of structure. Thus organizations as entities are groups of people bound together in a formal relationship to achieve certain goals.[3]

Organization as a process is the structuring of work, systems and people. Organization is the form of every human association for the attainment of a common purpose.[4]

If the work of running a business is beyond the capacity of one person to perform, it has to be shared out among other. This brings with it the problem of getting people to act in unison with each other. Organization is a matter of dividing work among people whose efforts have to be co-ordinated.

In practice, it is concerned with specifying objectives for the business and each of its sub-units, determining in broad terms the activities and decisions necessary to accomplish these objectives.[5]

There are three 'schools' of thought about the theory of organization as a process and in any study of management it is import to group these concepts. They are only concepts, not law as would apply in a physical science, and they are in many ways complementary. They will be discussed in turn.

The classical school

The theory proposed by the classical school on organization was first set down by F. Taylor but has since been modified and expanded by other writers such as Fayol, Urwick and Brech. The theory states that:

1. The activities for the purpose of carrying out the objectives set by the company must be determined.
2. These activities must then be arranged in groups which can be managed by one individual.
3. The groups are then joined to other groups in a hierarchy of importance until the structure of the company has been built.
4. People are now fitted into the structure according to their skills and abilities.

The over-riding sense of this theory is that organizations are formed to reach objectives and people must fit into the structure to enable the company to reach those objectives.

The general principles of the classical organization can be stated in this way:

1. *Specialization* of managers is very important. Each individual should perform a single function because this will enable that person to have a much greater chance of becoming settled at a particular job. It is this aspect of the classical theory which results in jobs within the company that can only be filled by specialists and makes for a lack of flexibility and job mobility within the structure of the company. Obviously, there are positions which require very specialist knowledge in any company, eg accountancy, but other jobs become specialized where recruitment is always from one branch of the company even though this may not be entirely necessary.
2. *Definition.* For an organization to work efficiently there must be a clear definition of the line of authority from the very top of the organization to the bottom. This line of authority must be known and recognized by all the people working in the organization. In other words, every worker must recognize who can give them orders and initiate action.

Authority and responsibility must be equal. If any worker is to be held responsible for the results of actions or decisions, that worker must be given the authority to carry out that action or make that decision. This means that the person being held responsible must be given sufficient information on which to base actions or decisions.

3. *Delegation.* Delegation is one of the hardest concepts to grasp in management and one of the most difficult to put into practice. Delegation means taking decisions as close to the activity as possible. It involves letting go of some authority and vesting that authority in a subordinate. It does not mean shedding accountability but creating new accountability. For example, the general manager of a road haulage company is accountable to the board for the success or failure of the business. He cannot shed that accountability even by delegating authority to other people to make decisions without consulting him. If those decisions subsequently prove wrong and affect the success of the business, the general manager will still be held accountable to the board. What he will have done is to create in others new accountability for their actions to him. In another sphere, the captain of a ship delegates the authority for good navigation to the officer of the watch but if the ship runs aground, the captain is still accountable to the shipowner for the accident even though he was not on the bridge of the ship at the time of the accident.

Three points must be noted when dealing with the concept of delegation:

(a) Delegation must not be carried too far by leaving decisions to people so low in the organization structure that the person asked to initiate the action or make the decision does not have all the facts necessary to make successful and proper decisions.

(b) It must always be made plain that any action or decision delegated must be taken in the best interests of the company, not to serve sectional interests. This in itself entails making sure that the company objectives are understood at all levels in the structure and there is a clear idea of how individual decisions affect the fulfilling of those objectives.

(c) The person to whom the authority is delegated must be competent and able to analyse all the facts.

Managers, no matter what their style or personal feelings, cannot escape the need to delegate some authority in most modern organizations. It is usually beyond the intellectual and physical capacity of any one person to make all the decisions necessary to keep even the smallest organization operating. The major problem involves the concept of accountability. Many managers have great difficulty in allowing subordinates to make decisions and initiate action without interference. This is because the manager knows that whatever happens, he is still accountable for those decisions and actions to a higher authority even though he had no direct involvement in the process. Delegation involves a fair degree of trust in one's subordinates and trust involves the lessening of control. The main point to bear in mind is the importance of mutual trust between the manager making the decision and the one delegating the authority. Without that trust, there is usually too much interference, or control, and delegation is really only a sham.

4. *Span of Control.* No one person can control or supervise more than a certain number of subordinates when the work of the subordinates is interrelated. The sheer size of the task of keeping track of the relationships between people in a group and being able to get those people working together is enormous. Many writers cite six to eight subordinates as the maximum size of group to be supervised but this is not always evident in practice. It is, however, important to recognize the problems associated with the span of control when examining the organization structure. There are historical precedents. The military have recognized this principle as far back as the Roman Legions, and the Jews used it when leaving Egypt to gain control of their march.

5. *Chain of command.* The chain of command is defined as the number of layers in an organization from the top to the bottom. The fewer levels there are, the easier it is for instructions to be passed from one level to the next and for information, especially oral, to flow without distortion taking place. Many readers will have played the communications game where a sentence is passed verbally from one person to another in a group. The more times the message changes hands, the more distorted it becomes and the less like the original it is when it comes back to the beginning of the circle. In a business environment, it is important that instructions are concise and accurate, leaving little room for error. The longer the chain of command, the more chance there is of the message becoming changed during its transmission.

The concepts of span of control and chain of command are often mutually exclusive because the fewer levels in an organization, the more subordinates report to each supervisor. The smaller the span of control, the longer the chain of command. What is important is that managers are aware of the problems when devising organization structures and that a balance is struck between these concepts.

6. *Unity of command.* It is held as axiomatic by the classical organizational theorists that each employee can have only one supervisor giving instructions. It is held that it is impossible for somebody to have to make a choice between conflicting instructions flowing from two supervisors. This situation results from confused organizational planning.

Line and staff

Line managers are those who have responsibility for those activities which are concerned with the prime objective of the company. In transport this is the function of transporting people or goods from one place to another.

Staff managers are those who contribute indirectly to the main function by providing services and advice to line management – for example the accountant.

Bureaucracy

Bureaucracy is defined as an integrated hierarchy of specialized offices defined by systematic rules, an impersonal routinized structure where legitimate authority rests in the office and not in the person of the office holder. The rules are rigidly laid down in writing and aim to provide for every eventuality. Commands are obeyed because it is laid down that it is within the competence of a particular office to issue such commands.

Bureaucracies can be efficient in that the means used can best achieve the objectives of the organization unencumbered by the personal whims of the office holder.

Bureaucracy suffers from excessive recording, ignores personal ideas and does not possess the means of resolving conflicts that are outside the rules. Communications can be distorted because they have to follow particular paths through the organization structure.

The classical approach to organization is a study of the activities that need to be undertaken to achieve the organization's objectives. Once these activities are identified, they are grouped to form individual jobs, work sections and administrative units.

The aim is to get efficient specialization of personnel and co-ordination of activities without overloading managers. Co-ordination is further facilitated by linking people together in a chain of command and ensuring that each person knows where his responsibility ends and another begins.

The classical approach attempts to establish rules to act as criteria in developing the organization.

The behaviour school

The problem of creating organizations which are efficient and which at the same time satisfy the desires, aspirations and interests of those who work in them has attracted the attention of many writers.[6]

Weber, writing about bureaucracy, saw the problem a one of constructing a rational system of authority for the efficient pursuit of defined objectives.

Many writers point out that it is *people* who are organized, yet the classical approach does not take into account people's likely behaviour under different organizational arrangements.

The classical approach concentrates on people's physical capacities and physical needs while ignoring the emotional, social side of human nature. People in an organization are viewed within the classical theory as passive instruments, content to act only in accordance with the rules and orders from higher authority.

In practice, people lead complex and interrelated lives which can make them pursue activities which do not conform to the official policy. Work groups develop their own social structure which may not relate to the official structure as laid out in the organization's structure chart.

The way in which people behave cannot be ignored. The behavioural approach to organization is an attempt to define what sort of social environment stimulates people to strive for the overall objectives of the company rather than their individual objectives which may be in conflict.

The behavioural approach tries to create an organization which:

1. Achieves the objectives of the company while at the same time satisfying the people who make up the organization.
2. Encourages high productivity and low absenteeism because people are stimulated by the work they do.
3. Enhances co-operation between managers and the workforce because everybody is pulling in the same direction. Everybody has a clear idea of the company's goals and their own importance to the attainment of those goals.

In this approach, the study of organization becomes basically a study of human behaviour. Understanding how people behave in given situations and why they behave in certain ways is important for efficient working. This understanding will enable predictions to be made of how people will react to future situations as they arise.

From studies of this kind, guidance about the best organizational arrangement for co-operation and good working practice can be implemented. The results of this line of research have been to stress three factors and their effect on the organization:

1. Individual and group productivity.
2. Individual development.
3. Job satisfaction.

These can be sub-divided into the factors which affect individual behaviour:

1. Needs and wants.
2. Behaviour in small groups.
3. Behaviour as a leader.
4. Inter-group behaviour.

Motivation

Every person has some idea of what he or she is at present, what he or she would like to be in the future, and how he or she fits into the world around them. Given this, there are still an awful lot of questions to be answered about what drives people.

■ Why do some people strive to be the Prime Minister of the UK or President of the United States, with all the the attendant pressures in both the job itself and the striving to get there?
■ What is the urge that drives some people to make a second fortune after the first has been safely accomplished?
■ Why do people move jobs and houses with all the upheaval this entails?
■ Why do people work so hard or so little?
■ Why indeed does anybody work at all?
■ There must be pressures which can explain specific actions in specific situations, but is there a common force within the set of individual circumstances which pushes people one way or the other?
■ Can a study of the individual decision process answer the questions about work in any given situation?

An investigation of these questions is usually called 'motivational theory'. It is believed that if only man could understand the ways in which individuals are motivated, their decision-making process could be influenced by changing the emphasis on different components of the motivational calculus.

The motivational theories stem from various underlying assumptions about man which have been derived through observation. They can be classified simply as follows:

Rational economic man. Man is primarily motivated by economic needs. He is fundamentally a passive animal to be manipulated, motivated and controlled by the organization. His feelings are essentially irrational; so organizations must be structured in such a way that feelings and unpredictable behaviour are controlled.

Now, behaviourists would argue that many people are not like this. It is only the classical theory of organization which dehumanizes workers. The classical theory writers answer this criticism by saying that those people who are self-motivated and self-controlled form the entrepreneurial, managerial and professional group of people.

Social man. Man is basically a social animal and gets his basic identity from relationships developed through joining other people. As a result, much of a person's meaning for living does not come from work but from the social relationships formed at work.

Organizations and management must mobilize these social relationships through the style of leadership and studies of group behaviour.

Self-actualizing man. Man is primarily self-motivated and self-controlled. He seeks to control his working environment and resents too much outside control, such control being a demotivator.

Management must give man a chance to work out his own solutions to the organizational goals, thus integrating his own goals with those of the organization.

Complex man. Man is a variable animal. He has many motivating forces acting on him at any one time, one of which may be dominant. Which this is will affect the way in which he reacts to any situation. He can be made to respond to a variety of management motivators but he may reject them if he feels they are not essential to his needs.

Psychological man. Man is a very complex animal who is evolving psychologically all the time. He manufactures ideals towards which he strives and the major motivating force is the need to bring himself nearer to the ideal. The gap between the perception of ourselves in reality and our ideal leads to feelings of frustration.

Whichever view you have of man will affect the way in which you view the nature of organization.

The behavioural approach is to maintain that organization cannot be a rigid structure but a system of inter-dependent human beings who affect the aims, functioning, principles and management of the organization.

The behavioural approach leads to the theory of the organic organization where jobs are loosely defined and everybody does what they can do best.

To get the best out of the organization, a study must be made of the attitudes, aspirations, expectations, tensions, conflicts and the effects these have on productivity, cohesion and the morale of the people working in the organization.

It has been found by many researchers that though this type of organization works well in small groups, the larger the organization the more need there is for a formal structure.

The systems school

The systems approach[7] to organization concentrates on decisions that need to be made to achieve the organization's objectives. Decision-making, rather than activity, is chosen for study because it is through this process that policies are laid down and actions taken that result in the future success or failure of the company.

The systems approach emphasizes that for any investigation there is an appropriate system to be studied and the purpose of the investigation decides both the boundaries of the system and the appropriate sub-systems. If the investigation concerns company organization, what is the system to be studied? The organization of the company is a means of achieving objectives. Thus the system must embrace the company itself and that part of the external environment, for example the market, that impinges on the objectives so that these can be set as the basis for organization.

What are the appropriate sub-systems to be studied? The sub-systems centre on the main decisions to be make to accomplish objectives. The organization should be designed to facilitate decision-making but since decision is dependent on information and information on communication, the organization is built up from an analysis of information needs and communication networks.

Decision-making is chosen rather than activities or departments because it is through the process of decision-making that objectives and policies are laid down and actions taken which result in success or failure.

The systems approach to organization consists of the following steps:

1. *Specify objectives.* Devising a system that pursues the wrong objectives, solves the wrong problem, may be more wasteful than choosing a system which fulfils the objectives inefficiently.
2. *List the sub-systems or decision areas.* In listing the decisions that must be made within a company, a difficulty arises in that all problems cannot be anticipated. This means that the appropriate decisions cannot be predicted with any certainty. Another difficulty lies in determining the unit of decision since almost all decisions are part of a system of decisions. The unit of decision must be a matter of judgement depending on the purpose of the decision and the detail of the analysis.
3. *Analyse the decision areas.* Decision-making means making a choice from a range of possible courses of action. Managers aim to be efficient at making decisions, ie choosing the alternative which, as far as they can tell, will give better results as measured against the objectives than the alternative course of action foregone. Indeed, ask any manager about management and they will put decision-making as the most important aspect of their job.

It is not immediately apparent in any study of managers that decision-making is any problem. Superficially, it appears to be merely a matter of getting the facts. Once the facts have been collected and analysed, the right solution will automatically present itself. Of course, decision-making is much more complex than this simple model implies. In all forms of business, and especially in transport, decisions have to be made quickly without a knowledge of all the facts, and are often more to do with the experience of the decision-maker than with any scientific analysis of the information. However, decision-making deserves detailed study since the success of a company depends on the quality of the decisions made by its management.

Briefly, effective decision-making depends on a disciplined approach and on how well the following steps in the decision-making process are carried out:

(a) Establishing the goals of the proposed action.
(b) Identifying the possible courses of action which can fulfil those goals.
(c) Identifying the consequences of any action based on the decision.
(d) Establishing criteria for evaluating the consequences.
(e) Establishing decision rules.

Obviously, the quality of the decision depends upon the quality of the information available as well as managerial judgement. In addition, because the information needs to be communicated, it determines the communications network, which itself is facilitated or hampered by the organizational structure.

4. *Design the communications channels.* Communication is the means by which information is passed from one person to another and can be carried out by a gesture, talk, instrument or the written word. It is through communication that information is passed to the decision-maker and resulting decisions passed to those executing them. Without communication there could be no organization since it would be impossible to get people to act in a co-ordinated way. People would be linked together by an abstract chain of command but acting without an abstract chain of understanding. Where communication is poor, co-ordination is poor. Co-ordination implies that people are being informed about each other's plans. Furthermore, co-operation presupposes co-ordination so that co-operation itself depends on communication.

5. *Group decision areas to minimize communications burden.* As specialization increases, inter-dependence increases, and with it the need for co-ordination. How much inter-dependence increases, and with it the need for co-ordination. How much inter-dependence can be tolerated without giving rise to a serious failure in assuming that people concerned are willing to co-operate? The answer depends on the channel capacity for information and the stability of inter-dependence.

The systems approach lays stress on minimizing the communications burden to improve co-ordination. Grouping people under a common supervisor and putting them close to each other may reduce the communications burden and may be one way to improve the co-ordination. Looking at the company as a whole, if co-ordination is the goal, groupings should be chosen which lead to more self-containment than alternative groupings. Information points, decision and action points most dependent on each other are grouped together. The pattern of inter-dependence between units may also be made more stable by grouping units under a common supervisor so that co-ordination is improved by having all units subscribe to a common plan.

Contrasting the theories

The classical approach attempts to analyse the activities, the behavioural looks at the people, and the systems provides a descriptive model based on the requirements of the information network. All three approaches attempt to see organization through a different viewfinder but each has important insights into what is important about organization.

One final word on organization can come from a study of the work of McGregor.[8] From its title you can see the degree of acceptance of the importance of manpower resources. McGregor presented attitudes to human resources and their practical implication as coherent theories which he called 'X' and 'Y'. They are outlined in contrasting models. Organizations tend to veer towards one model or the other and features of both may be found in the same organization, adopted by different sections of the management. They are simply given as a contrast to help the reader see the differences between them.

The contrasting models imply an authoritarian view of organization (theory 'X') and a more participatory view (theory 'Y'). McGregor did not judge either of these styles to be absolutely qualitatively better than the other. He considered them in terms of their suitability to the circumstances of the organization and examined their qualities in terms of this suitability. For example, theory 'X' type organizations are more likely to result in optimum efficiency in military type situations which often face conditions of intense pressure. The organizations must be able to act cohesively and quickly with obedience to clearly defined authority and clearly defined precise instructions. Theory 'Y' type organizations suit situations which need flexibility and individual commitment to objectives achieved through discussions and internal communications. In theory, 'Y' organizations there is likely to be far less threat of sanctions because the objectives are agreed by those involved in the enterprise.

ORGANIZATION STRUCTURE OF A TRANSPORT COMPANY

With the theoretical ideas about organization in mind, we will now look at the organization structure of a transport company, translate this into practice by looking at a shipping company and view some actual structures from the British Railway system and Associated British Ports.

As already stated, the primary objective of a transport company is to supply the utility of place. That means transport companies are engaged in taking people and/or goods from one place to another.

In simple terms, companies engage in three broad activities to carry out their business. They buy something, they transform that something to produce a product and they sell the product in the market place.

It is difficult to compare transport companies to manufacturing companies but the processes of business are very similar. A manufacturing company buys raw materials or components, undertakes work on the raw materials or components and then sells the production. This is a very simplified model because the company has to make sure that what it produces is wanted by its customers, but the concept of marketing will be covered in Chapter 5.

A transport company buys vehicles and buildings, in other words capital equipment, sets up an operating system using the vehicles to fulfil the major objectives of the company, and then sells the safe arrival which is the product of the operating system.

We can identify three factors which must be present for a transport company to accomplish these three phases successfully: finance, operating and marketing.

In most companies overall responsibility for co-ordination of the business activities is achieved by a board of directors, the board members as the heads of the various sections. In large companies, a chief executive or managing director with no departmental heads to act as a co-ordinator.

The first illustration of the structure of any company follows the simple model outlined in Fig. 3.1. For a small operation, these divisions are enough to carry out the management but with larger organizations each of these functions has to be further sub-divided. An understanding of how the sub-sections are formed can be gained by looking at the functions each of those areas has to fulfil.

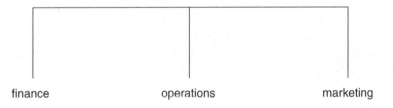

finance   operations   marketing

Figure 3.1   *Simple company structure*

Finance

The finance section has two main functions:

1. *Investment*: It has to raise sufficient finance to buy the equipment necessary for the company's operations and to allow for any future changes and growth.
2. *Accounting*: Controlling the use of the finance in making sure that the business is efficient is not only important for the success of the company but is a legal requirement.

Operations

There are three main functions of the operations section:

1. *Operating*: Working out and implementing the vehicle and personnel schedules to conform to company policy and legal requirements.
2. *Maintaining*: Making sure that the vehicles are maintained both from the point of statutory safety requirements and maintaining the value of the company's assets.
3. *Personnel*: Making sure that the right people are available to operate the vehicles which in transport means checking licences and qualifications.

Marketing

There are three functions associated with the marketing section:

1. *Advertising and publicity*: Informing the public about the services on offer.
2. *Selling*: Price fixing, contract negotiating and after-sales service.
3. *Market research*: Finding out what the customer and potential customers require from the company.

This explanation follows closely the classical approach to organization, by identifying the tasks and grouping the tasks into activities. For examples from shipping see Downard,[9] for air J.R. Wiley[10] and Smith, Odegard, Shea,[11] for the Bus Industry, see Hibbs,[12] and on rail, see Keys and Jackson.[7]

THE TRANSPORT COMPANY'S GOAL

We can look at this problem in a different way. As we shall see in Chapter 4, any company which is to have a chance of being successful must know the areas of operation in which it is most likely to find success.

A transport company operates within what can be called an 'open system'. It takes into itself from the surrounding environment resources both material and human, processes them, and returns them to the environment. The input of these resources is liable to cease if the service provided does not satisfy the needs of the outside environment.

The overall objective of the company must be that it is successful.

This does not mean that the company makes short-term profits to the exclusion of all else. In many cases, transport companies could sell their real estate and make substantial profits but they would not survive as transport companies. To be successful, the company must not only make a profit but also survive.

The transport company does not, in any physical sense, produce anything. It takes from the outside environment goods or other people, collects them together to form vehicle loads, transports them to another place and releases them out into the environment, hopefully unchanged. Therefore, the transport company provides a service to the community.

The major objective of a transport company must be to transport goods or people. In order to transport the people and/or goods, it must exist and fulfil the aims set out in Chapter 4. The goal of a transport company is to survive and grow in a changing environment by achieving a reasonable return on the capital invested by procuring employment for its vehicles at competitive rates. By this definition, all the objectives of the transport company are met. The company will survive, it will grow and meet the needs of the shareholders, executives and employees and it recognizes the need for planning.

THE COMPANY STRUCTURE

In a transport company, the activities can be broadly broken into four inter-relating parts (Fig. 3.2). At the top of Fig. 3.2 is the policy part. This is the group which formulates policy, in other words plans the carrying out of the company's objectives. In most companies, this

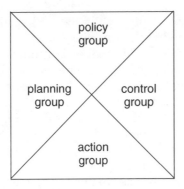

Figure 3.2 *Company activities*

group will consist of the board of directors answerable to the share-holders through a chairman. Any decisions of this group will be passed across the boundary to the action group.

The action group is the main task function group which carries out the main activities of the company. Furnishing the policy group with information to enable them to make decisions, and collecting relevant information from the action group, is the planning group. Checking on the effects of any policy decision on the company objectives and performance is the control group.

The transport company is an open system. As already stated, it takes in goods/people from outside, converts these into vehicle loads, transports them and releases them into the environment again. This system can be broken down into several task functions which all come under the umbrella of the action group. These separate task functions can be represented by a flow diagram (Fig. 3.3) showing that each function relies on the others to make up the overall action grouping.

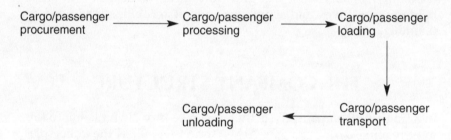

Figure 3.3 *Task functions*

The planning group could easily be called the servicing group because it is concerned with providing information and advice for the decision-making process. The planning group of activities includes advice on finance, technical developments and human resources. As one example, the changing environment within which the company operates will bring forth the use of new techniques. It is a function of the planning group activities to ascertain the likely path of technological developments and how these developments fit in with the company's existing equipment. They have to provide answers to questions about present working methods or whether new technologies will force the company to change working methods to accommodate developments. In order to stay competitive, companies have to invest and financial planning is needed to make sure the financial resources are available when required.

The activities in the control group area are those that oversee the broad day-to-day running of the company and look into the overall efficiency. This is the activity which sets standards and then measures the company's performance against standards.

Finally, a word about personnel. It is hard to fit personnel into the task service or control areas. At first sight, a personnel department or section looks superfluous as managers have the right and know-how to pick subordinates for their departments. On closer examination, it becomes apparent that a personnel department is essential to the overall performance of the organization. This department is not only concerned with hiring and firing but with the whole scope of the use of human resources in the company. The company structure can be built up around the task activities; aids to decision-making can be found with electronic machines; but the final decisions, policy directives and orders are made by people, and action is carried out by people. No matter which theory predominates – classical, behavioural or systems – the organization must be filled with people, with all the unpredictable behaviour this entails. The company will ultimately survive and grow on the strength of its human resources. It is through the personnel department that the motivational aspects of work can be fixed, look after labour relations in a co-ordinated fashion, lay down policy for handling discipline and grievances and institute training.

INFORMATION FLOWS IN A TRANSPORT COMPANY

Let us now return to the task activity and look at the flow of information between the various activities, using a unit of freight as an example.

The shipper or consignee of the freight will contact the company about the intended journey, how the freight can be loaded, the size of the consignment, the type of commodity and packaging and any special handling requirements. The consignment of freight is booked for loading and the information sent to the documentation section. The freight is collected, checked, loaded and despatched.

The flow of information between the various sections in the company can be illustrated as in Fig. 3.4. The arrows on the lines indicate the direction in which the information has to pass. Most of the information and communications in the action activity are concerned

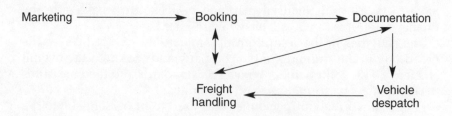

Figure 3.4 *Information flow in task function*

with the physical process of helping the flow of goods or people through the system.

Information will have to flow from all company sections and the outside environment into the planning activity, as illustrated in Fig. 3.5.

The personnel section will want information from all sections of the company on the ever changing human needs of the organization.

Information flow diagrams can be drawn for each function. By outlining the parts of communication within an organization between different departments and highlighting the areas where information is required, a picture of enormous complexity is constructed. If these flow diagrams are superimposed on each other, a picture of utter chaos seems to emerge though a three dimensional model would make the picture clearer. What these diagrams illustrate is the problems confronting people in an organization when trying to control the flow of information and communications so that they all work towards the objectives of the company. It also serves to expose the problems of the rigid classical structure.

One factor which does arise from attempts to show the flow paths of information and decisions is the importance of the type of people who fill the management positions in a company. For the company to be successful, all the human resources must be utilized in the best possible way. A square peg will not fit easily into a round hole, and, though it is not always as easy as behavioural theories would have us believe, to tailor the people/task exactly, there is a great need for a careful selection process to get the right type of people. Conflict arises in the job situation when the role image of the person undertaking the task does not fit the role image of the task held by the higher management. This conflict can be mitigated by job evaluation exercises where an explicit idea is formed of the nature of each task and the type of person required to carry out the task.

There must be a policy of getting people to ensure their objectives are in line with the company's objectives. The pressures on people at

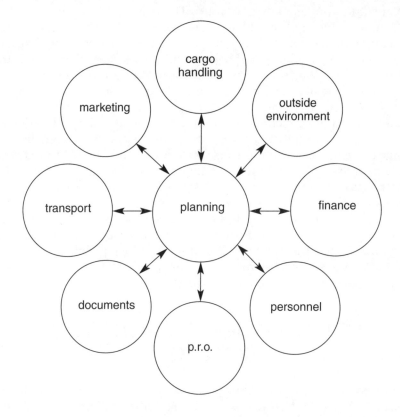

Figure 3.5   *Information flow to task function*

work are many and varied but a great many problems in the work place stem from people not being able to perceive that the company policy is in their interests.

This is particularly true in a strict hierarchical departmental structure where formal information transfer and communications with other departments only takes place through the departmental heads. If people at all levels can be shown that the overall objectives of the company are enhanced by the free flow of information, the communications flow will be freer from interruption. The problem is most apparent when workers in one department perceive that information supplied to another department is being used by the second department to enhance their own status rather than meet the objectives of the company.

It must be remembered that people rarely work as individuals in an organization but as part of a group. The company structure and the informal system will establish boundaries within which the group must operate in order to carry out the tasks that the organization sets the group. These groups will have an internal system that is built up around the personnel and their relationship to each other. It is very important to relate the internal aims and expectations of the group to the aims of the company.

Miller and Rice[13] point out that people may have difficulty in accepting the definition of their primary task as it is seen by the management: 'Groups tend consciously or unconsciously to redefine their primary tasks. Not infrequently irrational refusal to accept obviously rational solutions may be described as a failure to agree upon the obvious primary task. Workers, for example, may frequently oppose the introduction of lighter work and better wages. This irrational opposition is seen to have convincing logic only when it is recognized that the workers' definition of their primary task is to preserve the social system giving them satisfaction and security, rather than the carrying out of production.'

ORGANIZATION STRUCTURES IN PRACTICE

The objective of any transport organization is to facilitate the movement of people and/or goods. In terms of structure and control, this in itself causes problems. Unlike many other industries, a large part of the structure moves physically from place to place with the attendant difficulty with communications. As an example, we can look at the ship's crew.

In many instances, the ship group's primary task is seen differently by those in the shore office and by those on the ship. Let us take as an example a ship that has been worked hard for many months, giving very little time for crew relaxation, which arrives in port not long before a Bank Holiday weekend. There is a good chance, given co-operation and hard work on the part of the crew, that the ship can turn round and sail before the weekend. The prime objective of the shipping company is to have the ship at sea over the weekend instead of lying idle in port. Subconsciously, the ship group may accept the objectives of the shipping company but, if they are mentally and physically tired, they will see their main task as getting rest and relaxation. As Downard points out, ways must be found of integrating the ship group into the main organization structure to avoid this feeling of 'them and us'.

British Rail

The Railway Act 1993 and the Transport Act 2000 changed the structure of the railway industry by transferring British Rail assets into private ownership. The 1993 Act was intended to encourage profit seeking entrepreneurs into running railway services and to transfer the burden of financing the railways from the state sector to the private sector. The 1993 Act created:

1. Railtrack to own, maintain and operate the infrastructure charging train operating companies for the use of the infrastructure.
2. 25 train operating companies to provide train services.
3. Three rolling stock leasing companies to own the rolling stock and lease these to the train operating companies.
4. The Rail Regulator supervising competition between the operating companies and regulating Railtrack charges.
5. The Franchising Director who supervises the franchising of rail services to the operating companies.

The Transport Act 2000 set up the Strategic Rail Authority to deliver the government's Strategic Plan for the railways including meeting the government's performance targets. In addition the Strategic Rail Authority took over the responsibilities of the Franchise Director.

These Acts of Parliament have changed the railways from a one-company structure, where everything was under unified control of a central management, to a very dispersed structure with many companies connected to each other in the running of the railways by contracts and licences. Each of the separate companies has their own distinct company structure. Some commentators in the media and many politicians have commented that the structure has had serious consequences for safety on the railways.

Associated British Ports

Many British ports were owned by independent railway companies but in 1948 these ports were nationalized and became part of the British Transport Commission. In 1962, the BTC was abolished and the British Transport Docks Board was formed to manage the 31 ports of varying sizes. During the 1960s and 1970s some of the smaller ports were sold and Associated British Ports Holdings plc was formed in 1983 under the terms of the Transport Act 1981 to administer the remaining 19 ports.

The ports are divided into four groups, with the head office in London taking overall responsibility for the organization's broad financial, personnel and marketing policies. It is also the responsibility of the HQ to undertake negotiations with major customers, trade unions and large investors.

For day-to-day decision-making, there is a high degree of decentralization, with the port managers being responsible for the efficient running of their own ports. The management team take decisions on commercial, financial and personnel matters at port level and each port is organized as a profit centre. The group offices provide certain common services for the ports in their areas.

London Transport

London Regional Transport was created by the London Regional Transport Act 1984 removing responsibility from the Greater London Council (itself abolished in 1985).

London Regional Transport is divided into five divisions as shown in Fig. 3.6. Each bus division has a general manager at its head. The structure is designed to improve the system, reduce cost and improve efficiency, encourage private sector involvement and produce better management via smaller operating divisions.

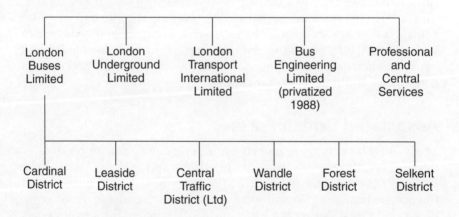

Figure 3.6 *London Regional Transport*

References

1. Hanson and Wiseman *Parliament at Work* Greenwood Press, London, 1976
2. Aldcroft, D.H. *British Transport Since 1914* David and Charles, Devon 1975
3. Sisk and Williams *Management and Organisation* South Western Publishing Co., Cincinnati 1981
4. Dale and Michelon *Modern Management* Methods Pelican, London 1969
5. O'Shaughnessy, J. *Business Organisation* George Allen & Unwin, London 1966
6. Handy, C.B. *Understanding Organisations* Penguin, England 1976
7. Keys, P. and Jackson, M. *Managing Transport Systems* Gower, England 1985
8. McGregor, D. *The Human Side of Enterprise* McGraw-Hill, New York 1960
9. Downard, J.M. *Managing Ships* Fairplay Publications, London 1984
10. Wiley, J.R. *Airport Administration* ENO Foundation, Connecticut 1981
11. Smith, D. Odegard, J. and Shea, W. *Airport Planning and Management* Wadsworth Publishing Co., California 1984
12. Hibbs, J. *Bus and Coach Management* Chapman and Hall, London 1985
13. Miller, E.J. and Rice, A.K. *Systems of Organisation*, Tavistock Publications, London 1967
14. Ballou, R. *Logistics Management* Prentice Hall, New Jersey 1973

4

Management Functions and Policy Formation

In Chapter 3, we discussed the concepts of organizational theory as outlined by contemporary writers and used these theories to construct the internal organization of a typical transport company. Within any organization there are many people with the title 'manager' and in this chapter we will discuss what is meant by the term management, and apply our conclusions to the operating of transport.

DEFINITIONS

As John Downard[1] points out, there are a vast range of books written about all aspects of management. These books describe the tools of management – planning, organizing, controlling, communicating – and the restraints placed upon managers by the operating environment.

Charles Handy[2] argues that it has never been easy, even with the help of such a wide ranging literature and the many experienced people who lecture on the subject, to define what a manager is and what he does. He goes on to point out that management is a useful concept: the missing 'x' which makes resources equal output (and leads to a profit).

Definitions of the manager and the role tend to be very broad and almost useless as an aid to understanding. Changes are occurring in technology and working practices at an ever increasing rate and the manager appears to be the lynch pin in the whole process of change in society, whether working as a civil servant for the government, in some large or small private company or in a state controlled enterprise.

The manager can influence three variables in the organization:

1. The people.
2. The work and the structure.
3. The systems and procedures.

Sisk and Williams[3] write that there are three aspects to any definition of management:

1. The co-ordination of resources, for example financial, physical and personnel.
2. The performance of the managerial functions.
3. The purpose of the management function.

Their definition states: Management is the co-ordination of all resources through the process of planning, organizing, leading and controlling in order to attain the stated objectives. [All organizations must have a set of objectives or goals to work towards and the setting of these will be looked at later in this chapter.] This type of definition is universal in its application and can be applied to any group of people who set out to reach a stated goal through group efforts. It applies equally to the small, local voluntary group formed to run a community transport service for the disabled as to the large organization of an airline corporation operating in an international environment. Everybody involved works towards the same goal.

Dale and Michelon[4] put forward the proposition that every manager can profit from studying the body of knowledge developed concerning management theory. By reading about the experiences of others, a manager will help himself to a better performance of his role, and will better understand the objectives of the company and the functioning of the organization for which he works. It will shed light on how the group being managed fits with all the other groups making up the overall organization.

Peter Drucker[5] takes up the theme of the universality of management and puts forward seven tasks that the modern manager must undertake:

1. He must always manage by objectives which he himself has had a hand in shaping. Knowing that the objectives set out for him and

his group are fair and obtainable (though not necessarily easy to accomplish) will help any manager to a better performance.

2. Management is becoming a far more risky occupation and all managers must learn to handle risk analysis. (This is difficult in transport where many of the risk-inducing variables are controlled by political processes.) By analysing risks, the manager is able to set up a control system whereby his expectations are measurable against events as they happen.

3. All managers must be able to make strategic decisions concerning the future of the organization and how they can help further the objectives of the organization.

4. Managers are responsible for setting up a team which can help them to satisfy the demands of the organization. In large organizations the functions of training, recruitment and development may be handled by specialist personnel departments but management must have some input into the process if the right people for their team are to be hired.

5. One of the biggest tasks facing all managers in the future will be the handling and communicating of information. The introduction of information technology equipment into transport companies is providing managers with a great deal of data. Managers must be equipped to sift out the vital information from the merely interesting, learn to use this information to advance the company's objectives effectively, and communicate this to their subordinates.

6. Traditionally, managers in transport companies have only been expected to know one or two aspects of that company's business but there is a growing need to appreciate the business as a whole and the part that the manager plays in the whole enterprise.

7. More and more, transport managers can no longer rely on a knowledge of their own particular mode. They will have to look at developments outside their mode especially economic, political and social developments that affect transport world wide. The bus industry manager contemplating the deregulation of his industry in the UK should study how the industry is organized and regulated elsewhere in the world and the effects of deregulation on domestic air services in the USA. The developing countries' shipping services would be well advised to study and understand the results of control in the international air transport sector.

Management is not an exact science like mathematics and there are no concrete sets of rules that can be laid down and learnt to be used in any circumstances. In other words, it is not possible in management to say: 'If I do X and Y, Z will automatically follow.' What can be said is that, from past experience and using the best analytical tools available: 'If I do X and Y, it is highly probably that Z will result.' It is possible to assess what is involved in taking steps X and Y and the probability of Z resulting. From any analysis of this nature, the worthwhileness of undertaking any course of action can be calculated.

Management is needed to run the business, to make sure that the organization moves towards the objectives set out in the plans. Management is also responsible for the success or failure of the business, whether it be a small provincial airline or a great international shipping company.

Whenever and wherever a group of people join together to pursue some stated objective, management is needed to direct and co-ordinate the efforts of the individual group members. It is often necessary for individual members of any action oriented group to subordinate their individual aspirations so that the group can reach its goals. To make the efforts of a group of individuals effective, management has to provide leadership and co-ordination to ensure everybody in the group works towards the stated objectives.

As we have already noted, there are many ways to look at management. Some of the writers dwell on the implications of management style – autocratic, democratic, bureaucratic, etc – and which style best suits the type of situation the manager is administering. Others write about management types – management by crisis, by default, by procrastination, etc – and how these methods of management interact with the problem-solving role of the manager. Peter Drucker believes that the key to good management lies in setting objectives, managing by results, and that managers learn best by learning to manage themselves before telling others. C.B. Handy finishes his book on management by giving advice that the only way to understand about management is to work as a manager and then write about it!

Again as we have already found out from this review of other writers, management is difficult to define, but we must try if we are to understand it. Downard suggests that one of the common strands in all attempted definitions is responsibility. Management overall is responsible for something, that responsibility being directed with and through other people.

In the past it was felt by many people that managers and leaders were born not made, and the concept of a hereditary aristocracy with all its nepotism and waste of talent it still prevalent in certain parts of the world and in certain professions – even in so-called democracies with supposed equal opportunities. Today, the majority of managers are trained and allowed to develop in the job. In transport, management means working with other people but it still requires the ability to make the right decisions from among a number of alternatives. The ability to make the right decision is gained through training and experience in using and developing the electronic aids to management. The manager has to make the decisions about the future requirements from an ever changing systems development, always with the fear that whatever he installs today will be outdated very soon.

Managers spend a large proportion of their time dealing with personnel matters, especially with how to help their staff cope with the subject of 'change'. In transport these changes in operating practices, employment levels and skill needs are often forced on the organization by outside bodies such as government departments, trade unions, professional bodies or pressure groups. The transport manager often has very little choice about whether to co-operat and obey their instructions – whether he believes the effect will be beneficial to his organization or not.

In Chapter 3, we looked at transport from an organization point of view, seeing the manager as part of the company structure. From this viewpoint, it would appear that managers undertake widely different jobs both in content and scope. Head of finance fits into an entirely different world than head of engineering. From this it would seem that it is impossible to discuss any general functional aspects of management but should concentrate on accounts or engineering.

However, Sisk and Williams point out that it is necessary to consider management as a process. If we look closely at what managers do every day, we can identify certain functions that all managers perform no matter what their exact job title. To make the study easier, each of these functions will be looked at as a distinct part of the process. Obviously, all of the functions may be performed at the same time and are part of a continuous process. The functions interact, but it is important to look at them separately. They can be categorized under various headings, but I will follow the pattern used in many other books, namely: planning, organizing, staffing, direction, control, innovation, representation, and communication.

PLANNING

Planning is generally regarded as one of the primary functions of management because it is the first function that has to be performed.

Planning encompasses all the tasks of management; the results of planning are plans which lay down the guidelines for action within the organization and serve as signposts for the organization's progress towards the fulfilment of its objectives.

Planning is an activity that is carried out at all levels in the organization. In fact it is fundamental to life itself, essential to everyday living. Consciously or unconsciously, we all plan our activities over time and use these plans to assess our performance in fulfilling our personal objectives.

At the top level of the organization, the overall objectives are worked out. From these strategic objectives, each manager has to plan how his actions can fulfil his designated part of the plan. This he will have to do through the group which he leads. He has the responsibility to make sure that his part is fulfilled so that the rest of the organization can reach its own planning goals.

Planning is not the strict prerogative of management, especially in transport. For example, each truck driver must plan his intended journey so that the goods he has to deliver arrive safely and to time.

The fundamental objective of any organization must be to survive, unless the group was formed to carry out one specific task and is then disbanded on fulfilment. In transport, as in any other industry, this means making a profit, ie income from whatever source must be greater than expenditure.

Each transport company must decide how, with regard to the sector of the industry and the operating environment, it can fit into and find a place in the market sector. For example, the company may decide that it is in the business to produce a very high quality passenger service catering for a very selective clientele at a premium price. On the other hand, the company may decide to provide a service carrying low value freight with a minimum quality of service. (The making of company plans and how the theory relates to transport operations is considered in detail later in the chapter.)

For the manager, planning is carried out in three stages:

1. Collect, analyse and set down all the relevant facts which have a bearing on the plan. This exercise enables the manager to have some certainty about the objectives of his plan and its feasibility.
2. Consider all the facts and work out the alternative courses of action which will fulfil the objectives of the plan.
3. Choose the best course of action in the light of all the facts gathered in 1 and considered in 2. It must be recognized that actions by one section of an organization will affect the actions of other sections. The best solution for a section may not be the one that produces the best results for the company as a whole.

There are many techniques available to help managers assess the likely outcome of different courses of action but, in many cases, the number of variables involved are such that the result of actions may still be uncertain. In these circumstances, the final decision on action will, to a large extent, depend on the experience and gut feeling of the manager making the decision. Often the room for action is limited by the constraints placed upon the organization by bodies outside the manager's control, and the reaction of these bodies to any proposals.

The plan must therefore be flexible, enabling the manager to change aspects as the plan unfolds. Planning is very much an on-going activity that does not cease with the publication of the corporate plan.

ORGANIZING

In the context of management functions, organizing is the dividing of work into manageable tasks. This process includes determining the specific activities necessary to accomplish the objectives of the organization, grouping the activities according to some logical pattern, and then assigning these grouped activities to the responsibility of a position or a person in the organization.

All companies tend to have a broad outline of the organization structure, as was seen in Chapter 3 for a transport company. It is the manager's function to make sure that the activities for which he or she is responsible are organized within his or her group. It is important that the group fits with the rest of the groups making up the organization, and that their efforts are all focused on the company's objectives.

It becomes obvious that any manager needs to organize the working group in such a fashion that the set tasks will be carried out efficiently and that the work load on individual people is as fair as possible. He or she has to make sure that the efforts of individual people or sub-groups under his or her control are co-ordinated so that everybody's effort is directed towards the same objectives. This also includes leading his group in such a way that their efforts are co-ordinated with the rest of the company.

Any manager must be aware when organizing people and sub-groups of the influence of informal links across the formal organization structure. The informal links can have both good and bad effects on the working of the group. It is the manager's job to use the informal links to enhance their good effects when they further the objectives of the company.

STAFFING

The positions highlighted in the organization structure must be filled with people with the required skill and qualifications to tackle the tasks. This staffing is a continuous function of management because people leave to take up appointments with other companies, are promoted to other work groups, retire or are dismissed. It is up to the manager to continually update the job descriptions of the people working for him or her and to ensure that these people are suited to the job that they are doing.

A major problem for all managers is being able to fill positions that become vacant in areas of national or local skill shortage. Often this can only be done against a background of local wage bidding – companies trying to attract scarce labour by offering higher wages and benefits than their competitors. This can upset the delicate balance of differential wage rates negotiated by the company. It may be necessary for the manager to take on people without all the advertised skills and help them master the job by training.

Training is an on-going part of the staffing function allowing junior management to develop and giving everybody the chance to anticipate changing technologies and working methods (see Cowling and Mailer[6] and Jinks[7]).

In large organizations, staffing and training are the responsibility of the personnel department but it is one of the tasks of management, indeed it is vital if the group is to be efficient, to liaise with the personnel department in drawing up job specifications and training programmes.

Transport staffing has two additional problems which many other industries do not have and which can restrain staffing decisions. In many cases, transport operates 24 hours a day or at every 'unsocial' hour. A lot of people see the industry as very unattractive as a career and there is a high incidence of people leaving to find other work. High labour turnover can lead to low morale and difficulties with recruitment.

As we shall see in Chapters 6 and 7, transport is one of the most highly regulated industries. This affects the discretion of the manager in hiring staff. Licences and certificates have to be held by people filling certain posts at all levels and this licensing is controlled by international, national and state bodies. It is part of the staffing function in transport for operating managers to make sure that all personnel who require them have up-to-date and valid licences.

The manning levels, ie the number of personnel needed to operate truck, bus, train, aeroplane or ship, are, in most developed countries, tightly controlled either by agreement between trade unions and employers or as the subject of legislation, leaving little room for compromise on the part of the manager. New technologies enhanced by new working methods can result in perfectly safe operation with reduced numbers of personnel but the implementation or adoption is often delayed because of protracted negotiations that have to take place before they can be started.

However, it is an important function of any manager, no matter how constrained by legislation and trade union agreement, to fill the positions under his or her control with properly qualified and licensed personnel, and make sure that they operate efficiently.

DIRECTION

Direction involves initiating the activities of a group as these are developed from the plan, laying down the order in which the tasks must be preformed and to what standard the end result should be achieved.

In much of management literature the central focus of direction is leadership. These theories are dominated by thoughts on how managers motivate their workforce to work. Part of this process which is important in transport involves encouraging those working for one to have a sense of responsibility for their particular tasks. For much of the time, transport operators are away from direct supervision of higher management and have to deal with developing situations as they arise by their own initiative.

It is felt that motivation can only be accomplished if the subordinate is instructed on the tasks to be carried out, allowed time to complete the tasks without interference and then held accountable to his superior for the results. For the manager this involves delegation and can only work if the subordinate has the necessary information, ability and authority to carry out the allotted tasks.

Direction, however, is more than leadership. It is closely related to the other management functions. The subordinates must be directed towards results that are regarded by the organization as both desirable and possible.

Direction in addition must be such that the subordinate values the reward he or she gains from work and sees the direction as fair.

CONTROL

The control function in management is very similar to the use of the word control in engineering. It means laying out standards of performance and measuring the actual performance against the standard. If there is any variance from the standard, it is a management function to take steps to investigate the variance and either correct the performance to match the standard or set new standards if the old ones prove inappropriate.

The control function calls for a continuous feedback on information on what is happening in the group. One task of the manager is to make sure that all the information gathered is relevant and useful. Much time and expense can be expended on collecting information that is interesting but of no utility.

A great many management control systems are based on measuring financial performance. This is executed by setting financial budgets and comparing the actual financial performance with the budget at the end of the control period. Budgets should be set by a process of discussion so that everybody involved has at least agreed that the budget is fair and accomplishable.

There are other control mechanisms – productivity, quality control, turnover of staff, etc.

INNOVATION

Many writers on management leave innovation to a discussion of the planning process and to the research and development department. Finding new areas of operation and integrating new technologies are part of planning. Planning need not necessarily involve innovation.

We live in an era of change – political, economic and social. The pace of change seems to accelerate at an alarming rate. Even in long-established and state protected organizations nothing stays static and organizations tend to fail if they try to stay exactly the same, working to the same methods, using the same equipment and following the same philosophy.

It is the research and development department's task to investigate and advise on new methods of operating and transporting goods and people. Equally, it is the function of management to try new procedures, new working methods and verify that their section is up to date and efficient.

By actually spending time thinking about better ways of carrying out the tasks assigned to their group, managers can gain valuable insights into the working of their group and highlight the areas that need improving.

REPRESENTATION

All people working for an organization represent that organization in some way. It is usual for top management to represent the organization to the outside world through the media, the government or other institutional bodies. Transport, being a very political subject, and affecting the social fabric of any country or community, tends to have the political spotlight focused on its activities for much of the time. There is no doubt that efficient transport brings immense benefits to a community, and it is essential to the workings of the modern world economy, as demonstrated in Chapter 1. It can have disbenefits that are used by critics to make operations, if not impossible, very difficult. It is very important that top management in transport organizations take their representative role seriously in order that the benefits of transport are explained to the general public and to counteract the criticism.

Internally in an organization, it is the manager's task to represent his or her group in discussions with other groups and to represent the organization as a whole back to the group. Managers must study and understand this representative function if they are to avoid problems when the time comes for them to carry out their representative duties.

COMMUNICATION

All the functions discussed so far are interlinked by communication. It is through communication – written, oral or electronic – that the manager manages. The ability to communicate concisely and understandably is at the heart of the management job.

The faculty to communicate ideas to the rest of the company, to give instructions to the members of the group so that they are easily understood and to communicate to individuals so that they are aware of their place in the organization and the importance of their work, is of paramount importance.

TRANSPORT MANAGEMENT

Managing a transport fleet is somewhat different to management of a number of other businesses. The main difference stems from the need for a great deal of delegation on the part of the management. The workforce, especially the drivers or vehicle crews, spend a great deal of their time away from the effective supervision of management and have to show initiative, especially in unplanned situations. This lack of control calls for a system of what could be called 'standing orders' or laid down procedures which are designed to help the driver complete the journey successfully, in line with the prevailing style of the company and to help the management retain some measure of control over their workforce. Supervision comes about by the keeping of records and comparing the records with the standards set by the management at the end of the journey. It is also helped in training the crews to carry out their tasks in an efficient and trustworthy manner.

Therefore, throughout the journey, a log must be kept of the actions taken during the journey. This log can either be in the form of written log books or by electronic recording devices. The following details should be included in the information depending on the journey and mode type: the driver, the point of departure and the destination, the route taken, start and finish times (where appropriate), passengers carried, type of freight carried and the weight of the load.

The roles and responsibilities of management are as follows:

1. Defining the job descriptions of the crew, checking competence levels and selection of the crew.
2. Defining vehicle specifications for the task in hand.
3. Setting out authorization levels and organizational requirements of the crews.
4. Setting performance targets and defining performance indicators.
5. Understanding the health and safety risks involves in the proposed journey and communicating these to the crews.

It has to be borne in mind that once the driver has left the depot, control is minimal and the management has to instill into the crews – through their instructions and training programmes – the way in which the company expects the crews to act while undertaking company business.

The role of supervision is as follows:

1. Setting out the instructions for the intended journey.
2. Checking the availability of vehicles and crews.
3. Checking the authorization for the intended journey.
4. Checking the authorization of crews and vehicles.
5. Monitoring performance and providing the first line of feedback to the management.
6. Ensuring that crews' needs on the journey are provided for.
7. Reinforcing the needs for good driver behaviour.

It has to be accepted that all of these points must be reinforced during the preparation for the journey and at the end, during the actual performance of the task, as in a factory.

The drivers or crews have some responsibilities:

1. Planning the journey in the light of the likely hazards which might be encountered.

2. Taking responsibility for the vehicle at all times they are away from the depot.
3. Making sure they fully understand the management and supervisor's expectations.
4. Providing feedback to supervisors at the end of the journey.

CORPORATE PLANNING

All organizations, as with all managers, make future plans as to which direction the organization will follow. The usual way of describing this type of activity in business is to talk to corporate planning.

Corporate planning is defined by John Argenti[8] as 'a systematic approach to clarifying corporate objectives, making strategic decisions and checking progress towards the objectives. Corporate objectives are the objectives for the organization as a whole, not parts of it; strategic decisions are decisions which affect or are intended to affect, the organization as a whole over long periods of time'.

A corporate plan is a set of instructions to managers of an organization describing what role each constituent part is expected to play in the achievement of the organization's corporate objectives.

THE NEED FOR PLANNING IN TRANSPORT

It is not very long ago that the majority of transport organizations, operating in a highly regulated environment, could count on a fairly stable market situation prevailing over an extended period.

In this situation traffic fluctuations tended to be small, mainly caused by changes in the economic health of a nation or the world economic state. Most changes were gradual and took place over relatively long time scales.

Given these circumstances, planning could be a slow, leisurely affair with ample time to change direction as economic, technical and social events unfolded. Mistakes could be rectified and new policy implemented without endangering the existence of the organization. Small companies could grow slowly with any increases in demand for their services. It was possible to allow competing companies to introduce new methods and operations, waiting until all the teething troubles were overcome and the results known before changing their own style of operation.

Three factors have combined to make forward planning not only necessary but vital to the survival of even the smallest transport company:

1. The increasing range and speed of implementation of technical and social developments.
2. The growing complexity of organizing a transport service, both administratively and in recruiting the right people with the required skills and experience.
3. The growing competition in both international and domestic transport as countries move to internal deregulation of their transport industries while at the same time moving to try to protect their shipping and airline interests from foreign competition by international agreements.

Technological change

The thrust of technological change affecting transport has led to a speeding up of that very change. The main advances in technology – jet aircraft, larger ships, quicker, more comfortable trains, larger, more efficient trucks – have led to the early obsolescence of other transport vehicles. New machinery purchased by a competitor can bring gains in productivity, advantages of reduced cost and a more competitive price structure.

The result of this is that some companies can be left with outdated, costly to operate equipment which is still serviceable but a liability in the new competitive environment. The only answer for companies caught out by a competing company in this way is to suddenly change their own equipment and working practices in order to stay competitive. This can be very expensive and there is always a time lag involved.

The shortening of the life cycles of machinery and methods of operation leads to a situation where strategic decisions must be made quickly and they must be right if the company is to survive. Detailed planning within the organization must be a continuous and careful process if the company is to take advantage of any technical developments or new opportunities.

In today's climate, it is no longer possible to let a competitor introduce a new service, sort out all the teething problems and then counter with a similar service of your own. The competitive advantage gained by the company first introducing new technology can, in a very short time, result in that company's market domination, leaving competitors with unprofitable leftovers while they struggle to re-equip. Indeed, even when they have the new equipment, competing companies may find market share hard to gain because of the dominance of the other company.

At this point it is as well to remind the reader of the fact, discussed in Chapter 1, that transport services cannot be stored when demand is low. Once a service has been provided costs are incurred whether anybody uses that service or not.

An example of technological innovation and the effect that this can have on an industry when it is introduced can be illustrated by a study of the introduction of long-range jet aircraft on the North Atlantic route in the late 1950s.

The international air transport industry has seen rapid technological change since 1945, and periods of severe financial difficulties for the airlines. The problems have been caused by the speed with which new types of aircraft have been brought into service.

The absence of price competition in a highly regulated market results in competition taking place in other forms. New technological developments can create a prestigious image as well as a less costly service and therefore a premium is placed on being at the forefront of new developments. Competition becomes not a matter of the most cost-effective service but of creating an image of the company in the view of the consumer. New technologies and products enhance the company's image and thus their competitive position.

The stampede into jets was occasioned by the decision of Pan Am in 1955 to order 45 large jet aircraft. All the world's airlines took note and started to order jets without the careful planning that had gone into Pan Am's decision. In 1959, the British European Airlines chairman stated: 'The whole airline industry has gone crazy about jets but we cannot be out of the race.'

By 1961 over half the world's airline capacity was in jets but the greater speed and capacity of these aircraft led to over-capacity on many of the world's most lucrative routes. Severe financial problems resulted for many airlines. It took a number of years for these airlines to get over the drain on their financial resources occasioned by buying new types of aircraft and the losses on the retirement or sale of still serviceable and undepreciated propeller aircraft. Indeed, a large number had to rely on government help to make them viable operations once again, illustrating the perception of most governments that their national airlines are too important to be allowed to fold.

The lessons to be learnt from this episode are that only by long-term planning can technological changes be accommodated successfully and financial provision made for those changes.

Complexity of business

The faster pace of technological change and the trend towards larger organizations has made the profitable running of a business very complex.

A fundamental principle of life seems to be that over any given time period, development leads to greater specialization. In the main, this is certainly true of transport. Technological development leads to vehicles being designed to carry narrower bands of commodities of particular groups of passengers. These developments are encouraged by the belief that greater productivity will result from designs which concentrate on a few limiting factors rather than trying to satisfy the demands of often conflicting criteria.

Increasingly specialization has profound effects on the transport industry, leading to a change in the way in which transport companies are managed. As vehicles and services become more specialized, it becomes more difficult if not impossible to find employment for the equipment outside of a specific market sector. For example, there is no other task that a fully cellular container ship can perform than to carry containers, leaving the company vulnerable to a downturn in their carryings (note the problems of US lines). Road haulage companies are having to concentrate on one aspect of their industry as a result of trucks being designed to carry specific types of freight. Some people feel there is no place for the general haulier in today's market place.

Transport managers undertake long-term plans to make certain that their vehicles and services match the requirements of the consumers in the specialist market in which they operate.

The trends towards specialization in vehicles and services coupled with the advances in electronic communications and office equipment have increased the number of specialists that the average transport company has to employ. It is difficult for the traditional transport manager to organize the workload of the company so that the specialist in one area works as part of the management team rather than concentrating on the narrow confines of his specialism.

It is important that operating managers have an understanding of the specialists that they have to employ so that they can assess the contribution that each specialist can make to the achievements of the company's objectives. A different recruiting system must be employed when assessing the background of new management trainees.

In a large organization, a greater effort has to go into organizing the information flow, breaking down the barriers between departments and making everybody aware of their contribution to the company's welfare.

The larger the company and the greater the market share, the more prominent the company becomes in the public consciousness. There is a need for large transport companies to satisfy demands concerning their behaviour and practices that come from outside the organization whether from governments, trade unions, consumer watchdog bodies or pressure groups.

In order to satisfy all of these conflicting pressures, the company must have a clear idea of where it stands at the present time, where it wants to be in the future, and how it is going to progress from one to the other without upsetting its image. Only meticulous and detailed planning will enable the company to overcome these problems and survive into the future.

Competition

Transport is a very diverse industry and it may not be apparent where competition lies. It is easy to understand competition in the tramp shipping industry where price levels tend to follow these classic demand–supply theory. In the tramp market there are many small shipping companies negotiating over contracts and rates with many small cargo shippers, and thus prices are set by prevailing market conditions. If there are a large number of ships ready for hire and only a limited amount of cargo on offer, the price will be low. If there is a lot of cargo and only a few ships, the price will be high. Even in this market, government interference, vertical and horizontal integration of large multi-national companies, and the use of flags of convenience distort the competitive picture.

It is often written that railways have no competition from other railways, running as they do on exclusive track, though in some parts of the world there is intense competition between railway systems. However, railways compete for passengers and freight with trucks, buses, ships, inland waterways, airlines and the private car.

Changes in technology in one mode can alter the balance of competition between modes. Government legislation can quickly alter the market environment. The railways in the UK were suddenly faced with fierce competition from long-distance coaches after the British government changed in the law in 1980. Again in the UK, the scheduled bus sector has been transformed by the passing of a bus deregulation Act from an industry which was highly regulated and virtually free from competition to one where competition can now flourish.

Competition calls for continuous planning if the company is to survive into the future.

Policy formation

It is a very obvious but frequently overlooked part of the planning process in any transport organization to ask the question as to what business the organization is really undertaking. It is of fundamental importance to define the answer to this question before going on to make plans for the future. Until a company understands the business it is trying to run, it is impossible to lay down guidelines on how to set targets for the future so that measurement can be made of the organization's progress towards its goals. We all have to know the point from which we are setting out before we make a journey so that we can plan the route and anticipate any problems.

A transport company's management has to be wary when answering this question of what business the company is running. On the one hand, by answering the question in too narrow a way, the company can constrain their room for manoeuvre in looking for new opportunities for expansion and change in the future. Company employees will be guided to concentrate on too narrow an outlook with regard to the company's field of operation. For example, a bulk haulage company could define its business objective as the bulk haulage of petroleum whereas they would be better served by having the objective of carrying bulk liquid products.

On the other hand, the business can be too loosely defined as a transport company when the management expertise is much narrower. This lack of direction and clear-sighted definitions can divert managers' attention away from areas where their knowledge is an advantage into areas which have little real hope of success.

The answer to any question such as 'What business are we in?' is not such a simple and easy proposition as some writers lead people to believe. Finding the answer requires a great deal of research, analysis and thought.

Having satisfactorily answered the question of 'What business are we in?', the next stage is to ask the further question. 'What business do we wish to be in in the future?'. On the answer to this question depends all the future planning process that the organization undertakes. By its very nature, planning means looking into the future and deciding what market sector the company will aim to serve, and the corporate planning process is the means used to make these decisions.

One way to illustrate the initial process is to draw a simple graph showing the company's current performance projected into the future (Fig. 4.1). As Fig 4.1 shows, a graph of present trends can be projected into the future to give a picture of the situation, all other things being equal, at the end of the planning period. This is what would occur if the company carried on in much the same way. By plotting an objective position over the planning time scale, in this case five years, it becomes obvious if there is a difference between the objective and the projected. The closing of the resultant gap is what corporate planning is all about.

Of course, in practice the model is far more complex because this presentation does not take into account the interaction of the variables but it is useful in illustrating the point I am making.

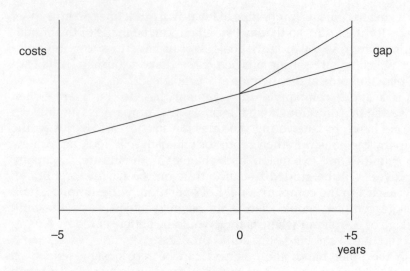

Figure 4.1 *Projections of future trends*

Objectives of a plan

There are three main objectives of a corporate plan:

1. To enable the business to survive in a competitive environment by introducing new methods of operation, new services and new technologies before the old ones become obsolete and uncompetitive. This will enable the company to remain competitive, to survive in the market place and grow, if that is desired.
2. To make a profit so that the various parts of the system can be replaced as they become worn out or obsolete, and to invest in new services. Profit in many transport undertakings is difficult to define, especially if it is looked at from a private business point of view. By profit is meant an excess of revenue over expenditure no matter where the revenue comes from – ticket sales, freight charges or some other source like operating subsidies or capital grants. In this sense all transport organizations must make a profit or the organization will become bankrupt.

   If any company can achieve success, satisfaction will be felt by all who have a stake in the business. (This is one of the reasons why in many countries subsidy is a word that is never used but some other form of words found to explain the giving of taxpayers' money to a transport company to cover loss-making services. The subject of subsidy is dealt with in Chapter 9.)

(a) The shareholders, whether private individuals, the government or local authorities, gain satisfaction from success because of the higher dividends that are likely to be paid.

(b) The managers gain satisfaction from managing a successful company and the added status this will give them in the community. For some of the higher management this will most likely make them more powerful.

(c) The employees gain satisfaction by identifying with a well-run and recognized company, with the prospect of stable employment and higher rewards for their efforts.

(d) The consumers gain satisfaction from the higher service that results from investment in new methods or technology.

3. One of the most important aspects of the process is that the plan is not only a look into the future but a guide to the direction of the company. It lays down signposts and sets out check points. It is the way in which the company's performance can be measured, it is used to test the soundness of the methods employed and the fitness of the organization structure.

Planning provides both a guide to the future and the goal towards which the company must aim if it is to be successful.

Making long-term plans

Corporate planning in transport organizations must be based on satisfying customer needs. It is people who sit on seats in trains, buses and aircraft. Other people make decisions as to which mode or company will carry and care for their goods. As explained in Chapter 1, the demand for transport is derived, and the transport manager is in business to provide the means for people to satisfy their overall requirements by the use of transport services. A paramount part of the process is for the company to ascertain the needs of consumers in any market sector within which the company wishes to operate services. (Market research is discussed in Chapter 5.)

Consumer needs are vital but there are no certain methods of calculating these future requirements. There are many indicators of long-term trends that can be used by the planner in drawing up his or her strategy. The main trends that affect transport provision are the location of new industrial plant, the growth or decline of towns and cities, the finding of new sources of raw materials, the growth of tourism and leisure, rising affluence and the general state of national and world economies. Statistics and forecasts concerning these factors are published by international organizations, government departments, academic research institutions and private consultancy firms.

Corporate planners must become familiar with these sources and learn how to use the information they provide.

There will always be risks associated with making long-term plans, the prediction of future events being rather unscientific, but the risks involved with any action must be carefully considered. As stated before, there are operations research techniques available which can be used to assess the risk and highlight the assumptions made during the calculations. A comparison between risk and likely reward has to be made and a choice of the best policy for the company made.

Another consideration for any transport company contemplating the future is to decide whether to control the whole process or only a small part.

Vertical integration involves the company buying into or controlling operations which immediately precede or follow the main services of the company. A railway company owning buses, or a road haulage group being taken over by a shipping company are examples of vertical integration. In some countries there are laws which make vertical integration difficult if not impossible.

Horizontal integration is where a non-competitive company is set up in another area of transport. For example, a scheduled airline setting up a charter company. Diversification into other areas of transport can pose problems for the parent company in the field of management expertise. These can be overcome by training or by buying into the company experienced personnel to manage the new business. Reverse diversification has taken place in the shipping industry where large corporations have taken over shipping companies without any previous expertise in shipping. The prime example of this trend is Trafalgar House which took over Cunard. The motives for this vary but in the case of the UK the important factor was the tax advantage accruing to the take-over company stemming from the method of calculating depreciation allowances against tax.

Once the area of operation is known, the goal to set over the planning period can be ascertained. It is necessary to work back from this goal and delineate the steps that must be taken, and the times at which decisions have to be made to reach the set goal. Each of these steps can then be broken down into factors and results needed in terms of finance, manpower and equipment. Once the resource needs are known, the source of these resources can be decided, ie whether from within the company or from outside.

A revenue forecast must be made to ensure that the return on investment is adequate. No revenue forecast is possible without knowledge of likely demand. This can only be calculated by using published statistics, market research and demand forecasting techniques. It is important that as many sources of information as possible are used regarding market statistics, market trends, the extent and nature of the competition, the prevailing and future projections of costs and prices.

At this stage in the planning process it is good policy to look at all the work undertaken so far and check that any assumptions made are valid in the light of the data collected.

The plan

The factors which make up a detailed plan can be summarized as follows:

1. What course of action the company is to take in the light of all the research and forecasts which have helped lay down the objectives and focused on the direction in which the company should move.
2. How the resources are to be obtained, utilized and allocated during the life of the plan.
3. The responsibilities of each manager in relation to the various aspects of the plan enabling each manager to work towards common objectives with all the other managers.
4. A complete structure for the plan laying down when each phase must be implemented and completed, which will provide the guidance for management. This structure will help to co-ordinate the activities of the various groups involved by setting out what has to be completed before subsequent actions can be undertaken. Some form of critical path analysis will help with this co-ordination.
5. A projection of the incidence of cost for each phase in total and for each group. This is the basis of control, allowing budgets to be agreed and published. Coupled with a projection of revenue, standards can be set against which to measure performance.

The foregoing factors can be split into three distinct levels:

The strategic, which sets down the overall objectives of the company and highlights new opportunities. This has to do with the company's place in the market.
The corporate sets out the use of resources within the company.
The operations lays out in detail what each section of the organization must do to fulfil the organization's objectives. It is at the operations levels that the plan splits the overall objectives into assignments for the various groups and gives guidance through the setting of standards by which performance can be measured.

References

1. Downard, J.M. *Managing Ships* Fairplay Publications, London 1984
2. Handy, C.B. *Understanding Organisations* Penguin, London 1976
3. Sisk and Williams *Management and Organisation* Southwestern Publishing Co., Cincinnati 1981
4. Dale and Michelon *Modern Management* Methods Pelican, London 1969
5. Drucker, P. *The Practice of Management* Pan Books Ltd, London 1955
6. Cowling and Mailer *Managing Human Resources* Edward Arnold, London 1981
7. Jinks, M. *Training* Blandford Press, Poole 1979
8. Argent, J. *Systematic Corporate Planning* Thomas Nelson and Son Ltd, Surrey 1974

5

Marketing Transport

INTRODUCTION

Marketing is the management function which organizes and directs all those business activities involved with assessing customer needs and converting customer purchasing power into effective demand for a specific product or service. It is also involved with making sure the product or service is moved to the final consumer in such a way that the profit or other objectives set by the company or organization are achieved. This definition has three important implications. It is a management function within the organization which underlines and provides a framework for all the activities which the organization undertakes and it lays emphasis on the central point of putting the satisfaction of customer needs as the starting point of any business. This emphasis on satisfying needs is vital to any successful transport undertaking.

From this definition it can be seen that marketing covers a number of activities:

1. Identification of customers, their needs and wants and the various market groups and segments which exist to attempt to satisfy their needs and wants.
2. The creation, production and delivery of products and services which will satisfy those customer needs and wants.
3. Setting the correct prices in relation to the customers and to the fulfilling of the organization's objectives.

4. Communicating to the customers what products and services the organization is offering in the market place.
5. Ensuring that all activities impinging on customer relations are successful in meeting the identified customer needs.

Transport is a service industry. In other words, transport is an act or performance which is intangible and does not result in the customer owning anything. This is in direct contrast to a product which, on buying, the customer owns. There are a number of significant points which must be borne in mind when thinking about the marketing of services which makes the marketing of transport services different from product marketing.[1]

Services like transport are intangible in that customers must experience them to really know them. Service marketing is much more complex than product marketing.[2] This product cannot be defined as easily as tangible goods and the whole organization, including its personnel, and the physical environment serve as promoters of the service. The buyers of transport products have to look for physical evidence of service quality. Customers will have to look for evidence of service quality from the place where the transport is consumed, from the people running the transport, from the state of the equipment, from publicity material issued by the transport organization or an intermediary, from the organization's symbols and from the price they are asked to pay.

Transport services are typically produced, purchased, used and evaluated at the same time. In other words, the customer buys a ticket, sits on a bus, undertakes the journey and gets off the bus to fulfil some objective. The customer cannot try the bus journey without consuming it. Thus, the organization and the customer interact throughout the process and the production of the service is not only visible to the customer but often requires, or is the result of, customer participation. Since the customer is present when the service is being produced, the interaction between customer and provider is vital to the success of the venture. In this way, both the provider and the customer can effect the service outcome by their behaviour.

There are problems in making sure that the transport service is being delivered in a manner consistent with the way it was originally planned. It is difficult to achieve standard output from a transport service. Even though standard systems, vehicles and personnel can be used, the other variables in providing a transport service are so many, each unit of the service may differ to a lesser or a greater extent than the other similar units. The customers' expectations, however, are that the service should be performed in a consistent way, these expectations being formed through service design, promotion and price. If the outcome of the journey does not match the expectation, then either the expectations were too great and have to be changed, or service performance fell below what is required.

Transport services are what is known as perishable. In other words they cannot be stored. Mistakes made in the production of a good can be corrected by inspection before the product is placed for sale or, if a mistake gets past the inspection process, it can be put right by replacement. With transport, a mistake ruins the whole product and replacement is not possible. There is in transport always the problem of fluctuating demand levels, in other words the problem of the peak. Decisions have to be made by the organization about what capacity levels the organization will make available to take account of the peak problem. In production it is always possible to store products at slack times so that peak demand can be met from a level of production schedule.

Lack of ownership is the basic difference between production industries and services. This is because when a product is purchased the buyer owns the product. With transport services, the buyer pays to use the service. It must be remembered from Chapter 1 that people use transport to satisfy their desires in other areas, in other words the derived demand nature of transport. This concept has a bearing on transport marketing.

THE MARKETING MIX

An essential part of any marketing strategy is the concept of the marketing mix. The marketing mix is the set of controllable elements with which an organization can influence customer responses to their services. A major task of the marketing management of an organization is to blend these elements in such a way that they fulfil the needs and wants of the customer. Within this framework attention must be paid to those elements over which the organization has very little control. These are factors like cultural and social differences within the market, political environment, the existing market structure, the resources and objectives of the organization and the economic environment. These variables must be recognized and the organization put into a position to respond to them by altering the marketing mix over time as the situation changes. The process of marketing mix formulation and balancing is unique to any organization marketing services but the concept is vital to an understanding of marketing strategy.

In many books the marketing mix is explained in terms of the seven 'P's', namely, Product, Price, Place, Promotion, People, Physical

Figure 5.1 *Marketing mix*

Evidence and Process.[3] In order to emphasize the importance of these variables we will deal with each separately.

Product

The initial stage of any attempt to market a transport service must be to try to ascertain the business which the organization is in. This question should have been answered during the corporate planning process as explained in Chapter 4. The transport product requires the consideration of the range, quality and level of service provided. In addition to these there is the question of branding and after-sales service which have to be taken into account. Branding is the situation where customers perceive significant differences in your product over the market as a whole. There is always a question as to whether the concept of branding can apply to transport.

Price

All organizations must set a price at which they are willing to sell their service. Price considerations include levels of prices, discounts, allowances and commissions, terms of payment and credit. It must be remembered that in transport, price is one of the major influences on buyer choice. Many areas of transport offer standard products and the customer often perceives price as the sole indicator of service quality. There are other aspects of consumer choice which are important but the level of prices, especially in a competitive market, is vital in transport. It must also be remembered that the revenue or earnings of the organization are dependent on the prices charged.

Place

Direct customer accessibility is important to transport due to the need for direct customer/organization contact. Accessibility in transport does not just mean being able to get to the transport but to other means of communication for inquiries or through intermediaries like travel agents and freight forwarders. It is important that the transport service is presented at the right place or the customer will not use the services provided but find alternative means to satisfy their needs.

Promotion

Organizations, after designing the product, pricing it and making it available, must tell their customers and potential customers that the service is available. Promotion is concerned with converting customer needs into positive patronage of the service. There are two levels of promotion. First, there are the traditional methods, like advertising and publicity. Second, there are the clues to the service, like design of the organization's building, the organization's name and logo, the contact personnel and the process of gaining access to the service.

People

The nature of transport demands that there is direct interaction between the customer and personnel representing the organization. It is because of this interaction that marketing management is involved in the operational aspects of transport, because the staff often play a critical role in the relationship between the organization and the customer. In making sure that the service is performed to meet customer needs, the marketing management must have a say in the area of employee selection, training, motivation and control.

Physical evidence

Components of the physical evidence of a service will influence customers' and users' judgement of the service that the organization is providing. Physical evidence includes elements like the physical environment, the vehicles and the personnel. The customer feel for the service is important.

Process

The behaviour of people in a service organization is vital to the success or failure of the organization. The process of how the service is delivered to the customer, its performance and how it is monitored must be a concern of the marketing management.

These seven P's represent the variables which an organization can, in the main, control and which have a great bearing on customer responses to the service. Decisions cannot be made on one element in the mix without considering the impact of that decision on the other elements.

There are some external forces[4] exerting influence which cannot be controlled in the same way as the seven P's. These can be summarized as follows:

1. *Competition.* The supplier of a transport service cannot directly control the strategies and tactics of the competition. A prediction can be made of the way in which competitors will react to any market strategy and take pre-emptive action but that is all.
2. *Commercial environment.* Lifestyles differ, social and family codes are diverse and so are the ways in which consumers decide on which service to use. For different ethnic and cultural groups the cultural environment is a significant factor in transport choice. While the basic customer need may be similar, how the customer wants that need translated into a service can be vastly different.
3. *Legal constraints.* There are laws related to health, safety, environmental issues, consumer protection and financial practice. These laws provide protection to the customer, the employee and third parties, and can affect the way in which a marketing strategy is developed.
4. *Institutions.* Institutions are those organizations which support customer rights. It is important to react to any customer representation quickly because a bad reputation can quickly affect the business.

CONCEPT OF MARKET SEGMENTATION

Marketing in transport cannot be concerned with meeting the exact requirements of all customers in a precise manner. The reason for this is that all customers have their own unique requirements and it is therefore impossible to meet these unique requirements in any mass form of transport. Marketing in transport therefore has to be a process of compromise, whereby an organization will seek to group together as many customers as possible with broadly similar wants and needs. This process is known as market segmentation.

There are three steps to the market segmentation process:

1. Finding the relevant characteristics that divide a market into smaller consumer groups. For example, by trip purpose, traveller characteristics, length of stay, type of freight, importance of time, just-in-time needs.
2. Using these characteristics to identify all the significant market segments and relating these systematically to the services each segment requires.
3. Collecting the market segments most consistent with the organization's objectives and capabilities and then choosing which market segments to serve.

The market segmentation process determines an organization's competitors. The organization has to research the competition and decide how best to position the organization in that market sector. This is called positioning and is the act of designing the organization's image so that the customers understand what the organization stands for in relation to its competitors.

THE EXTENDED ROLE OF MARKETING IN A TRANSPORT ORGANIZATION

In order to satisfy customer needs in transport, the organization must first understand customer expectations of the service and match these to the actual experience when the service is provided. Internal marketing is a system of employing motivated and customer conscious staff. Staff need to appreciate that they are part of the service and they must be encouraged to perceive the service as their service, which makes them committed to the organization's goals. Employees will be more committed to customer satisfaction if they realize what impact and control they have over it.

In the enthusiasm for marketing new products and services, marketing to existing customers must not be forgotten. This is used to convince them to use the service more often and to create loyalty to the organization. It must be remembered that it is often more cost effective to hold onto customers who already use the service, because they often represent a good opportunity for profit growth and an increasing market share. It is also important to take account of the way in which transport services are publicized through customer to potential customer contacts, so keeping existing customers satisfied with the service and aware of new opportunities is vital.

Another part of the marketing effort must be monitoring customer satisfaction. Customer satisfaction and quality control can only be assured through monitoring the services. Procedures should be set up to monitor the services on a regular basis.

Marketing must be based on the principle of customer service which is critical to the success of all transport. Customer service begins with the fundamental principle that the customer is the most important person in the business system. Most transport organizations use, apart from price, quality of service as a way of differentiating their service from others in the same market segments. Making sure the quality of service levels are set up and maintained and that the level of customer service is high is the main way to generate repeat business. The role of operating staff in this process is vital and training in customer handling and relations should be given to all staff who may come into contact with customers and potential customers.

MARKETING STRATEGY

A marketing strategy indicates the specific markets towards which activities in the transport organization are to be targeted and the types of competitive advantages to be exploited. The overall market strategy must be to use all the resources of the organization to identify the needs of the customers in the chosen market segment and then bring customer satisfaction from the services offered. One important aspect is to identify the organization's strengths and weaknesses (in the same way in which modal strengths and weaknesses were identified in Chapter 2) for the task the organization has set itself. The strengths can then be used to promote the better services, while the weaknesses must be recognized and overcome.

It takes a great deal of courage on the part of managers to acknowledge weaknesses in their organizations. It is far easier to discover and exploit the weaknesses of others. All managers of transport organiza-

Figure 5.2 *Market strategy*

tions operating in a competitive market can be certain that if they do not recognize their organization's weaknesses and devise a strategy to overcome them, their competitors will discover them and use that knowledge as a marketing tool. The strategy requires clear objectives and a focus in line with the organization's corporate goals. The right customers must be targeted more effectively than by the organization's competitors and the associated marketing mixes developed into programmes which successfully implement the market strategy.[5]

The marketing techniques discussed make up the components in the marketing strategy and all of them must be considered when planning to carry out a successful marketing scheme in a transport organization.

Redefining marketing to fit transport services, we can come up with the following definition: 'Getting the right sort of transport to the right place at the right time in the right quantities and at the right price.'[6]

The right sort of transport

In order to provide the right sort of transport, the organization must involve the marketing manager in the decision-making process of vehicle organization. With the trend towards specialization in transport, it is important that any transport company uses properly designed equipment for the task that they have planned. This requires investigation of market requirements for equipment, a study of what equipment is being utilized by competing organizations and research to ascertain what developments in products and equipment are likely to take place in the future. For a transport organization to be successful in a highly competitive situation, the management of that organization must make sure that the services they are offering are the services the market requires.

To the right place

The right place implies that the marketing management have a knowledge of where the market lies and who their customers and potential customers are in the market place. This requires market research to help identify customer needs as regard the location of transport services and the use of advertising and publicity to inform the customer and potential customer of the location of transport services on offer.

At the right time

The right time is part of the organization's efficiency equation. It is vital to ensure that any proposed transport service runs as promised, that delays are avoided and that the scheduled or contract timing is that required by the customer. It must be borne in mind that the customer is really interested in the safe arrival so that other desires can be fulfilled. Of paramount importance in the safe arrival is the time of arrival. Marketing practice must ensure that timings of services are such that they are attractive to the customer's needs to reach other goals than the transport itself. This has become especially important in logistics with the concept of just-in-time manufacturing.

The right quantity

The right quantity is concerned with matching the space available on the service to the demands for space at any particular time. This is a very complex transportation problem involving the economic trade-off between having vehicles in the fleet matched to the specific demands of individual services, and maybe having those vehicles under-utilized, and having flexible vehicles which can accommodate a number of different services but which do not exactly match customer requirements. The problem can only be solved by a compromise between that which would ideally suit the customer and the level and type of service which is economically prudent for the company to offer. This can be overcome by entering a dedicated transport contract, where the emphasis is on service quality to fit the requirements of the customer rather than pure economic operation. Clearly, the provision of transport services stems from people's desire to move their goods or themselves from one place to another. The nature of this demand often peaks either in one-day cycles or at more lengthy time periods. The most researched aspect of this peak problem is in urban areas where the journey to work in the morning and back home at night means great disparities in demand for public transport and for road space at different times of the day. The urban transport official has to decide whether to purchase enough capacity to cover the peak, with the problem of under-utilization at off-peak times, or to only cater for average loads with the subsequent deterioration in service quality and levels due to overcrowding or long waits for passengers. This question also arises in vehicle purchasing decisions: acquiring vehicles fitted for peak operation or for average loads. These problems can only be overcome to a great extent with a thorough knowledge of the services required by the customer, the financial viability of the organization and the organization's operating philosophy.

The right price

The price charged for any transport service is the result of a number of factors dependent on the service mix that the customer requires. Of importance is an understanding of how much the customer would be willing to pay for any rise in service quality. It is of no benefit to any transport organization to run a service where the costs of operation far outweigh the likely revenue, unless the management have some strong evidence that the resulting goodwill earned will lead to more revenue in the future, or add to the revenue earned from some other part of the system. (Obviously included in the term revenue is any subsidy or revenue support payment paid by the government or any other body.) On the other hand it is not good practice to fully cost a service and then still run this service if the price that brings a financial return to the company is so high that the customer cannot afford to travel or the goods cannot absorb the transport cost in the final selling price.

In defining a marketing strategy, all the inter-relationships in the marketing mix between the various elements must be understood and used to enhance the attractiveness of the transport service. This can be a problem area. Measuring how much of an organization's success can be attributed to individual elements in the marketing mix requires very complex analysis. It can be done using the latest 'multi-variate' analysis techniques but this is time consuming and needs trained personnel: it is usually not cost effective. It is often only possible to say whether the overall approach is correct or incorrect.

In essence, what the marketing manager has to do when devising a market strategy is decide on the transport needs of the chosen market segment, ascertain the price/quality criteria for that market segment and arrange the information requirements. The simple flow diagram in Figure 5.2 (page 117) illustrates the factors which make the market strategy. As this shows, when building the strategy, any transport organization must endeavour to become completely familiar with the market segment in which they are operating or in which they plan to operate.

Information is required on the type of consumer, the size of the market and the relative standing of competing organizations. It is also essential to gain an insight into the market potential, ie the size of the latent demand for services which could be activated by a careful combination of price and quality.

As can be seen from diagram 5.2 the process relies on the collecting and analysing of data:

1. The *true costs* to the organization of operating services in the chosen market sector, including capital costs, labour costs, over-head costs and running costs. These should then be compared with the costs of the leading competitors as far as is practical.
2. The prevailing pricing policies of the leading competitors. This can be difficult in freight transport because rate levels used by any organization are closely guarded, but in passenger transport, especially scheduled, it is easier.
3. It is imperative to keep under review the type of equipment used by competitors and any new developments in the equipment used.

MARKET RESEARCH

Elvey states that 'market research involves the systematic collection and interpretation of all relevant data about the demand for an organization's services and the means of satisfying that demand.' Market research which is undertaken for manufacturing companies, which involves testing the products in the market place, may not be suitable or relevant for a transport organization, but market research is important.

The marketing process must be continuous, with each cycle starting and finishing with an analysis of the potential market and the organization's position in that market. The reason why the process must be repeated regularly is that markets are dynamic, not static. Markets are ever changing due to the efforts of all the organizations seeking to serve that market segment and to external factors. There are those social, economic, technical, political, international and competitive forces which are linked, directly or indirectly, to the markets for transport.[7] Because of the dynamic nature of the market for transport, marketing managers must have continually updated information which is accurate in order to set the right strategy to meet customer needs and competitive pressures.

Of overriding importance for market research is to find out why a customer uses one transport organization's services rather than a competitor's service.

The factors which make up the answer to this question can be grouped under three main headings:

1. *Service Quality*. The service quality, whether freight or passenger, is generally taken to mean the way in which the transport organization looks after the goods or people in its care during the journey. It is often forgotten by transport managers that quality of service plays a large part in the decisions of customers on whether the transport organization's services are patronized in a competitive market. Quality of service is difficult to define, made up as it is from a combination of factors like price, comfort and reliability.
2. *Price*. The price charged for any transport service is a product of many factors, some financial, some technological and others political. What must be remembered is that the price charged for the service is one of the most important considerations when potential customers make choices between competing services. If there are no competing services, often the price affects the decision whether to travel or not. The price charged can be distorted from the true economic cost by the use of subsidies or economic regulation. Price, however, has always to be considered in relation to the quality of service on offer.
3. *Image*. Brand loyalty is well known for products but it is less well known in a service industry like transport. It is important that brand loyalty is built by transport companies so that customers make repeated use of the services on offer.

A great deal of marketing information is available to transport managers from within their own organizations. The precise nature of the services offered by the organization or the mix of different types of operation can be found from organization records. Existing customers can be classified according to the type of service they use, the extent of usage and the profitability of carryings. Periodic analysis can give insights into changes in customer profiles.

This is entirely different from finding out the customer's specific requirements for any future transport service but, by analysing the different types of traffic and how profitable each type is, the organization has the basis for comparisons between different traffics and some knowledge of the likely effect on the organization's business of changing customer profiles.

In order to find out what will be the customer requirements in the future and to plan a strategy for meeting changing customer needs and wants, the organization must undertake market research. Only very large organizations can afford to use a market research company or employ their own staff to carry out market surveys. If a small organization has exhausted the amount of time its staff can spend on research, both internal and external, but still wants an in-depth market survey, there is no choice but to go to some outside agency. Small firms could approach a local college for help. Some transport professionals tend to be rather sceptical about the results of in-depth market surveys and this is understandable when the organization operates in a limited local market. What an outside agency can do is devote their whole time on collecting and analysing the data about competition, prices, contracts, changing customer demands and report on the changes in the organization which will result from particular proposed service changes. One of the things that has to be identified is who is actually responsible for the decision to change patronage from one transport provider to another, how these decisions are taken and when. A lot of careful planning can be wasted if the message about changes never reaches the person in the target market who has the authority, power and day-to-day responsibility for making decisions on transport usage.

Market research must, however, be seen as part of the total business effort. The findings and conclusions must be presented in such a way that they can be easily interpreted by operating management. Only if the decisions based on market research are seen as part of the organization's objective achieving process, will changes envisaged be accepted by the operating management.

There are problems which make market research more difficult in the freight business than in the passenger business. Answers must be found to questions about who the customer really is – is it the consignee or the consignor who makes the decision about modal choice? This question is very important. The person who books the space could be a clerk comparing transit times and prices or the logistics director whose position in the organization depends on the organization's investment in its own transport fleet. The approach adopted when seeking business from these two people must be different.

PRICING THE SERVICE

The price charged for the service is the instrument by which the organization seeks to fund its activities and ultimately gain a financial return on investment in the form of a profit. The correct pricing decision for each of the services on offer can be the difference between the success or failure of the business.

The factors which have a direct bearing on the prices charged are bound up with marketing, namely demand, elasticity and cost.

The various characteristics of demand all have effects on the pricing of a service. The variability of demand combined with the provision of capacity to meet peak demands results in the under-utilization of capital equipment and staff at off-peak times. The expenditure on vehicles and other equipment can be considered as a sunk cost. This means that the operation will be paying for the vehicles and other equipment over their planned lifetime, regardless of whether they are being used or not. The only profitable way to recover these costs is through productive use. Hence the well-established transport industry maxim that it is better to use the investment and put any revenue towards overheads. As long as the revenue exceeds the additional running costs, a contribution is being made towards sunk costs and is preferable to an idle vehicle.

The multiplicity of demand patterns affects pricing decisions because different people use transport for different reasons and therefore have different reactions to pricing levels. It is essential for the operator to know how these variations of price for the services on offer affect the level of business. If there is no elasticity, it would be bad practice to reduce prices because no extra business would result. The only certainty would be a loss of revenue. If there is some elasticity, a knowledge of this will enable an operator to charge the correct price.[8]

From the foregoing it must be concluded that the price charged for the service is but one input into the marketing mix. It is very difficult to measure the importance of price in getting a potential customer to use the service.

INFORMING THE CONSUMER

Having analysed the market sector and planned how best to meet the needs of that sector, the company must devise the best method of informing potential consumers of the planned service. Any operator can plan the best service to meet the needs of a large market, and determine the price which will both satisfy the need for a return on investment and which the customer is prepared to pay, but unless potential customers know that the service is available, they will be unable to use it. It is one of the tasks of the marketing department to inform potential customers of the service and persuade them to use it.

Marajo[9] puts forward six promotional objectives for a transport company:

1. To create awareness of a company's services among potential users.
2. To generate detailed knowledge of the company's products and services.
3. To improve the company's image among existing and potential users so as to improve the customers' attitude towards the company.
4. To eliminate perceive misconceptions.
5. To advise existing and potential customers of special offers or modifications to the services.
6. To advise the market place of new sales channels.

It is as well to remind the reader of what it is that a potential customer wants from a transport company. At the operational level the requirement is a seat or cabin, some cubic space in a freight vehicle or inter-modal transfer facilities at a transport terminal. It is this that is costed and paid for but, as we have seen before, above this the customer requires a safe arrival.

There are two factors involved in informing the potential customer – company image and advertising. These can be broken down into sub-sectors such as personal selling, press advertising, public relations, etc.

Company image

Before we address the subject of advertising, it is important to look at the subject of the company's image. A great many of the potential customer's impressions of any transport company are based on the sight of the company's vehicles and operating staff.

All members of the staff who have contact with potential customers have an important role to play in promoting the company. This is especially true of the telephone switchboard operator, who in many cases is a potential customer's first contact with the company. As John Silberman recommends, 'A customer on the telephone must be greeted cheerfully, promptly and helpfully, stating the name of the company and avoiding the "hold on" situation. Once the caller has been connected to an enthusiastic negotiator who can answer the customer's queries, the customer will gain a feeling that he is important. This sense of personal treatment is vital because there is nothing worse than making a customer feel that he is not important. This making customers feel important is a "need" just as basic as the safe arrival and must be satisfied on the first contact with the company.'

Many potential customers' first impressions concerning a company are based on the sight of that company's vehicles. This is true as much for a large international airline as for a one-man road haulage business. The vehicles must be used to promote the company's image and should as far as possible always be clean and well maintained. Dirty or badly looked after vehicles allied to scruffily dressed employees cannot fail to give a bad impression. One has only to contrast the vehicles of firms with good reputations with those of poor reputation to see the truth of this statement.

The image of the company can likewise be enhanced or damaged by the design and layout of the company's documents. Stationery should be clean and simple with the identification of the sender clearly shown. The identification of the company is often served by a 'logo' which is used on the vehicle, in advertisements and on all documents. Of course, documents are not mainly concerned with creating an image: their main purpose is to convey information. This information should be set out clearly, concisely and making sure that the recipient will understand.

Finally, public relations and promoting a favourable public image is something that the transport operator cannot ignore.[10] The nature of transport, the image in the public mind, have far-reaching effects on the community. The dilemma of 'living with the costs of transport' has to be recognized by the operator. A great many people are against the inconveniences ('disbenefits' to economists) of many forms of transport in their locality but are quite prepared to reap the benefits of the overall system. It is part of the operator's responsibility through a trade association or other pressure group to counterbalance the criticisms by highlighting the enormous benefits of transport in all its forms to society. It is also important for any operator to make every effort to keep inconvenience to the public to a minimum by ensuring that vehicles, plant and equipment are well maintained and that *all* regulations are adhered to. Nothing has done more to promote a bad image of the road haulage industry world wide than noisy, dirty lorries trailing smoke around the countryside, paying scant regard to traffic regulations or other road users.

Advertising

Advertising is the use of paid messages communicated through the 'media'; as Elvey says, 'when we think of advertising it is natural for our thoughts to turn immediately to the promotion of consumer goods. It is in this form that it appears to dominate our daily lives. It is a mistake, however to overlook its importance for all commercial enterprise.'

It should always be remembered that advertising alone does not sell a product, especially a transport service. At best, its function is to stimulate interest among potential customers. It is therefore important that advertising is fully linked with other elements of the marketing mix in trying to achieve customer satisfaction.

Advertising to fill passenger facilities must be centred on creating attitudes in the minds of potential users about the type and nature of the service on offer. There are a number of factors that must be pursued at the same time.

Of over-riding importance is to make all potential consumers aware that the service exists and that it fulfils some need of the consumer. This involves enabling people to recognize the service whenever it is seen. This is achieved by the use of identification symbols and co-ordinating these symbols with the advertising campaign. Some part of the campaign must be directed at persuading people to try the service. This must be linked to a knowledge of what the type of passenger the service is aimed at requires from the company. Lastly, advertising must endeavour to retain the customer's loyalty to the service by making customers want to use the service again and again.

Scope

The scope for advertising will depend on the number of factors. The market segment at which the advertising is to be directed is one of the most important ones. The social status of the people the advertisement is seeking to influence will affect the choice of media to be used. This target group will affect the type of information to be presented, the emphasis of the copy and the timing of the advertisement. Careful selection of the promotion has, therefore, to be linked to a detailed knowledge of the potential customers' information sources and their ability to absorb information. The consumers will want to know about the service, its price in relation to quality, the reliability, flexibility and ease of gaining access. It is no good advertising economy class travel in media which is only seen by those requiring luxury and willing to pay for the privilege.

The size of the market to which the advertising is directed will affect the scope. Only when the potential market is large should advertising be directed generally at the public at large as, for example, by a railway operating company for their intercity services. In many cases, research will show that the market is restricted to particular groups or by location. In these cases the advertising must be finely targeted so that effort is not wasted.

It is not often forgotten that advertising costs money and the process must be costed to make sure that the money spent is repaid by patronage. It is very difficult to measure the effectiveness of advertising in terms of increased revenue but it is possible through surveys and other techniques. Companies must attempt to measure the amount and cost of advertising needed to put the desired message before the public. Only if it is judged that the costs involved are justified should an advertising campaign be mounted.

Freight advertising

In contrast to passenger transport, freight companies have a problem in trying to advertise their services. It is often stated that the advertising needs are different because the market is more segmented and the consumers are easier to identify. But it does not necessarily follow that in a more segmented market, the consumer is easier to identify. Although there are broad categories of need and service qualities that every transport user requires, it is the appropriate mix of service qualities that are difficult to identify.

A major difference between service advertising and product advertising is the question of branding. Consumer product marketing is very concerned with brand loyalty which helps to protect market share from competition and generate repeat purchases. In many sections of transport there is strong competition and the industrial buyer of transport service can choose between a number of operators to carry his freight or set up his own transport fleet. Why then should not a transport company try to create a brand image, thus gaining loyalty from regular customers and helping to protect the business from competition? The brand image is obviously different from the brand image of a consumer product but it is used to create a feeling of well-being for the carrier in potential customers. If a manufacturing company decides to use a transport service, there is potential for repeat business and the marketing manager must try to ensure customer loyalty by making sure the company gives the best service possible.

The main thrust of freight space advertising must be to elicit enquiries from potential customers for the company's services. A space salesman or manger can then convert these enquiries into firm bookings. Advertising rarely creates the demand for freight space but provides the key to potential customers translating their perceived need into fulfilment.

The following question is often posed by operators: 'Is the advertising of freight space really necessary or is the service promoted by other means?' With ever increasing competition, it is necessary for transport companies to inform their potential customers of the services they offer the market. The following objectives can be identified as the major factors in freight advertising:

1. There can be no hard and fast rules about whether a company needs to advertise its services. This is also true about the amount of money spent on advertising. What is right for one company is not necessarily right for another.
2. Advertising is used to create awareness of the company's services among potential users or to increase this level of awareness if the actual penetration of the market is known.
3. Advertising is used to provide information about the service, to enhance the advantages of using the service and to give an idea of the cost. Detailed information can only be provided at the time of an enquiry, especially where the exact type of service is the subject of negotiation.
4. Advertising is often used to improve the company's image among existing and potential users in an attempt to change customers' attitudes to and awareness of the products on offer. This aspect is especially important when a company is trying to recover from any bad publicity that may have arisen for a number of different reasons.

    The importance of informing existing customers and non-users of changes in the company's organization and business philosophy must not be underestimated. Advertising can help to eliminate perceived misconceptions concerning the company and its products. An example of this type of advertising can be seen in British Rail Freights' recent adverts which have attempted to show that the company have learnt the lessons from the reputation gained in the 1960s and 1970s of inefficiency and lack of management control in freight operations.
5. 'Effective advertising means attracting attention, arousing interest, creating desires and stimulating action.' This achieves nothing if

the appropriate media are not selected. As with passenger advertising, this means identifying the proposed recipient of the advertisement and selecting the media which will most likely be seen by that person. All of this is important but of over-riding importance is making sure that the advert is put out at the right time.

Selling freight space

Some large companies recruit sales persons to fill the space on their vehicles and to add the personal touch to their company's image. The following points should be borne in mind when considering the employment of space salesmen:

1. The level of product knowledge is a vital factor in recruitment even if the sales person is to be recruited from outside the organization. There are many potential customers who prefer to deal with a person who has worked in operations and is knowledgeable from experience rather than training.
2. If the sales person is selling a specialist service to the managing director or some other director, the need will be to use the language appropriate to that situation. Not only must the service be explained but also the advantages to the customer in terms of cash flow, stock holding and avoiding stock-outs. These aspects may be irrelevant or meaningless to a despatch manager whose main task is making sure the company's products are delivered to the customers on time.
3. The type of sales person employed depends on the complexity of the product, the level in the hierarchy of the customer company to be dealt with and the preferences of the sales manager. The last is important because, even though selling is an individual task, the sales department must work as a team.

Direct mail advertising

Direct mail is simply the sending of advertising matter to named recipients through the post. The size of the operation may be either modest or intensive according to the coverage of the market required and the financial budget available. One of the greatest advantages of direct mail advertising is the ability to target specific groups and measure the response rate as a proportion of the number of items posted. The effectiveness of direct mail advertising is dependent on an up-to-date mailing list which identifies the individual who has most influence on the target company's transport or traffic decision.

THE RELATIONSHIP BETWEEN MARKETING AND OPERATIONS

This is one of the vital issues on which the whole concept of marketing is tested in the working environment. The marketing concept creates a service by studying consumer needs and setting out to satisfy those needs for providing services which match consumer demand. The snag in this concept arises from the nature of transport operations. From the moment a service is in existence – ie the route planned, the vehicles purchased – it can be modified by improving the quality of the service variables but any generated sales must fit into the operation which is already running. The *quality* of the transport company's service, such as better reliability, less damage, etc, can only be improved by staff training, better and planned maintenance and operationally efficient decision-making by management. The role of marketing is to channel customer requirements so that efficiency can be achieved. In many cases, the impetus to change the operational methods comes from increased competition or the changing needs of the consumer. Therefore, it is vital that all transport managers keep abreast of current developments in their mode and in other modes, attempt to cater for the needs of both the shipper and receiver of goods or changing needs of passengers, but still make sufficient profit from the service.

A note of caution must be entered about the relationship between operations and marketing, especially when relating this to costs. Lawrence,[12] writing about the ship operating costs, illustrates this point. 'There is a special case of a vessel speeding to marketing requirements which merits attention because it is very common, often marked in the effect (on running costs of a ship) and difficult or impossible to quantify when a senior marketing man claims that a vessel must wait (or arrive early) for a parcel of cargo, because the effect of non-compliance with the shipper's request will put the loyalty of a valuable customer at risk. [For the operations staff] to take a hard line (about the extra cost) would obviously be unwise; the marketing man might very well be right. The effects of market risk versus vessel operating costs are not comparable. Someone has to make a decision. It has to be the marketing man (since vessel costs are quantifiable, while marketing risks are a matter of judgement). An elegant solution is offered; let the marketeers delay whenever they will but let them request by means of a recorded instruction, costed at a pre-agreed rate, and let this amount be debited to marketing (along with entertainment and public relations and similar costs, for that is what we are talking about) and, at the same time, credited to vessel costs.

'No one except the marketing director need complain about any cost so vouched for.

'The cost of vessel delays (or premature arrival) should be known and visited upon those who caused them.

'There is a minor administrative difficulty in adopting this approach – the first operations manager who suggests that the marketing department should pay for delay will be murdered. It may, therefore, be necessary – until policy is accepted as reasonable and normal – to approach the matter cautiously. The operators could, for example, simply picket the (no doubt) four star hotel where the sales people are having their monthly get-together.'

The lesson illustrated by this quote is that the true costs of any marketing effort should be known and apportioned to the marketing department budget. By making other sections or departments bear the costs of factors over which they have no control, the marketing department calls into question the very nature of what they are trying to achieve.

PASSENGER INFORMATION

Closely allied to the subject of marketing is the provision of information to help passengers successfully complete their journey. Some of the principles involved are equally important, though of a different nature, for freight transport operators.

There are two essential requirements for successful passenger information systems:

1. To provide clear and precise information which the traveller requires and which the totality of passengers are able to understand.
2. To ensure that the information provided by the carrier is made readily available to passengers.

The former is related to the amount, presentation and contents of the information material which is produced by a carrier; the latter to the techniques and processes used to distribute and present the material to the general public.

The types of information required by a passenger making a journey can be broken down into three broad categories:

1. Information which helps the passenger follow through the process of making the journey from origin to destination. This includes such items as route to be followed, tickets needed, times of departure and arrival and any connections *en route.*

2. Information about passenger facilities *en route* which are not essential for the journey process and may even be optional.
3. Information on changes from the normal such as to timings and route.

The process of making a journey can be laid out as a series of actions which lead the passenger step by step through the journey. It must always be borne in mind by the transport manager, especially those most intimately involved in the provision of services, that a large proportion of passengers will be nervous about the planned journey. These people need reassurance at each stage of the process, that what they are doing is correct.[13]

The first step in any journey is finding the terminal. Irregular travellers require guidance about the location of terminal buildings in relation to other landmarks. Motorists and pedestrians may use different routes to reach the terminal from any one place and this must be catered for by the relevant authority. It is good policy to make sure that the terminal building itself is easily identifiable. Information should be provided about how to reach other transport facilities.

On arrival in the terminal, the potential passenger must be guided towards the departure point. This includes the location and procedure for car parking, how to purchase a ticket and what to do with luggage. Clear visual information linking the journey details with the departure point are required not only as guidance but for confirmation and reassurance to the passenger.

One of the basic fears of even the most experienced traveller is that they will unknowingly board the wrong vehicle and discover this too late to avoid a great deal of embarrassment and inconvenience. It may not be a very big problem in the case of the airlines or shipping where the passenger is personally guided to the vehicle but it is a problem for coach and rail passengers.

Obviously, the best method of giving reassurance to passengers is to have employees making sure that passengers get into the right vehicles. At a time of cost-cutting by manpower reductions, however, other methods must be found. The vehicle should be externally identifiable, this information being reinforced by a public address system where practicable. The main difficulty for many modes is to identify all the stopping points on a route. Merely being informed of the final destination may not be sufficient for occasional travellers, and the best opinion is to identify as many intermediate points as is practical.

The next worry for the passenger is finding a seat on the vehicle. With reserved seating there is not much the passenger has to worry about except the occasional overbooking practised by some airlines.

The main problem is with trains, where, even when a passenger has reserved a seat, many people have great difficulty in identifying the correct one.

Just before reaching the destination, passengers need a warning so that they can mentally and physically prepare for their arrival. This warning must be given neither in so short a time before arrival that the passenger has to rush to gather luggage, nor so long before that he or she has to wait after getting ready to leave. On arrival at the terminal, the passenger is concerned with finding the way to the final destination which may mean using another vehicle.

The available media

There are three ways to classify the media available to transit passenger information:

1. The means of transmission, either verbal or visual.
2. The way in which the information is transmitted, either general or personal.
3. The place where the information is received, either public or private. The main forms of information transmission can be highlighted in terms of their advantages and disadvantages.

Radio and television can give a wide coverage of the potential market but can only give general information to the public at large. These media are also relatively expensive if paid advertisements are used, although broadcasting time can be obtained at little cost through news items, announcements of service changes, notification of emergencies or breakdowns. A great number of radio and TV stations run transport items during morning and evening peak periods.

Newspapers and magazine have wide circulation but, again, they are geared to give only general information. They are a useful medium in which to highlight long-term changes in services but useless in emergencies.

Telephone information is possibly the easiest to obtain and can be right up to date. There are very few people who are without access to a telephone. The transport company must make sure that their number is easy to identify in the telephone directory, and where practicable, a separate telephone number should be issued for all enquiries. All staff assigned to deal with enquiries should be adequately trained in the techniques of giving concise and unambiguous information over the telephone.

Offices and agents are essential for transmitting specific information, and all enquiries must receive proper attention. Business can easily be lost through staff not dealing with tentative enquiries adequately, making the enquirer go elsewhere. Display information and leaflets dealing with routine matters are helpful in busy offices. What is important is that the potential customer leaves with the exact information that is required.

Operating staff comprise the largest and, in many cases, the most easily recognized source of information for the travelling public. In many cases they are grossly under-utilized. However, if they are to be used to their full potential, it is important that they are trained to carry out this function and motivated to see information giving as part of the job. Any information given must be accurate, up to date and with a clear explanation of the reasons for any major changes.

Timetables and printed information

The timetable is common to all modes of transport and is by far the most frequently used public information tool. It is often defined as a 'list or table of events arranged according to the time at which they take place'. In its simplest form, the timetable provides information on how to get from one place to another, how long the journey will take and when it will occur.

In most forms of passenger transport, the timetable is derived from the documents used to plan the total service. It is developed further by providing the schedule of both vehicles and crews for the operating management.

The extensive use of timetables results in the production of a vast amount of material which has to be constantly updated. Timetables are presented with different formats not only by various companies within a mode but also across modes. They are variable in comprehensiveness and understandability. This lack of a standard layout emphasises the problem facing both regular and potential passengers. There seems to have been little attempt to co-ordination between operators to produce a standard format which would benefit both users and operators.

The lack of standardization has been paralleled by the reluctance to undertake research on public transport information requirements. This is true of evaluating the usefulness of existing information designs and of testing passenger reactions to innovations in information layout. As with marketing itself, the passenger transport industry tends to provide the information which the operator thinks the public need and can understand. The modest method would be to find out by research what information the public require and then to attempt to supply that type of information.

There are three major considerations in the design of a timetable:

1. The layout of the table to be chosen.
2. The notation to be used.
3. The amount of information to be included.

The format dictates how the list of stopping points and their timings are to be laid out. There are only two alternatives with a two-dimension matrix timetable. One is to have the stopping points arranged vertically down the side of the table with the columns of times depicting the services read vertically. The other is to have the stopping points along the top, the horizontal lines of times showing the services. From this format the passenger has to grasp all the destination and timing material required.

The understanding of timetables is often complicated by the need to use additional notations to denote variations in service at different times of the day.

The amount of information included in a timetable is directly affected by the layout adopted. An alternative to the two-dimensional matrix is the one-dimensional table which lists departure times from the origin point. These have advantages in areas where destinations are few and most passengers are familiar with the route.

In many modes of passenger transport, it is now commonplace to produce timetable leaflets from small groups of inter-related services rather than a booklet of all services. The passenger can collect leaflets directly related to requirements rather than purchase a booklet full of information which will never be used.

Timetable leaflets have a dual advantage over timetable books. First, they are cheaper to produce and easier to alter than the timetable book. Revision of one service renders the book out of date whereas the leaflet offers the operator a flexible system which saves printing time and cost.

Second, it is more convenient for the intending passenger, as leaflets are distributed free of charge. It has always seemed illogical to me that an intending customer has to pay to find out details of the services he might wish to use. Would a shop make potential customers pay for any publicity material they produce? It is both practical and vital for any passenger transport operator to market the service, and charging for information goes against the whole concept of marketing.

The timetable book showing the whole range of services does have its uses, however. It contains details of all services on offer and is essential in enquiry offices. It also gives the operator an opportunity to promote other services which the potential customers for one service may not otherwise be aware of or have brought to their attention.

Other travel information

It is very important for operators to publicize fares, as the price of the service can be a major factor in the decision on whether to travel. Unfortunately, many operators either do not produce fares information or publish it separately from the timetable. There are two practical factors which discourage the printing of fares on timetables:

1. Fare changes tend to occur at different times from service revisions. The printing of fares in the timetable would require frequent updating.
2. Fare tables can be complex, which makes them difficult to understand, and tend to require a large amount of printed space. Accordingly, the majority of operators produce fares information separately.

Fare concessions, whether social or commercial, need to be brought to the attention of customers. Publicity ranges from the use of space on the timetable to wider media coverage. It is important to make sure that the publicity about concessions reaches the market for which it is intended.

Onward connections by other modes of transport receive varying attention from the different modes. Some bus and rail stations have extensive displays indicating the best methods of reaching selected destinations and the services available from other operators. In other cases there is little or no display information and staff show little inclination to help. There is a need for agreement between operators about the level of information and the method of presentation of one mode's service by another mode.

Conditions of travel (in the legal sense) are of direct interest to a limited number of passengers and it is normally left for them to enquire for a copy of the exact conditions of carriage. Specific conditions are often summarized in various notices inside the vehicle – succeeding in the aim of bringing the conditions to the public's attention but often appearing officious, impersonal and legalistic.

Operational changes

Operational changes from the advertised service can take the form of:

1. Long-term alterations.

2. Short-notice changes.
3. Emergencies.

Long-term changes to services, facilities or conditions are not easy to communicate to the customer. The regular is not looking for any change, while the occasional passenger is difficult to contact.

Major changes can necessitate reprints of timetables and fare schedules and involve media advertisements. Both reprinted timetables and fare schedules should contain an explanation of the reason for the change and, if appropriate, a summary of their effects. It is essential for those people handling enquiries from the public to have this information well in advance of the change so that they can answer any questions prior to the occurrence. Extended press publicity can be obtained by a press release or news story. Caution is needed because the press are notorious at using this type of information in a way which may not be intended by the operator.

Short-notice changes include cancellations, delays, diversions, breakdowns, additional stopping points and so on. Of all the various aspects of communication that we have been looking at, it is of this aspect that the travelling public are most critical.

Most passengers are prepared to accept breakdowns and other causes of delay. From experience of their daily lives they know that incidents are bound to happen to interrupt the smooth flow of transport services. The vary nature of transport with its reliance on moving vehicles testifies to this. What these same passengers find frustrating and hard to understand is the lack of even basic information about short-notice changes. In addition, many feel that the transport operator is unconcerned about the passengers' welfare during these times. This often focuses on the operating staff being 'offhand' and officious.

Any information, no matter how incomplete, is a valuable demonstration that the operator is concerned about the welfare of the passengers. Obviously, the more accurate and comprehensive the information the better, though it must not be too technical or alarmist. The use of generalizations like 'weather conditions' or 'technical fault' can lead passengers to believe that management and operational inefficiencies are really responsible.

One of the major causes of this seeming lack of efficiency and inadequate caring for the passengers is the clash of priorities for the staff. At the time of an incident it often happens that the same staff member is responsible for both reorganizing the operation to overcome the fault and instituting information promulgation to waiting passengers.

Communications with passengers experiencing delays should be made at reasonably frequent intervals, even if there is no change in the situation. The passengers will then feel that they have not been forgotten and that steps are being taken to rectify the situation. It must be remembered, especially with long-distance travel, that many passengers' greatest anxiety will be over possible missed connections and the inconvenience of relatives or friends waiting at destinations.

The biggest problem in this area is for the bus companies. Passengers are spread over a large area at sometimes very isolated bus stops with no chance of being informed of changes. If the bus does not arrive and they miss their appointment or are late for work, the company could very well lose passengers. This is a problem that all bus operators should study, using the knowledge gained in other modes or in communications technology to try to overcome the problem.

What really counts is the ability of the transport company's employees to act on the information available. This can only be improved by training.

Emergencies are covered by procedures which are in most cases laid down by government regulation and legislation. These regulations include the training and competence of operating personnel.

Information as reassurance

Infrequent travellers tend to lack confidence in their ability to absorb travel information. As stated earlier, they need reassurance that they are following the correct procedures both at the time of starting a journey and during the journey itself. Some operators fail to pay sufficient attention to these feelings of insecurity. Indeed, many transport professionals find acceptance of the need to reassure passengers very difficult to grasp. This is especially true in the bus industry and to a lesser extent on the railways. An overwhelming sense of insecurity can be a great deterrent to some people using public transport.

The greatest help to uncertain passengers is friendly personal assistance from passenger transport staff. Many staff are very competent at reassuring passengers that their journey is going well but others find this the most difficult part of the job. This difficulty can be overcome by training programmes specifically designed to help operating staff feel more comfortable when dealing with passengers' problems. One problem facing all operators is the trend towards greater productivity by employing fewer staff, which reduces the number of staff available at any given time to help and reassure the public.

The passenger or potential passenger is often ill-informed or misinformed about constraints, problems and policies affecting the operations of passenger transport and transport in general. In many cases, the passenger or potential passenger has a very biased, over-simplified or naive view of what certain transport modes can achieve. They feel that management of transport companies could be more effective and that they, the passenger, could run the system more effectively than the professionals.

A great deal more could be done in the general public relations area to explain the basic facts about passenger transport in language that is easily understood.

Conclusions

1. Passenger information needs must be clearly identified by all passenger transport companies. It must always be acknowledged by staff and management that, in addition to actual travel information, passengers require reassurance about their progress through the journey process. A passenger has placed him/herself in your care and it is up to everybody concerned to make their journey as comfortable and trouble-free as possible.
2. The methods of communication of passenger information are complex and imperfect. Each passenger is an individual with different needs from those of fellow passengers. Access to passenger information and the passenger's ability to understand the information provided varies widely between individuals.
3. There could be much greater efforts by operators to co-ordinate and standardize their information services to passengers. This is especially true in the case of small-scale operators.
4. There is a great need to provide information for underdeveloped areas os passenger demand. Growth comes from attracting new users to a system.
5. Public transport has a case to put forward to gain support in the public interest and this case must be presented in a positive and on-going campaign.
6. The high level of staff/customer contact inherent in the passenger transport business should be enhanced by systems of positive recruitment and training. All staff should be trained to deal with information-giving, especially in the event of changes to the service.
7. The layout and presentation of passenger information should be designed more specifically for the ease of absorption by the intended customer.

References

1. Berry, L. and Parasuraman, A. *Marketing Services: competing through quality* Free Press, New York 1991

2. Reis, A. and Trout, J. *Marketing Warfare* McGraw-Hill, New York 1986
3. Cowell, D. *The Market of Services* Butterworth-Heinemann, Oxford 1991
4. Kaiz, B. *How to Market Professional Services* Gower Publishing, UK 1988
5. Westwood, J. *The Marketing Plan* Kogan Page, London 1990
6. Elvey, *Marketing Made Simple* W. H. Allen, London 1972
7. Farms, M.T. and Harding, F.E. *Passenger Transport* Prentice Hall, New Jersey 1976
8. Thomson, J.M. *Modern Transport Economics* Penguin, London 1974
9. Majaro, S. 'Transport needs marketing' *Journal of General Management*, Vol 1, No 3, 1974 (p. 121)
10. Wragg, D.W. *Publicity and Customer Relations in Transport Management*, Gower Aldershot 1981
11. Wood, E.G. *Marketing Guide to Small Firms* Small Firms Information Service, No 5 1976
12. Lawrence, C.A. *Vessel Operating Economics* Fairplay Publications, London 1984
13. Clayton, D.G. 'Communications with passengers' *Transport* March, 1976

6

Safety Regulations

INTRODUCTION

All methods of transport are inherently dangerous, in the sense that transport involves moving vehicles. A mistake by the driver of a vehicle or a mechanical failure of one of the many components can have catastrophic consequences. The over-looking of some vital steps in procedure by a person far removed from the actual vehicle can result in an accident. One of the factors which makes transport almost unique is that transport vehicles move among innocent bystanders who are equally at risk from an accident as the crew, driver and passengers.

Throughout this chapter, I will use the term 'driver' in its widest sense to mean the person in charge of the vehicle. It includes airline pilots, ships' captains, lorry, bus and train drivers in this definition.

A quick glance at the newspaper over only a short time scale will remind us how dangerous transport can be. These spectacular crashes which grab the headlines are only a small fraction of the daily toll of injuries that transport inflicts on its employees and the public. These accidents are a reminder of the paramount importance of establishing safety standards, and the need for strong enforcement of those standards.

A plane is taking off from an airport when, during take-off, one engine becomes detached from the wing. Unfortunately, in breaking away from the plane, the engine damages the control surfaces which are needed for safe take-off. The plane crashes, killing all those on board. Some competent body then has to ask why the engine became detached. Was it a design fault or human error? The real reason for the accident must be ascertained so that it can be avoided in the future.

A ferry leaves port crowded with passengers, their cars, freight lorries and their drivers. Within a short time, while everybody is still getting used to the ship, it has turned on its side, killing many of the passengers. It is found that the bow doors had been left open when the ferry put to sea, a common practice on the shorter routes. Why were the doors left open when putting to sea? Was it some mechanical failure, a breakdown in the usual procedures, or the commercial pressure from head office to save time?

A lorry leaves a motorway because the driver feels that the brakes are failing. It is going too fast when it enters the town and crashes into an ice cream parlour, killing many children. Why did this accident occur?

A coach carrying people back from a day trip runs into the back of a line of stationary cars waiting at a contra-flow system on a motorway. Many people are killed or injured. What caused this accident?

A train crowded with commuters is standing at a station when an express train runs full speed into the rear. Who or what caused this accident?

What these examples prove is that no method of transport is immune from incidents leading to death or injury to passengers, crew or bystanders. The toll of human suffering is immense for the few people involved. In a well-run industry accidents should never happen, but in transport they occur with a certain regularity. As has already been stated, they are accompanied by spectacular headlines in the press, on the radio and television.

Collins[1] states: 'No accident should happen but occasional ones are inevitable, part of the price of moving around. The goal should always be absolute safety. Absolute safety is not obtainable in any form of transportation. Somewhere, sometime, all the bad factors are going to come together and result in an accident.'

Ramsden[2] writes: 'Safety begins with the design of an overall system to encompass the overall requirements.' Safety in transport is not only concerned with the design and maintenance of vehicles but includes the infrastructure, the organization, the law and the people. It is to do with processes, both physical and social.

The subject of safety in transport is usually treated in terms of the three E's: enforcement, education and engineering.[3] Enforcement involves the setting of standards, both technical and behavioural, backing these standards by a system of penalties if they are breached, and providing some form of enforcement agency to apply sanctions to those who break or defy those standards.

Education and training are vital and well recognized in the matter of transport safety. Education must have far wider implications than simply teaching to attain competence. It must include alerting everybody involved in transport operations to the risks inherent in poor procedures and in deviating from the safe forms of operation. As has been pointed out many times, though engineers can design high levels of safety into their vehicles and infrastructure, it is people who ultimately build, maintain and operate transport systems. Human lapses can only be eradicated by proper education and training – education and training which not only teaches them how to perform their tasks but makes people aware of the risks involved in any action that they may undertake.

Engineering for safety is one of the major concepts in the design and construction of both vehicles and infrastructure. In many instances, engineers hold the key to transport because much safety regulation is the result of engineering analysis.

However, accidents do happen, no matter how careful people are to follow the practices inherent in the three E's. There are a number of factors which, combined or individually, are present in all accidents.

Chance is the random happening which could not be foreseen by even the most safety-conscious individual. In legal language this is often referred to as an 'Act of God'. The sinking of a ship by a freak wave which could not be predicted, the crash of an aeroplane after hitting a flock of birds, the washing away of a coach by a flash flood, these are examples of the chance occurrence. Even these types of accident are becoming less frequent. As scientists gain knowledge about the dynamics of ocean systems, the generation of weather patterns and the way in which chance happenings arise, fewer and fewer accidents can be attributed to 'Acts of God'.

By far the largest cause of accidents in transport is classified as 'human error'. Indeed, many researchers contend that all accidents are the result of human error. If the nature of the cause and effect can be traced far enough back along the path of actions leading to the accident, it is usual to find some human action or omission which led to the accident. For operators it is easy to blame human error as the cause of an accident, especially if the error can be attributed to the driver of the vehicle. The ship's captain takes the blame for the ship running aground because he did not have the correct charts or had to stay on the bridge in fog for too long because he was not confident in his junior officers' ability to look after the ship. The airline pilot overruns the runway during landing at an unfamiliar airport. These are example of '*human error*' but some people would question the assumption that the only human making the error was the captain or the airline pilot. What of the managers who sent the captain to sea without the required charts or competent crew, the pilot without proper guidance about a particular airport? As Ramsden stated, 'Safety begins with the design of the overall system'.

Inherent faults in the engineering of both vehicles and the infrastructure can cause accidents. Engines fall off planes because the maintenance was not properly carried out, ships are designed with inadequate strength, cars explode when struck in the rear because the petrol tank is vulnerable, bridges collapse under the weight of traffic. All engineering industries present dangers to both employees and customers but transport has a potential for inflicting death and injury to innocent bystanders which far exceeds that of any other industry. Faulty design and maintenance can be a major contribution to accidents.

Because transport involves moving vehicles controlled by a driver, *alcoholic drink* is a special danger. In 1965, 7,952 people were killed on Britain's roads, in 1984 this had decreased to 5,599 and by 1992 to 4,229. There has been a similar decrease in the number of injured. Many commentators claim that as many as 40 per cent of these casualties can be regarded as alcohol related. The decline can be viewed in the light of government moves to both impose penalties on drink drivers and through the government's anti-drink/driver advertising campaigns. Drink can be a major factor in accidents in all forms of transport and its control is vital for the safety of passengers, freight, crews and third parties.

These factors combined to make the search for complete safety regulation a joint effort by governments and the industry. The remainder of this chapter will deal with the regulation of transport by mode and conclude with a comparison of the regulatory frameworks.

REGULATION

With all modes of transport, there are three elements to be considered when contemplating legislation to regulate the safety of transport operations: the operator, the driver and the vehicle. These three elements interact to form the total operating system and the cause of accidents can often be traced to the boundary between these subsystems. All three must be considered together to ensure the greatest possible safety:

1. *The operator.* The operator is usually defined as the individual or company that controls the management of the vehicle and operating crew. It is the operator who determines the operational ethos of the company, schedules the vehicles and plans the total system.

The operator has a significant effect on the safety of the transport operation which he controls.

In many modes of transport, the operator of the vehicles has to have a licence to run the business. To gain a licence, the operator must satisfy some licensing organization that:

(a) The applicant is a fit person to run the business. This usually means that he has had no previous convictions for contravening regulations in that industry.

(b) The applicant has a thorough knowledge of the industry. In some cases this means passing an examination to provide his competence.

(c) The applicant has adequate financial resources to run the business. This means proving by a business plan that the business will start on a sound financial base.

(d) The applicant has facilities to maintain the vehicles. This does not mean that any aspiring operator has to have maintenance facilities at the base but that adequate arrangements have been made for maintenance either by the company or by contracting out the work to a competent engineer.

2. *The driver.* In all modes of transport, regulations cover the competence and working load of the driver:

(a) Drivers must have a licence to drive a particular type of vehicle. This involves passing a set of examinations and tests.

(b) Regulations restrict the hours worked by drivers.

(c) Drivers are empowered to keep records of the hours they have worked in order that the authorities can check that the hours regulations are not being exceeded.

3. *The vehicle.* In all modes of transport regulations have been formed to ensure the safety of the vehicle:

(a) Design and construction of vehicles are the subject of extensive sets of rules.

(b) Regulations lay down the procedures to ensure that vehicles are maintained adequately throughout their working life.

(c) Legislation has been enacted to make sure that operators and staff load and use vehicles in a safe fashion.

To ensure that the regulations are adhered to and enforced, organizations have been established to administer these functions.

The main conclusions to be drawn from the rest of this chapter are how similar the regulations are across all modes of transport. Where there are differences, it is usually due to different operating circumstances or the custom and practice in that section of the industry. As with most functions in transport, each mode tends to view its circumstances as unique. The prevailing view seems to be that one mode has nothing to learn from a study of other modes. A review of safety regulations will show that this is far from the case. Obviously, in a book of this nature, detailed regulations are not reproduced, only sufficient detail for highlighting the similarities and differences. For a more detailed study of a particular set of regulations, the reader should consult the references provided and the statutes covering that area.

ROAD TRANSPORT

Operators' licences

Road haulage[4]

The main objective of the operators' licence system is to ensure the safe and proper operation of heavy goods vehicles by suitably qualified people. There is the added need to protect the environment from the potential harmful effects of heavy goods vehicles, especially in the vicinity of the operators' base.

The regulations cover goods vehicles over 3.5 tonnes gross vehicle weight, ie the weight of the vehicle and its load.

There are three types of licence:

1. *Restricted*, for the carriage of own goods in own vehicles for own business and trade.
2. *Standard national*, to carry for hire and reward in the UK.
3. *Standard international*, for the carriage of goods for hire and reward both in the UK and abroad.

The licence will be issued if the applicant can prove to the Licensing Authority, that he:

1. is of good repute, ie does not have a past record of contravention of goods vehicle regulations;
2. has the appropriate financial standing to run and maintain the vehicles;
3. is professionally qualified (or will employ somebody who is professionally qualified). This means holding a certificate of professional competence (CPC) issued by an approved body. To gain a certificate, the applicant must pass an examination or gain exemption from the examination through a recognized professional institute.

The Licensing Authority has powers to ensure that the licence conditions are adhered to by the holder, by:

1. Refusing an application on the grounds of not meeting the original conditions.
2. Attaching additional conditions to the licence regarding operation of the licence.
3. Granting a licence for fewer vehicles than the applicant requested.
4. Granting a licence for a shorter period than the usual five years.
5. Withdrawing or suspending the licence if the operator ceases to meet the original issuing conditions.

The Licensing Authority must be notified if any operators' licence holder wishes to change any aspect of the licence.

Road passenger[5]

The public service operators licensing system is much the same as road haulage except in a few particulars.

A public service vehicle is defined as a vehicle adapted to carry more than eight people for hire and reward though this is qualified in some cases:

1. A restricted licence is to carry less than eight people in the UK, less than 16 abroad if not in the passenger business.
2. Standard national to carry more than eight people in the UK.
3 Standard international to carry more than eight people abroad.

The body responsible for the licensing process in the case of road passenger transport is the Traffic Commissioners.

Drivers

Any person wishing to drive a mechanically propelled vehicle on the road must have a driver's licence and, for both heavy goods vehicles and public service vehicles, a heavy goods vehicle driver's licence or a public service vehicle driver's licence in addition.

The various classes of these licences are covered by Acts of Parliament which lay down the conditions to be fulfilled before qualifying for a licence.

Information required when applying for a heavy goods or public service vehicle driving licence includes:

1. Past medical history, with a current medical certificate from the doctor.
2. History of any previous traffic convictions.
3. Type of ordinary driving licence currently held.

4. Public service vehicle/lorry goods vehicle licence as may be appropriate.

This information serves to satisfy the Traffic Commissioners or Licensing Authority that the applicant is a fit and proper person to drive a public service vehicle or heavy goods vehicle. Any change in health or traffic convictions during the validity of the licence period may cause the licence to be revoked by the authorities. This includes convictions for traffic offences when driving a private car, not only for offences when driving public service vehicle or heavy goods vehicles.

Rules and regulations concerning working hours and the recording of that information can be divided into three sections, different regulations applying to each section:

1. British domestic operations.
2. Operations between EU member countries.
3. Operations between EU member countries and other European nations.

Tachographs – recording devices which automatically register time, speed, distance travelled and type of driver activity – must be fitted to most heavy goods vehicles and certain public service vehicles. They must be of an approved EU design and manufacture.

The driver is responsible for making sure that name, date, start and finish places, vehicle registration, and distance travelled are entered onto the disc. Charts for the previous two working days on national journeys and for the previous seven working days on international journeys must be carried and enough spare charts to complete the proposed journey. The completed charts must be handed to the employer within 21 days of the finish of the journey. The driver must notify the employer of any failure of the equipment during the journey. For journeys where tachographs are not needed or where the equipment malfunctions, a written log sheet must be kept.

Employers must ensure that the tacograph is sealed and calibrated. This involves a check every two years and re-calibration every six years at a calibration centre. When the charts are returned by the driver, the employer must check the entries and retain the charts for one year ready for inspection by Vehicle Inspectorate agency inspectors.

The vehicle

Construction and Use Regulations[6] are made by the Secretary of State for Transport exercising powers granted by sections of the various Road Traffic Acts.

The regulations covering motor vehicles and trailers are made with respect to the following factors:

1. The width, height and length of the vehicle, and trailer, and the load, diameter of wheels, width, nature and conditions of tyres.
2. The emission of smoke, vapour, ash, sparks and grit.
3. Vehicle noise.
4. The minimum weight unladen of all vehicles, maximum weight to be transmitted to the road and the condition under which these weights may be required to be tested.
5. The particulars that are to be marked on vehicles and trailers.
6. The towing or drawing of other vehicles by the motor vehicle.
7. The number and nature of brakes.
8. The testing and inspection of vehicles by authorized persons.
9. The appliances fitted for signalling the approach of a motor vehicle.

Regulations specifically for goods vehicles are made with respect to:

1. Prescribing other descriptions of weight which are not to be exceeded.
2. Providing for the marking on such vehicles of weight and other particulars by a fixed plate.
3. The manner in which these particulars are to be marked.

Different regulations may be applied to different classes of vehicle in different circumstances with regard to different times of day, night or locality. For public service vehicles[7] similar types of regulation apply.

Regulatory organizations[8] exist to administer these regulations: the Traffic Commissioners for the bus and coach industry, and the Licensing Authority for the road haulage industry. They work closely with the Department for Transport in all aspects of safety.

AIR TRANSPORT

It is very hard to realize that the first tentative flight in a heavier than air machine was made in 1903. The expansion and development of the air transport industry has been rapid since that time. Currently, millions of passengers and tonnes of freight are carried across national boundaries and between continents, travelling at up to twice the speed of sound and heights of up to 11 miles.

The international nature of air transport as a mode of travel, not confined within national boundaries, necessitates that the support systems must be compatible, no matter where on earth they are situated, in the interests of safety and efficiency. In air transport the safety of the passengers and crew of the aircraft must be the prime consideration of all those people concerned with the industry. Indeed, when comparing the air transport safety record with other forms of transport, accidents as a percentage of miles flown are few, but they invariably lead to fatalities. It has been found by investigation and research that, in all but a very few cases, accidents were preventable by the application of the proper procedures.

To try to ensure the safety of air transport, every aspect of airline operation is covered by rules and regulations which should be properly observed by all personnel involved. These necessary constraints on free operation, impose high financial obligations on airline and airport operators but safety must never be compromised by commercial decision-making.

The aviation industry comprises three separate entities, each independent: the aircraft manufacturers, the airline operators, and airport management. As in all walks of life, there are constant conflicts between these separate industries, but national governments have aviation ministries to help resolve the conflicts in the interests of safety. The problem of international flight over and between countries with different language and cultural backgrounds is alleviated by international organizations such as the ICAO.

ICAO[9]

The International Civil Aviation Organization (ICAO) was established on 4 April 1947 after a conference decision reached in Chicago. It is now an agency of the United Nations.

The aims and objectives of the ICAO can be summarized as follows:

1. To ensure the safe and orderly growth of civil air transport throughout the world.
2. To encourage the development of airports and navigation facilities for international civil aviation.
3. To reduce wasteful competition.
4. To ensure that all nations have a fair opportunity to operate international airlines.
5. To avoid discrimination between the contracting nations.

Membership of the ICAO comprises more than 140 sovereign states, meaning that the organization is an inter-governmental body, not an association of airlines. The headquarters is in Montreal.

The sovereign body of ICAO is the *assembly* on which each member state, no matter how large their air transport industry, has equal representation. Meetings of the assembly are held at least once every three years and must be attended by a least 50 per cent of the member states before decisions can be taken. Decisions are by simple majority.

The governing body of the organization is the *council* which comprises one representative from each of the 30 states elected by the assembly. The council directs the working of the organization through a committee structure. Each committee is composed of qualified experts appointed by the council from persons nominated by the member states. The committee members do not function as national representatives but as international experts. There are five committees:

1. Air Navigation Commission.
2. Air Transport Committee.
3. Legal Committee.
4. Committee on Joint Support of Air Navigation Services.
5. Financial Committee.

Annexes to the convention contain the International Standards and Recommended Practices as laid down by the Technical Divisions of the Air Navigation Commission. These have been ratified by 50 per cent of the member states by passing their provisions into national law. (In simple terms, the annexes define what should be done in any particular case and these are followed by Procedures for Air Navigation which explain how to go about implementing the practices.)

Due to the rapid development of international civil aviation, the ICAO is conscious of the need to adopt in its specifications modern systems and techniques.

Many subjects are considered on a regional basis and the ICAO recognizes nine geographical areas for planning the provision of air navigation services and facilities required on the ground by aircraft flying across these regions.

The ICAO provides the machinery for the achievement of international co-operation in the air, but successful results depend on the willingness of the nations of the world to make concessions and work together to reach agreement. All ICAO recommendations must be turned into binding legislation through each member state's national legislative machinery.

The CAA[10]

In the UK, the organization responsible for the introduction and monitoring of the ICAO provisions and procedures is the Civil Aviation Authority (CAA).

The CAA is both a public service enterprise and a regulatory body. Its responsibilities include:

1. The national air traffic services, both air traffic control and telecommunications.
2. The economic regulation of civil aviation including air transport licensing, approval of air fares and the licensing of air travel organizers.
3. Air safety, both airworthiness and operational safety, including the licensing of flight crew, and aircraft engineers, licensing of aerodromes and the certification of UK airlines and aircraft.
4. Advice to the government on civil aviation matters, both domestic and international.
5. Consumer interests, private aviation requirements, economic and scientific research, the collection and publication of economic and statistical data, consultancy and training with overseas administration.
6. Ownership and operation of aerodromes.

British civil aviation regulation

The operator[11]

All UK registered aircraft can only be operated anywhere in the world if the operator holds a licence and the terms of that licence are followed. This licence is called an air transport licence. The *air transport licence* must be held by a person who has the management of the aircraft and the applicant must be a UK national or a company incorporated under UK law.

Applicants must satisfy the CAA that they:

1. Are experienced in air transport and fit to operate aircraft.
2. Have the financial and other resources to operate aircraft.

The licence can have specific terms attached to it by the CAA when it is granted. During its currency, the CAA can revoke, suspend or vary the licence conditions by giving the holder 21 days' notice with reasons. The licence holder has the right to appeal to the Secretary of State over any decision of the CAA with regard to the licence.

The air transport licence applies to all UK registered aircraft which means that any foreign operator wishing to use a UK registered aircraft must have an air transport licence. In law, this can only be accomplished by the foreign operator incorporating a company in the UK but the Secretary of State has the power to allow foreign operators and nationals to operate British aircraft if it is thought to be in the public interest.

The operator has certain responsibilities which must be fulfilled when operating the aircraft:

1. Each aircraft must have a designated commander.
2. It is the duty of the operator to make sure that all radio stations and navigational aids along the proposed route of the aircraft are adequate for safe navigation.
3. The operator must ensure that the airfields en route are adequate to accommodate the aircraft in its likely loaded condition. This includes any likely emergency airfields.
4. It is the operator's duty to ensure that all personnel employed on the aircraft as crew hold the required licences.
5. Operators must ensure that no simulated emergency manoeuvres will take place during the flight.
6. Before the flight, it is the operator's responsibility to ascertain that the aircraft is loaded properly.
7. Each aircraft must have on board a flight manual which includes all intended airports' operating minima.

Aircrew licensing[12]

An applicant for an airline pilot's licence has to satisfy the following CAA standards:

1. Medical requirements: all applicants must undergo a medical examination to obtain a medical certificate. Applicants must be free from physical disabilities, defects of sight, hearing and colour vision. This examination must be repeated at six-monthly intervals.
2. Flying experience: applicants must have satisfactorily completed a set number of hours' flying including night flying, pilot in command hours, cross-country flying and overseas flying.
3. Flight test requirements: applicants have to undergo a general flight test, an aircraft type test and an instrument rating test.
4. Technical examination: this includes examinations on aviation law, flight rules, navigation and aircraft performance.

Schedules regarding flying hours and duty time are laid down by the operator for each route. These must be approved by the CAA. In addition, the pilot cannot fly if the total flying hours in the past 28 days was more than 100 hours or if the total for the past year was more than 900 hours. Every pilot is required by the CAA to keep a personal log book which records dates of flights, type of aircraft and actual flying time.

The commander of the aircraft has the following duties:

1. Before each flight:
   (a) To check that the flight can be safely made.
   (b) To check that all the necessary equipment is on board the aircraft.
   (c) To check that the aircraft is fit for the intended flight.
   (d) To check that the balance and weight calculation has been fulfilled and that the results are within the specified laid down limits.
   (e) To check that there is sufficient fuel on board for the flight, including enough reserves.
   (f) To make sure that all the pre-flight checks as laid down in the operations manual are carried out competently.
2. During the flight:
   (a) To ensure that one pilot remains at the controls at all times.
   (b) To ensure that passengers understand the emergency procedures.

The aircraft

The regulations concerning the safety of aircraft are known as airworthiness regulations. The main concern of the airworthiness system is safety. ICAO standards are adopted by the CAA and laid out in the Air Navigation Order. (The latest volume of the ANO should be consulted for the most up-to-date information.)

The CAA is responsible for the issue of airworthiness certificates to British aircraft which meet the British Civil Airworthiness requirements.

The certificate of airworthiness is issued to any aircraft which meets the prescribed airworthiness conditions. It is basically the same for all aircraft although different procedures must be followed when applying for certificates for different types of aircraft.

For foreign constructed aircraft, the aircraft must first be registered in the UK or must already have a UK type certificate. The application must provide the certificate of airworthiness, the type of certificate issued in the country of manufacture and the flight manual to the CAA. The CAA uses these documents to decide whether the aircraft is designed and tested to the level of safety equivalent to British airworthiness requirements standards. The CAA in these cases relies heavily on the foreign country's investigation of the aircraft design but these invariably follow the procedure laid down by the ICAO. This means that the CAA can be fairly confident that an aeroplane given an airworthiness certificate by another country has been well tested. If it is decided that the evidence is not enough to show that the aeroplane reaches British airworthiness requirements standards, the CAA will require additional tests to be fulfilled before a certificate of airworthiness is issued.

For a prototype aircraft, the organization responsible for the design must issue a certificate of design for the aircraft concerned. This certificate testifies that the aircraft has been designed to British airworthiness requirements standards. Once these designs are approved by the CAA construction can go ahead with inspection by CAA, inspectors throughout the building period. The workmanship must reach an approved standard, the engines be of an approved type and all the equipment tested. Once built, the aircraft is finally inspected and flight tested. If satisfied that the aircraft reaches the standard, the CAA will issue a certificate of airworthiness.

A type certificate is issued by the CAA and states that the design and construction of a particular class of aircraft is approved by the CAA. Once issued, further aircraft of that type qualify for a certificate of airworthiness provided they are in good working order.

The certificate of airworthiness is valid for a limited period. Renewal procedures involve an engineer checking the relevant maintenance records determine what work is required on the aircraft to maintain its airworthiness. For public transport aircraft, reports from regular maintenance checks are used, these maintenance check periods being statutorily laid down. Account is taken of such items as the area of operation and the flight manual. If modifications are necessary, these must be completed before final inspection and flight tests are carried out. If all is satisfactory, the certificate of airworthiness is renewed.

Maintenance engineers must be licensed by the CAA to issue certificates of aircraft maintenance. The type of maintenance they can certify depends on the classification of their licence.

Airports[13]

At UK airports the ICAO operational standards, as laid down in Annex 14 to the convention, are enforced through CAP 168. Airport operations must satisfy CAA operations inspectors that the local facilities and operational procedures meet the requirements of CAP 168 before an aerodrome licence is issued. Annual renewal of this licence is subject to satisfactory reports from regular CAA inspections.

One of the conditions of the issue of a CAA aerodrome licence is that the holder is required to produce and maintain an aerodrome manual for that airport. Copies of the manual should be available for ready reference by all airport staff responsible for the management and operational use of the airport. The aerodrome manual is the means by which all airport operations staff are fully informed as to their duties and responsibilities, the aerodrome services and facilities, all operating procedures and any restrictions on airport availability to air traffic.

The exact form of the operations manual is now laid down but a typical aerodrome manual includes comprehensive sections under the following headings:

1. Technical administration.
2, Aerodrome characteristics.
3. Operational procedures.
4. Rescue and fire fighting services.
5. Medical facilities.
6. Aerodrome lighting.
7. Signals and surface markings.
8. Air traffic services.
9. Communications and navigational aids.

Each section lists equipment, procedures, areas of responsibility and availabilities applicable in the airport. The manual is the local application of the nationality accepted ICAO agreed criteria.

SEA TRANSPORT

The safe operation of ships includes safety in three vital areas:

1. Safety of human life and health.
2. Safety of the ship and its cargo.
3. Safety of the environment.

Safety in sea transport, as in other modes, involves not only shipping companies but governments and international agencies whose task is to set and regulate agreed standards over such a large and diverse industry. The diversity, both in type of operation and in locality, of the industry coupled with the sheer size of the world fleet and the record of maritime safety, has led to the establishment of a number of regulatory bodies. Their dual roles of work and regulation are, in the main, complementary, each organization playing its own part in the development and implementation of safety criteria.

Ship registration

All ships are registered in some country but the legislation and criteria for the registration of a merchant ship varies from country to country. There is no commonly adopted standard throughout the world except that each ship carries a document of identification issued by the country of registry. This document is commonly known as the ship's 'certificate of registry' or the 'ship's register'.

The ship's register contains a full description of the ship, type of construction, main dimensions, official number, place and date of building, description of engines and boilers, details of gross and net tonnages, master's name and certificate number. It also contains the name of the owners.

Most established maritime countries restrict registry to individuals residing or companies incorporated in that country. 'Flags of convenience' countries are those which have no such requirement and allow any individual or company to register a ship under their flag.

The UK restricts ownership of British ships to British subjects or companies incorporated under British law. All seagoing vessels must be registered except certain small coastal vessels, fishing boats, barges and Her Majesty's ships. There is no other requirement such as an operator's licence as there is in other modes of transport.

Ship classification

There are a number of ship classification societies world wide, of which Lloyd's Register, based in London, is the oldest and largest. The main function of a classification society is to assure the owner and other people that the ship has been designed, built and maintained in accordance with a set of rules. These rules, which cover the hull, equipment and machinery, reflect international agreements, national legislation and proposed legislation in addition to the classification society's own experience and technical expertise.

A classification society is an organization of technical experts and achieves their aim of ensuring that ships are constructed and maintained to high standards by examining and approving designs for new ships before construction commences, examining the materials used in the construction, surveying the ship and engines during building to check the workmanship and surveying the ship at periodic intervals during its working life.

These periodic surveys can be 'running surveys' carried out on parts of the ship whenever circumstances allow, provided that the whole ship is surveyed over a specific time period. On the other hand, the ship can be taken out of service for a few days and every part examined in that time. All societies require ships to undergo special surveys at four- or five-year intervals, the severity of these surveys increasing with the age of the ship.

There is no direct counterpart to the classification societies in any other sector of the transport industry. They are non-governmental, independent organizations set up solely to serve the interests of shipping and its customers. Why this is so is a matter of historical fact. Lloyd's was established at a time when governments and politicians maintained that industries should regulate themselves with only a minimum of political interference. It is significant that societies are concerned with the safety of the ship's structure and its equipment but not with safety of life. The concern for the lives of seafarers arose when governments were becoming more involved with social issues, and safety of life is a part of the governmental regulation system.

The classification society approach to ship safety is not simply concerned with rigidly applying their rules. These rules are backed by extensive research departments which keep under constant review new developments in technology, international agreements, and casualty investigation, and they give other wide-ranging services to the shipping industry.

Although the Department of Transport in the UK and government departments in other countries are responsible for issuing load line certificates, the standards set by the major classification societies are so high that a great deal of this type of work is delegated to their surveyors.

All societies keep register books which list details of the ships classed by themselves. Each society has its own shorthand method involving letters and numbers of notating the standard of the ships they have registered.

The Maritime and Coastguard Agency

Although the classification societies play a leading role in ensuring ship safety, their primary function is to oversee the standard of the ship's structure, equipment and machinery. The Maritime and Coastguard Agency is responsible for implementing the shipping related legislation concerned with safety of life, crew licensing and pollution from ships. It also has other wide-ranging duties which have a bearing on marine safety and pollution prevention. In this context, the Department provides the UK representatives to IMO (see p 160) and the International Labour Organization. Guidance about compliance with the regulations and information on matters not covered by the legislation is widely distributed through the Department's 'Merchant Shipping Notices'.

The Department for Transport through its local marine offices, performs a number of duties which relate to the safety of ships and which are not undertaken by the classification societies:

1. Certification of UK flag ships.
2. Investigation and reporting of casualties.
3. Random general inspection of both domestic and foreign ships.
4. Surveys of life saving appliances, radio equipment and the issue of certificates.
5. Surveys of passenger ships and the issue of certificates.
6. Surveys of crew accommodation.
7. Surveys of structural fire protection arrangements.
8. Examination of ship's officers and the issue of licences (called certificates of competency).
9. Prevention of accidents to seamen.

Certificates required by merchant shipping legislation provide international legal evidence of compliance with IMO conventions. The certificates which relate to ship safety include load line, radio equipment, safety equipment and safety of construction. Certificates have to be kept on board and be made available for inspection.

In July 1982, 14 European states brought into effect an agreement to allow inspections of ships in their ports no matter which flag the ship was flying. The signatories agreed that the national surveyors from each state will endeavour to make visits to 25 per cent of the foreign flag ships visiting their country. Inspections are recorded in an information bank, along with the results. Each of the signatory countries has access to this data bank. If the ship's certificates are in order and the surveyor has no comment on the ship's condition, then the ship will not be inspected again in any of the countries. In any other case, action will be needed by the shipping company to bring the ship up to standard and the proposed action is fully reported through the data bank. Ships which are allowed to sail on the understanding that defects will be rectified can be inspected in one of the other signatory countries to check that the repairs have been carried out. If the surveyor thinks that the ship is unsafe, it can be detained until the surveyor is satisfied that the ship is no longer in danger. It is hoped that this system will help to make the shipping industry safer by providing a check on those flags which do not have the administrative resources to control their shipping.

Manning scales

'Manning scales', the number of crew members needed per ship, are laid down for vessels flying the British flag and every vessel must carry a minimum number of duly certified British deck and engineer officers. The total number of personnel on any particular ship depends on the size and type of vessel in addition to the trade route on which the ship is engaged.

The Merchant Shipping (Certification of Deck and Marine Engineer Officers) Regulations 1977 contain the regulations regarding certification requirements. All UK registered ships of 80 gross tonnes and passenger ships must carry a specified number of deck officers determined according to tonnage and the type of voyage. Certificates of competency are issued by the Department for Transport after an examination. Additional training is required for certain deck officers for ships carrying bulk cargoes of specified dangerous chemicals and gases. The same applies to marine engineers. Overall, the standards of certification broadly reflect the outcome of IMO resolutions.

In sea transport there is no legislation regarding the hours that personnel can work, these being the subject of agreement between employers and the trade unions. This is in direct contrast to other modes of transport and means that seamen do not have to keep personal log books.

International Maritime Organization[14]

The most important inter-governmental organization with particular responsibility for promoting safety and pollution control is the International Maritime Organization (IMO). IMO was formed in 1948 as a specialized agency of the United Nations and is the sea transport equivalent of the ICAO.

The role of IMO is that of a consultative and advisory body for member states. As an inter-governmental entity, it has no legislative, executive or judicatory powers over member states. As with the ICAO, IMO provides the machinery for governments to co-operate and exchange information which relates to the standards of marine safety and the prevention and control of marine pollution from ships, with a view to obtaining international regulatory agreement. How it achieves these aims is closely related to its organizational structure.

The principal organs of IMO are the *assembly*, the *council* and the committee structure, as with the ICAO. The maritime environment protection committee deals with environmental protection. The committees are required to submit through the council to the assembly the proposals for new regulations and amendments of existing regulations, together with any comments and recommendations.

IMO is empowered to call international diplomatic conference at which proposed conventions, protocols, amendments and other aspects of safety are brought before member states' representatives for final consideration. The procedure is for conventions and protocols to state that the proposed regulations are to come into force after, for instance, a given number of states have become signatories, together with a qualifying minimum of registered tonnage. The past record for amending or updating conventions has been found to be unsatisfactory and amendments are now subjected to a 'tacit acceptance' procedure. This means that for future conventions, amendments will automatically enter into force within a prescribed time unless a minimum stipulated number of objections from contracting parties to the convention are received.

IMO seeks to establish the highest practical standards of safety in shipping. It is felt, though, that there is little practical benefit to the world shipping industry in establishing standards based on the most advanced technology if these standards cannot be attained on the world's fleets within a reasonable time scale. Unrealistically high standards only result in prolonged delays of entry into force of the instruments concerned. In effect, the standards lie unused and unobserved, having no impact on the day-to-day activities of the shipping industry. On the other hand, low standards may gain early global acceptance but do little more than reflect the generally accepted practices of the industry and do nothing to raise the standards of safety. IMO standards tend to be pitched at a level which can reasonably be attained by all fleets, not just the most advanced. IMO feel they have been successful in striking a reasonable balance in their standard setting activities.

As stated before, IMO is not a supranational authority and has neither the means nor the power to enforce convention standards. IMO standards, as with the Annexes of the ICAO are implemented through the actions of the member government. It is sovereign states which incorporate the international standards into their national statutes. National governments then have the power to take all the necessary action, including enforcement, to give full effect to the requirements of the conventions they adopt. IMO therefore, like all international organizations, depends on the ability of individual members to effectively implement the various standards and enforce their observance. This means that even those member states with the smallest of national fleets must pass the required laws, regulations, administrative instructions and guidelines. Each country has to develop a viable maritime administration embodying the wide variety of skills and disciplines employed today in the technological regulation of shipping.

The main conventions dealing with maritime safety are:

1. Safety of life at sea (SOLAS).
2. Load line rules.
3. Anti-collision regulations.
4. Standards of training and watch keeping.
5. Marine pollution from ships.

The role of IMO in establishing safety practices and policies in shipping can be summed up as follows:

1. IMO provides a forum through which all necessary measures can be discussed and decisions taken to establish the highest possible international standards. These can take the form of conventions or protocols which can be passed into law by all member countries. Because all countries are represented, from the most advanced to the least developed, IMO standards are not so high as to make them impossible to attain by some countries.
2. Through the various committees, to encourage all member states to adopt as speedily as possible the relevant international standards.
3. Through advice and assistance from experts, to allow all member states to succeed in their efforts to implement international standards by incorporating the necessary provisions into their national legislation and develop the appropriate administrative organization.
4. By making it possible for those administrations' officials, given the responsibility of implementing and enforcing international standards, to receive adequate training of a technical and administrative nature.
5. By providing a forum for the establishing and maintaining of international provisions and guidelines so that port state control (inspection of foreign ships in a state's ports) may be exercised in an effective and equitable manner.
6. By monitoring and analysing through its component bodies the deficiency reports from flag states and the responses received from flag states to maintain awareness of the problem of ships not up to standard. Where necessary, to enhance the efficiency of the flag state control procedure and practices.
7. By obliging parties to a convention to apply the requirements of that convention to ensure that no 'more favourable' treatment is given to non-party ships. In effect this means that the ships of

countries which refuse to apply the standards laid down in a convention must comply with these standards if they are to visit ports in a country that is party to the convention. This has far-reaching consequences for the shipping companies which flag their ships in non-party countries in order to try to avoid international standards.

RAILWAYS

The British government exercises technical supervision of the safety standards of railway construction and operation through Her Majesty's Railway Inspectorate. The Railway Inspectorate is part of the Health and Safety Executive.

The Railway Inspectorate's role is to secure the proper control of the risks to health and safety of employees, passengers and others who might be affected by the operation of Britain's railways. It monitors safety on the railways by:

1. Approving and inspecting all new railway works and rolling stock to ensure they meet acceptable safety standards.
2. Considering, accepting and monitoring railway safety cases as put forward by the train operating companies.
3. Instituting a programme of planned inspections of the railway to make certain that all the organizations involved in constructing, maintaining and operating the railway are complying with health and safety legislation. They have a system of enforcement for any non-compliance with the regulations.
4. Investigating accidents and dangerous occurrences on the railway.
5. Reports on trends in accidents and incidents on the railway.

The Railway Inspectorate has jurisdiction over Railtrack, the train operating companies, Eurostar UK, Eurotunnel UK, London Underground, Docklands Light Railway, and Tyne and Wear Metro. In addition there are the tram systems in Manchester, Blackpool, Sheffield and Nottingham and other minor railways.

The Railway Inspectorate produces 'Railway Principles and Guidance' which establishes the benchmark against which new developments on the railway are judged.

Accident investigation

The following types of accidents on the railway must be reported to the minister:

1. All accidents to passenger trains.
2. All accidents to goods trains which occur on or affect passenger lines.
3. All cases of trains becoming divided.
4. Mechanical failures that have caused or may have caused an accident to a passenger train.
5. Fires on trains, at stations or affecting signalling and telecommunications.
6. Failures of structures and rail breakages on passenger running lines.
7. Accidents to any person working, travelling, having business or trespassing on the railway.

All accidents reported to the minister are given out notices to the inspectorate where they are studied by an inspecting officer. Serious accidents are handled by the Chief Inspecting Officer who initiates action to obtain the details.

Ministerial inquiries are held into the most serious accidents. When the Chief Inspecting Officer has decided that a ministerial inquiry is necessary, he appoints an inspecting officer to carry out the inquiry. An inquiry is held in public but is not a court of law and there are no strict rules of evidence. The inquiring officer may exclude the press and the public if the evidence may prejudice a future court case.

Inquiries are not concerned with establishing criminal negligence or civil liability; that is for the courts to decide. The inquiry is set up to ascertain the causes of the accident and make recommendations with a view to preventing the same sort of accident occurring again.

The inquiry is held independently of any internal investigation held by the railway management but any evidence gained by the railway can be called by the inspecting officer. Representatives of the railway management and trade unions attend the inquiry to give evidence and assist the inspector. The inspecting officer hears the evidence and cross-examines witnesses. Council representing witnesses or people injured in the accident can put questions to witnesses through the inspecting officer.

Following the inquiry, the inspecting officer must submit a report to the minister 'stating the causes of the accident and all relevant circumstances, attaching observations on the evidence or matters arising out of the inquiry'. Copies of the report are sent to railway companies and their management's comments on the recommendations of the report are returned to the minister.

This procedure for inquiry into the causes of accidents is found in all forms of transport. The railway example serves to illustrate the process and the form.

SAFETY IN OPERATIONS: COMPARISONS BETWEEN MODES

In the field of the design and construction of vehicles, the comparison between modes is easy to make. This is a matter of engineering in its physical sense. Engineering principles and development are applied to the needs of each mode and a design is developed which will solve the problems of operation peculiar to that mode. It involves the application of engineering principles not only to the building of a vehicle but also to making sure that the vehicle can be maintained during its lifetime or that component parts can easily be replaced. The aspect of safety is inherent in the engineering design.

Operations involve human beings and the taking of decisions on incomplete data bases. An operating system consists of vehicles, people and the environment in which they work. All three subsystems interact. In considering an operations system which involves moving vehicles and human decisions, it can be confidently predicted that:

1. 100 per cent safety of the vehicle and people is not achievable because the unexpected is likely to occur. Thus, nuclear power stations have built-in safety features unheard of in other industries but even in this industry catastrophic accidents have happened.
2. There is a level at which the risk of an accident becomes unacceptable to the public at large. This usually occurs when similar accidents involving similar vehicles occur frequently, thus gaining the public's attention. This shows up when accidents are not perceived as random but follow a perceived pattern.

Casualties in the transport system can be the result of material or human failing. As stated at the beginning the chapter, a great deal of research has shown that a large proportion of casualties, even when materials failure was the primary cause, are of human origin. These accidents usually involve the ignoring of safety procedures by one or more people. There is a growing fear in all modes of transport that commercial pressures are forcing employees of transport companies to 'cut corners', leading to unsafe practices.

All modes of transport have one factor in common. They are all operated by people subjected to normal pressures, temptations and weaknesses. People under stress sometimes take chances, do things which are contrary to the regulations or neglect the proper procedures learnt in training. Ships' officers fail to reduce speed in fog even though the regulations are very specific on this point. Lorry drivers break speed limits or drive too close to the vehicle in front. We rarely hear of airline pilots or train drivers taking liberties with the regulations but when we do, it is front page news. Is there something different about the procedures in air transport or on the railways?

The following points of comparison between shipping and air transport can serve to illustrate some of the differences:

1. Ships can be seen at a great range by radar but the only means of identifying them positively is to get within visual range and read the name. Aircraft are fitted with radar transponders which identify them to ground radar. Indeed, for much of an aircraft's flight, the aircraft is closely monitored and controlled by air traffic control. Once a ship leaves port, the decision on how to proceed is largely up to the master.

2. Events on a ship are recorded in a manuscript log which may or may not be written up accurately at the time of the action. Some ships do have automatic helm, course and engine revolution recorders but in most cases these are accessible to the crew. Aircraft have sealed flight recorders which automatically record the multitude of events, and voice recorders which record a continuous record of the crew's orders and conversations.

3. Availability of enforcement of operational safety standards is different. All aircraft have to land within hours of an incident at a limited number of airports. A ship can be at sea for weeks after contravening regulations or good seamanship and, when it does arrive in port, the authorities in that country may be unwilling to act on matters which happened some time before and half the world away.

These factors alone point to the mariner having a greater chance of getting away with an act contrary to the regulations than his airline counterpart – which makes the seafarer far more likely to cut corners. This points to the conclusion that an important factor in maintaining safety standards is the likelihood of detection for contravening the rules.

The technology is available to produce transponders and recorders suitable for marine use, to provide similar data to that of aircraft. Two factors stand in the way of the introduction of such measures, factors which are significant in all modes of transport when considering safety devices on their vehicles. One of these is the cost of introducing measures which would seem to be of no immediate value to the company itself: for example, the fitting of effective spray suppression equipment on trucks can make motorway driving safer for other road users, but cost is the deciding factor for many road haulage companies. The other factor is the reluctance of transport operators to have their freedom of operation compromised by the fitting of such devices. One has only to recall the problems that had to be overcome with the fitting of tachographs to trucks, even when they were the subject of government legislation, to understand the difficulties.

Two factors may eventually occur to make the detection of deviations from regulations more certain in those modes which are harder to control. One is the probability that these devices will be built into vehicles as a result of the electronics revolution. The other is that there will be government legislation to compel their use as there is in the airline industry.

Accidents often occur through misunderstanding or misinterpretation of the information supplied to the driver by machines. Vehicle control in times of crisis make considerable demands on the driver. In aircraft the problem is to retain the alertness of the crew during long periods of inactivity. Current developments in information technology give great scope for improvements in safety.

It is clear that to push comparisons between the modes to absurd conclusions is silly – eg controlling road vehicles in a similar way to aeroplanes. However it is important for each mode to learn from the experiences of other modes.

CONCLUSIONS

This chapter has outlined the scope of the safety problem facing the transport industry. It has described the manner in which regulatory organizations seek to maintain and improve the standards of safety by international agreement and national legislation.

It should be clear that the approach to safety adopted by different sections of the industry has produced significant improvements in most areas. Many accidents result from human errors but the standards of training and licensing are making a major contribution to reducing accidents caused by human error.

It must be borne in mind that the cost to an individual company of implementing safety legislation can be high. A vast legislative and administrative bureaucracy has been built up, calling for the expenditure of government resources. As safety levels improve, it is apparent that future legislative and regulative requirements will have to take notice of the costs of implementation within the likely risk/benefit equation. It is no good pushing safety legislation so far that the costs cause transport to stagnate. From this it follows that we may be entering a period when it is necessary for the experience gained in operation of the current framework to be consolidated before any far-reaching changes are made.

Accidents, near misses and technical problems will occur in any dynamic industry and, though they will be used to highlight deficiencies in the regulations, they will not easily be remedied. A rational approach to safety is required which looks at the inter-related causal factors and assesses the impact of innovation and changes. One such change which will need close watching are the moves to deregulate the industry, which may lead to commercial pressure to neglect safety in the interests of profit.

References

1. Collins, R.C. *Airline Crashes* Macmillan Publishing Co, New York 1986
2. Ramsden, J.M. *The Safe Airline* Macdonald and James, London 1976
3. Leeming, J.J. *Road Accidents* Cassell and Co Ltd, London 1969
4. Lowe, D. *The Transport Managers Handbook* Kogan Page, London (yearly)
5. Department of Transport, *A guide to public service vehicle operators licences* HMSO, London
6. Consult the latest edition of the Construction and Use regulations for clarification of the latest position
7. Consult the latest edition of the Public Service Vehicle regulations for up-to-date information
8. Stewart-David, D. *The theory and practice of transport* Heinemann, London 1980
9. ICAO *Memorandum of the ICAO* ICAO Montreal
10. CAA *What it is, what it does* CAA London
11. Department of Transport *Air Navigation Order* HMSO, London
12. CAA 'Professional Pilots Licences' *CAP 54*, HMSO, London
13. Ashford, N. *Airport Operations* J. Wiley, Chichester 1984
14. Branch, A.E. *Elements of Shipping* Chapman and Hall, London 1981

7

Economic Regulation

The operation of transport vehicles within any particular market sector, whether on land, sea or in the air, can take place within a highly competitive environment. Whenever there is an opportunity to exploit a transport need, there always seem to be business people willing to institute a service to satisfy that need. This is true even though the transport industry has a reputation of difficulty in making a success of any new venture. As an example of new business people exploiting a transport opportunity, we have only to look at London passenger transport during the early 1920s. The London tramway network suffered competition from motor buses run by private companies. These companies were attracted into the market because they saw a demand for a more flexible service than that provided by the tramway company and calculated that they could exploit this opportunity profitably.

Besides the potential for competition, transport is for the most part small scale, though some individual companies are relatively large in comparison to other transport companies. Over any particular route, the size of the market depends on other factors than just the efforts of a transport company. The location of homes, offices, factories or raw materials, ie the landuse patterns in any area, are a major influence on the size of any transport market. Where the size of the market is unlikely to attract many services public authorities may have to give some financial support in order that transport be provided.

Entry of companies into any transport market sector is relatively easy, both financially and technically. Financially, the sums of money needed to start a transport company are not large when compared with the capital requirements needed to start in many other industries. The purchase of a coach or a truck is within the reach of almost any person willing to take the risk of repaying interest charges on a loan. Even an aircraft or a ship can involve the direct investment of only modest sums of money when compared with other industries. To make a successful business venture from the investment requires additional skill and expertise but this seems to be no bar to the number of people willing to try to operate transport companies.

It is technically easy to start a transport business because vehicles and systems can be purchased in the latest version from the vehicle manufacturers. Even if one company gains a competitive advantage by introducing technically advanced vehicles, it is not long before other companies can avail themselves of most advanced equipment. Technically transport is an open industry in that any technological development can be utilized by all companies. In most sectors of transport there is separation of the operating company from the vehicle manufacturers and no one operating company can ever gain complete unique control over new technologies or operating methods.

These conditions of easy entry to sometimes limited markets, and shared technology, carry strong inducements for established operators to seek protection from competition. The history of transport operations is one of both operators and governments restricting entry of new competitors and restricting competition between established operators. This is true of all modes of transport.

In very recent times, this picture of transport has changed. The major policy issue which has dominated both national and international political debate for the last 25 years has been the issue of free competition versus some form of economic control. Though there has been competition in all modes of transport and between modes, this competition has been highly regulated. Now, almost all governments in the developed world are examining ways to ease the regulations and introduce true competition.

There are many points of view on both sides of the debate about economic regulation and we will study these points in detail.

SAFETY

As was discussed in Chapter 6, all methods of transport involve an element of risk during the operation of moving vehicles. It has long been accepted by all those involved that in order to protect the environment, the employees and the passengers, an extensive system of regulations and restrictions concerned with safety is necessary. These restrictions are forced on operators by governments and international agencies.

For the majority of transport operators the provision of safety equipment and procedures is a major cost item. To many, it is seen as a cost which has no direct benefit operationally except in terms of customer goodwill. Commercially, high safety standards imposed by regulation are a drain on the earnings potential of any company. These operators argue that to maintain high safety standards, they need protection from competition. The direct result of competition will be a lowering of prices, price being the main competitive device open to most companies in the short term. In order to compete on price, companies have to cut their costs in an effort to maintain their market share or even to survive. In any cost-cutting exercise, companies identify cost centres and act to reduce costs through these centres. One easily identified cost centre is safety measures. Costs in this area can be saved by postponing replacement of equipment, increasing the interval between maintenance periods, employing cheaper, under-trained labour, making the labour force work longer hours and ignoring safety procedures to gain more productive time. On the surface, these arguments are very powerful but they are countered in two particulars by those arguing for more competition.

In the first place, it is asked, can any operator afford to gain a reputation for a bad safety record, even in a highly competitive market? In passenger transport it may very well be true that no operator can afford to gain a reputation for poor safety standards. If the vehicles of any passenger transport operator are frequently involved in accidents resulting in death or injury to the passengers, the public are likely to become wary of using that service. As regards goods transport, this type of argument may not apply with the same force. Goods are invariably insured during transit and the financial loss to the shipper may not be great in the event of an accident. There is, obviously, some loss of goodwill between the shipper and the consignee when goods do not arrive as promised, but this can be overcome in time. With goods transport it is usually the vehicle crew which are the human sufferers in accidents. Overall, the argument has some validity even with goods transport, indicating that free market competition will not have a dramatic affect on safety standards.

A much stronger reason for believing that economic regulation or the lack of such control does not have a bearing on safety standards is that governments pass legislation to control safety in transport. The legislation not only lays down minimum standards but also puts in place a regime of inspectors to make sure that the standards are upheld. There is no evidence to show that the absence of economic regulation results in higher safety. Even in highly regulated sections of transport, safety regulations are regularly developed to meet the needs of changing technology and vigorously monitored. Though transport is difficult to regulate because the main object of the regulation, the vehicle, moves from place to place, it is possible to regulate for safety without resort to economic regulations imposed on the industry.

PUBLIC UTILITY

To many people transport should be treated as a public utility like water, electricity and sewerage. Transport is essential to the maintenance and well-being of any nation. The benefits of a well-planned transport system spread far beyond the transport field. Transport is essential for industry, for people's mobility and for good communications. In any civilized society, people are entitled to mobility in the same way as they are entitled to sewerage and fresh water systems. The benefits deriving from the public utility nature of transport can only be realized if the system is planned and regulated so that all members of society benefit – not only the rich.

To economists, transport cannot be thought of as a public utility in the sense of being essential to the welfare of the community. New services and innovation will only take place if entrepreneurs are allowed to experiment with services offering different mixes of comfort and price. If there is not enough demand to make some services profitable, these services should be discontinued.

What of people who are reliant on public transport for their mobility, especially those who live in remote areas or places where there is little demand? Are they to be left without, in some cases, the economic and social lifeline which public transport represents? Should we not regard transport in such a way that these vital services can be provided as part of an overall network?

Countering these arguments, those who oppose the idea of transport as a public utility say that these are political questions and should be approached from a political viewpoint. Services which the political process deem essential but are non-commercial can be supported by subsidies. By opening transport to commercial competition, these services will be identified and their true nature recognized, rather than constrain the whole system with regulation to make sure that essential non-commercial services are provided.

AN INTEGRATED TRANSPORT SYSTEM

The essence of economic control is to harbour resources and prevent waste by integrating or co-ordinating transport services. For example, if two services compete for custom along a route where there is only sufficient demand for one service, wasted investment will result. In fact, the revenue will be low for both services because there must be a sharing of potential customers between the services. It is believed that co-ordination of transport by common ownership or a system of economic licensing will eliminate this waste.

This argument is equally valid when applied to intra-modal competition as to inter-modal. By a system of control, investment and demand can be channelled towards those modes which serve the public need most adequately in any particular circumstances. Thus, buses should be used in major conurbations to take people from their homes to the main transport arteries served by some form of mass transit system. The timetables of the mass transit system and the buses are co-ordinated to provide a properly integrated system of passenger transport. The same case can be put forward concerning freight transport, where rail is used for trunk haul and road for local delivery. Indeed, the whole transport sector can be viewed in this way, with some competent body, like the British Transport Commission, having the power to plan transport for the national benefit.

A further point used to back up the perceived need for integration is the belief among a certain group of people that investment by individuals is often misdirected. Individuals lack adequate data on which to base investment decisions, especially in a sphere as vital to national well-being as transport. The only way to make sure that resources are not wasted or investment misdirected is to carefully control transport. This contention is backed up by showing the numbers of companies optimistically entering a sector of transport, providing services often in an innovative nature and then leaving the industry after making losses on their investment, as proof of the need for a planned co-ordinated approach.

Just as passionately, the belief that competition is healthy for the development of any business is held by many advocates of the free enterprise system. They believe that the principles of open competition applied to other sectors of the economy are just as valid when applied to transport. Indeed, competition itself ensures correct investment because investment will only be undertaken if there is the chance of a return. On any given route, competition will ensure that supply meets demand in a way which satisfies customers' needs. Competition is not merely concerned with lower fares; it can bring other benefits to the user of a transport service. Operating transport in a competitive environment ensures that managers have to research the needs of their potential customers. By experimenting with the marketing mix, competition will be the spur to customer satisfaction.

Transport policy should be aimed at satisfying user needs in exactly the same way as in other businesses. Economic regulation which enhances the status quo by favouring the established operators has the effect of making people choose between using the service which is offered or not using the service at all. In some cases, rather than use services which only partially meet their requirements, people will find ways other than using transport to satisfy their desires. If parts of the system are insulated from market forces, the needs satisfaction becomes very difficult to fulfil. Managements have no incentive to innovate, no spur to better operational methods and lack any measurement of success. They do, however, have a strong sense of social duty which may be missing in a very competitive company.

LOAD FACTORS AND SCHEDULED SERVICES

The load factor of a vehicle is the ratio of the vehicle's actual load on any individual service to the designed or optimum carrying capacity. The load factors for individual journeys can be averaged over any period to arrive at the average load factors figures. The load factor is obviously a measure of the operational success of the service. Unit transport costs diminish with rising load factors because costs are spread over more units. Operators of transport services strive to achieve the highest load factors possible in order to keep unit costs low.

The achievement of high load factors is incompatible with many transport users' desire for frequent and regular services. These customers require that the transport they use will operate to an established schedule. They want the schedule adhered to even though the vehicle may have to leave the terminus almost empty. This means that at that time, in order to provide a schedule service, the operator has to accept lower average load factors. In calculating his fares or freight tariffs, the operator will have to take this into account and charge the appropriate rate.

With a rate structure which reflects the low average load factors, the scheduled operator, during times of high demand for his services, is vulnerable to competition from a non-scheduled operator. The latter is unburdened by the need to account for low average load factors at non-peak demand times, and can therefore charge lower fares. The scheduled operator is then placed in an impossible position: in order to fight off the competition at peak times, he must lower his prices at these times, but he will still have to maintain the frequent service demanded by the consumer.

In all branches of transport, the scheduled operator is at a disadvantage when competing with the non-scheduled operator. The scheduled operator looks to some form of protection from competition through economic regulation. He wants his regular services protected against the irregular services which are possible at peak times and argues that the regulations are a small price to pay for the benefits of regular and efficient services of a scheduled nature.

This is one of the main arguments in favour of economic regulation and it is difficult to construct a case to refute the necessity in such cases. It is argued, however, that transport users are not all the same and do not have the same demands. The only way in which the real preferences, as opposed to perceived preferences, of customers and potential customers can be established is by some form of competition between operators. The market is the best judge of its own needs. There is no real evidence to suggest that the market place should not be able to accommodate carriers offering different types of service in competition. If a scheduled carrier designs the service well, costs the operation effectively and satisfies customer needs, he should be able to compete with the non-schedulee carrier.

STABILITY

Stability of the route structure and of the operators of transport services is preferable to frequent changes of services and operators. Competition risks the creation of an unstable environment where the customer is never sure what services are on offer or what the charges are likely to be for a given service. In a freely competitive market there is always the risk that a carrier will cease to trade, leaving some parts of the market without services.

Small companies lacking financial resources can be drawn into transport at times of economic boom and then fall victim to a financial crisis during a contraction in the market. The entry of marginal carriers during good times is followed by a period of struggle during bad economic conditions. During the down-turn too much transport supply chases a diminishing transport demand resulting in even lower rates and bigger financial crisis for all carriers. It is argued that to avoid the risks of instability, the survival of transport in a comprehensive and easily understood form depends on careful planning and economic regulation.

The main danger of this argument is that it enhances the status quo. Regulators have tended to confuse the sound development of the industry with making sure that established transport companies avoid bankruptcy. As a result, regulation has tended to shield inefficient companies from the necessity to undertake changes to meet the changing needs of the customers. This in turn has engendered a very conservative view of developments as companies are reluctant to change. The most striking illustration of this was the upsurge of technical and operational innovation which flooded the coach industry after the 1980 deregulation.

EXPLOITATION OF MONOPOLY

Many scheduled routes can barely support one regular scheduled operator, let alone competing services. On such routes, periods of intense competition are usually short until one dominant carrier emerges. Once this carrier has overcome the opposition, it will substantially raise prices using its new monopoly position to make up for losses during any period of intense competition. The monopoly position will enable the carrier to build up reserves which can then be used against any attempt by another operator to compete. The only way to avoid this situation is to overcome the danger of exploitation by regulation which controls fares in exchange for monopoly.

It must be acknowledged that transport is an 'easy' industry to enter and any transport business charging monopoly prices invites competition unless protected by regulation. Even under strict modal regulation, there can still be fierce competition between modes. There is in the modern era very little danger of any carrier being able to charge monopoly prices. There is also the theory of 'contestability'. With easy entry to markets, no carrier can charge too high a price for a service because that would invite competition. An established operator on a highly used route will price his service at the level just below that price at which competing operators would move in to compete. In this way, prices are always set in a freely competitive market at the correct level.

DISPARITY IN SIZE

It is argued that the relative sizes of carrier in any market sector can lead to unfair competition. The larger operator can dominate the market by drawing on vastly superior resources to those of a smaller operator.

The disparity in size of different companies within any market sector is a positive advantage if there is competition. Large companies can build up a network of routes and benefit from any economies of scale. Small companies can innovate more easily, specializing in exploiting narrow sectors of the market while benefiting from low overheads and intimate management.

CROSS-SUBSIDY

One reason for requiring protection of regulation claimed by many transport operators stems from the widespread practice of cross-subsidy. Cross-subsidy is defined as the practice of averaging costs over a network of services. In practice, this means that although some services may be running at a loss, these loss-making services can be supported by the profits earned in other parts of the network. There is nothing intrinsically wrong with the practice of cross-subsidy. It is normal practice in many businesses to market some products at a loss in order to attract customers and help sell more profitable items. Supermarkets do this all the time.

In transport, cross-subsidy occurs for three main reasons:

1. *Public service requirements.* Operators of passenger services (though some freight services have the same characteristics) are expected to maintain a minimum schedule of services regardless of how profitable individual services prove. This is often a requirement for obtaining a licence. What this means in effect is earning greater than need-be profits on some routes in order to make up the losses on others.
2. *Standard fares systems.* In many cases, the public and politicians believe that the fare should always be the same for a given distance travelled within a network. The costs of providing services are different in different parts of the network according to the time of journey, the nature of the route and the type of vehicle used. If a standard fare system is used, the most costly routes must be subsidized by the less costly ones.
3. *Temporary losses.* Transport is not a product that can be stored or offered when it suits the operator. Permanency and reliability are essential to the customer and operators are obliged to persist with loss-making services by cross-subsidy from other routes.

To make a policy of cross-subsidy viable, operators claim that they must have protection from competition on their profitable routes. If competition on the profitable routes results in lower rates and squeezed profit margins, the only way the operator can survive is to cut the number of unprofitable services. Taken to the ultimate extreme, this will result in a break-up of transport networks and grave inconvenience to the transport user.

Critics of this stance by operators contend that cross-subsidy used as a method of sustaining unremunerative routes is undemocratic. It represents, in a lot of cases, a shift of resources from the poor to the rich. In many large cities, the profitable routes are those which run through inner city areas where car ownership is low and people rely on buses for their mobility. The unprofitable routes are to the outer suburbs where the income levels are higher. The fares charged on the profitable inner city routes have to be higher than needed in order to subsidize the outer suburban routes. Thus there is a shift of resources from the poor to the rich.

What is needed is a system where an operator knows the true costs of providing any service and bases his pricing policy on those costs. It is argued strongly that although cross-subsidy is not necessarily bad, the building of a protective licensing system on this proposition is bad. Monopoly rights given to an operator over a network can blur the perception of the true costs of any system. This in itself is bad management practice.

PREDATORY PRICING

There are two aspects to this argument. On the one hand, the large company can use its greater financial strength to offer artificially low fares in order to force a smaller competitor out of business. Thus survival is likely to be merely a reflection of financial strength rather than of operating efficiency.

On the other hand, new operators can often be drawn into market sectors with limited resources and basic operating knowledge. In many cases, the size of the market is too small to accommodate many operators. The only way open to a new entrant is to try to attract customers is by undercutting the rates charged by operators already established in that market sector. The result is often a 'price war' as the established operators cut their rates to meet the competition. In a very short time, the situation arises where no company is able to earn adequate profits. The road haulage industry is very susceptible to this form of competition. Very little capital is required to start a business, and it can provide self-employment for the lorry driver.

It is natural for companies to complain of excessive competition leading to instability and lack of resources. Excess capacity occurs in all branches of transport, especially in times of economic recession. Capacity can be increased fairly rapidly during times of economic expansion, drawing new operators into the industry. It is harder to decrease capacity in times of economic downturn because operators stay in the market place hoping that the economic situation will improve. The direct result of over-capacity is very low rates and increased bankruptcies.

The perception of this type of situation leads to calls for at least co-ordination between operators in an effort so share out the available work. In many cases it leads to calls for restrictions on entry and to harsh standards of quality licensing. The established operators always believe that this will help solve their problems.

PRICE FIXING

The alternative to 'price wars' which occur when competition gets too intense is some form of price fixing arrangement covering transport operators. Price fixing in cartels is a method of avoiding price competition between operators. Price control can also be supported by government legislation or by inter-governmental agreement in international transport.

The danger of price fixing agreements is twofold. The price has to be fixed at a level which allows even the most inefficient operator in the group to make some sort of profit. Efficient operators will go along with the agreement, certain that they will be able to make superprofits. Within any price fixing system there is no incentive for managements to be particularly innovative. Indeed, because of the disparity in efficiency of the different operators, what were initially purely price fixing arrangements often lead on to restrict other forms of competition. In some instances, especially in air transport and sea transport, price fixing includes pooling agreements and sharing out the service between the operators.

The other danger is that all operators' market mixes become the same and competition is no longer a matter of real factors but of image. Product differentiation is no longer a matter of price and service quality, but of trying to convince the customer that your service is different, although all the characteristics of the service are the same as everybody else's. The air transport industry suffers a great deal from this type of competition where, as an example, the only way some operators can think of differentiating the service is to claim that their air hostesses are prettier than all other air hostesses.

PUBLIC SERVICE

The notion of public service has been a part of the culture of transport management for a long time. It has often been suggested that where communities have been established, transport should be provided. Transport, especially passenger transport, is a public right. This again emphasizes the political dimension of transport provision.

The central controversy is how best people's needs for mobility for themselves or their goods can be met. As we have seen, there is in all branches of transport the tendency for the established operators to try to protect their position by some restrictions on the free entry into their particular market and the controlling of competition between operators in any particular market sector. It is a matter of political conviction as to which way any one person views the controversy.

As has been demonstrated, there is enough evidence to support either the case for restriction of competition or the case for a free market approach. The restrictionists argue that to allow market forces a free reign would leave many people without transport services and cause damage to the environment. This shows a lack of social responsibility. The free market advocates reply that once the commercial network of services is established, the question of how unremunerative but socially necessary services can be provided then requires political decision.

The rest of the chapter will examine each mode to follow the trend of regulation in that mode. It will become increasingly clear that, although the scale of operation may be different, the regulations and debates are very similar.

ROAD HAULAGE

Between 1933 and 1968, the UK had a rigid licensing system to control road haulage. In many ways, the system was a reflection of the perceived importance of the railways and was used as much to protect the railways from competition as to regulate the industry. There were three types of licence covering the road haulage industry.

An 'A' licence entitled the holder to ply for 'hire and reward', with very few restrictions.

A 'B' licence entitled the holder to ply for 'hire and reward' as well as carry goods on own account. The licence was restricted to certain types of traffic and in geographical areas.

Companies wishing to transport their own goods in their own lorries without restrictions did so under a 'C' licence. This licence was restricted to own account transport. 'C' licences were granted automatically if provisions on safety and quality were met by the applicant. To gain a licence 'for hire and reward' applicants had to demonstrate a need for their services. Existing operators and the railways could raise objections to the application.

As Aldcroft[1] states, 'The main effect [of the licensing system] was to freeze the status quo. The system favoured the existing operators and made entry into the industry more difficult, with the result that growth in the industry occurred mainly in the own account sector.'

In the USA[2] there are three major segments: the regulated motor carriers subjected to licences to allow them to carry regulated commodities: private motor carriers, the private fleets of companies 'not primarily engaged in transport' and which do not offer their services for hire; and exempt motor carriers hauling for hire commodities exempt from regulation.

All these systems fall short of full-blown quantity licensing by leaving some room for competition. Full quantity licensing would only allow carriage if the licensing authority or regulating body authorized such carriage. In some countries carriage can only be undertaken by nominated carriers or modes. This is the system which was the ultimate goal of the British Transport Commission (see Chapter 3) but which was never fully realized.

The Transport Act of 1968 practically deregulated the road haulage industry in the UK. There are now no restrictions on operating or entry. The quality provisions of operating licences are intended to make sure that only responsible people are operating road haulage companies.

BUS AND COACH INDUSTRY

Economic regulation of the bus and coach industry was first introduced in the UK in London in 1924 and in the remainder of the country in 1930. It was the type of regulation which is found throughout the world.

The central feature of the system was the road service licence. This was based on the concept of licensing exclusively specific routes to specific operators. It enabled operators to build networks of services especially in major towns and other geographical areas. It was instrumental in the growth of the municipal operators and the territorial companies eventually absorbed into the National Bus Company.

There were three types of road service licence – stage carriage, express carriage, and excursion and tours. Contract hire was not controlled. Any bus company could apply for a licence to run a particular service but various organizations, other passenger transport operators, local authorities and designated bodies could object to the granting of a licence. This resulted in operators being able to build almost vertical monopolies within their operating area.

The main criteria used by the traffic commissioners when deciding the question of a licence application was whether the service in question was in the public interest. To decide on the principle of the public interest, the traffic commissioners took into account the public transport need of the area as a whole and the level of provision within that area. Thus, if a new service was proposed which, though not directly in competition by using exactly the same route, was still expected to take traffic from an established route, the application would be refused. It would be deemed to be against the public interest for any new service to gain passengers from an existing service.

Public interest in transport implies the husbanding of scarce resources so that unnecessary duplication of services is avoided. This is taken to mean that services which are unnecessary because there is no need or because there is already provision should be eliminated. This, in effect, gives the established operator in an area a real stranglehold on the bus services. The husbanding of scarce resources and the public need criteria meant that after an application was turned down, the established operator could make a successful application by incorporating the proposed changes into his network.

Finally, public interest was taken to mean that services should be provided where there is a need but little hope of making a profit. This led to the emphasis on cross-subsidy in the bus industry. This formed part of the feeling that bus services should be co-ordinated along with rail and air. Co-ordination never worked properly between bus and rail because the ownership of the modes was different and they saw themselves serving different markets.

As Moir Lockhead[3] sums up the situation: 'There is evidence to suggest that in the last decade (1975–1985) the bus industry failed to read the signals of discontent and was slow to respond to this and the continuing decline in passenger demand. The aim of the 1985 Transport Act was to introduce free market competition into the highly regulated environment of bus operation. The Act provides for the transfer of existing municipal bus undertakings to companies wholly owned by the regional authorities and the privatisation of the National Bus Company. Where the local authority require to provide services without the free market which are socially desirable, tenders must be invited to ensure value for money against the subsidy provided. There are risks in the new legislation.'

The Transport Act of 1985 practically deregulated the bus industry in Great Britain, following the path of the 1980 Act which deregulated express coach services. All that remains of the old regulation is the need for a bus company to inform the traffic commissioners of the services they wish to run. Anybody who meets the criteria for an operator's licence (see Chapter 6) can now start and operate a bus service.

In addition, the Greater London Council and the Metropolitan Councils covering the major conurbations have been abolished. In 1984 the government took control of London Regional Transport from the Greater London Council. The passenger transport executives in the Metropolitan nominate representatives to sit on the executive. All municipal bus undertakings have been transferred to companies in which the former controlling body, the local authority, hold the shares. The government hope that this will open the way for private share capital. The National Bus Company is being sold piece by piece, ie each operating company independently, rather than as a whole.

Following the coming to power of the Conservative Government in 1979, the bus and coach industry transformed from a highly regulated, rather introspective industry into a free market with managements pushing innovation to the fore. Whether the change can be sustained into the future is a matter for debate. It must be constantly borne in mind that, just as in 1930, the whole system could become highly regulated in a very short time.

SHIPPING

It is only in the scheduled liner shipping services that economic regulation is relevant. In bulk shipping[5] there is unregulated competition where a large number of small size buyers and a large number of small-size sellers are in the market. At most times there is no organization which can dominate the market and, therefore, influence the prices paid for shipping services. There are few barriers to entry into the market and new entrants can produce identical services to the established firms. Any technological innovation must prove its worth to the shipowner by enabling him to secure a better price in the market and to the shipper of the cargo by providing the service required. There is no point in building highly advanced ships if the shipper does not require them or is unwilling to pay higher prices for higher quality services.

The majority of bulk shipping is undertaken under the terms of a charter agreement between the shipowner and the shipper. What the terms of that contract are is a matter of negotiation between the shipowner and the charterer, not the subject of third party regulation. It is in this part of the shipping industry that there are a number of merchant traders (own account operators).

Shipping conferences

Shipping conferences are the main method of economic regulation in shipping and are associations of companies serving a distinct route. Shipping conferences are maintained with the intention of protecting scheduled shipping from competition from non-scheduled shipping. It is firmly believed that by using the combined strength through a conference, scheduled lines will be able to withstand price or any other type of competition.

Shipping conferences were first formed as a result of severe competition between steamship lines when advances in technology led to enormous increases in capacity on some routes. The first conference, the Calcutta formed in 1875, fixed equal rates from each of the ports from which the vessel was despatched. A deferred rebate scheme was introduced whereby shippers were granted a rebate for constant patronage over a period but the rebate was not actually paid until they had shown their goodwill by shipping all their freight by the conference lines for a further period.

Membership of conferences is international and shipping companies can belong to several conferences at the same time. This is because conferences are route-based, not company-based. There are also in existence several inter-conference agreements which regulate the relationships between conferences.

Conference policy is decided at meetings of the member lines, hence the origin of the name conference, and by the votes of the conference members. Because of their nature, conference rights have a market value, so they can add to the value when a shipping company is sold or taken over.

In some conferences, pooling agreements have been negotiated. With these agreements traffic and gross or net earnings on the total trade route are pooled, members receiving agreed percentages of the pool. Under the gross earnings agreement, each shipowner bears all the costs of operation and pools his gross revenue. With a net earnings agreement, each operator pools only his net earnings, meaning that the more efficient low cost operator is penalised when his performance is compared to the more expensive and less efficient operator. No individual shipowner has control of other operators' expenditure and this also tends to favour the less efficient shipowner. With these arrangements there is no real incentive for any shipowner to control his costs. Indirectly, any excessive costs by one member of the conference will be borne by all the other members collectively. The objective of these arrangements is to guarantee to members a certain share of the trade and to limit competition between the members of the conferences. Pooling agreements are becoming more common even among British shipowners through traditionally British shipowners have preferred to use the conference arrangements to establish an agreed scale of tariffs but to permit competition between members in quality of service.

An excess of tonnage on a particular route is likely to lead to an agreed reduction in the number of sailings and a pooling of receipts. Often, when conferences perform special services such as lifting unprofitable cargo or resorting to chartering in tonnage to cover temporary peaks in demand, the conference members pool the resulting losses or profits even though they do not have an overall pooling agreement.

A further example of a liner conference stopping competition is where each member agrees to operate a percentage of the sailings and take an identical percentage of the total pooled income. Hence, in a conference of four members, two may agree to provide 20 per cent of the sailings each and get 20 per cent of the income. The other two may provide 30 per cent of the sailings each and get 30 per cent of the income. With this type of agreement, each operator is responsible for his costs, thus the lowest cost operator would make the highest profits.

The objectives of conferences are to restrict competition in scheduled liner shipping on specific trade routes by restricting entry, agreeing rate scales and gaining loyalty from shippers. There are two types of conference, open conferences and closed conferences. Open conferences are conferences where membership is open to any shipping line using a route. These apply to all lines to the USA. Closed conferences are where entry can only be gained if all the members are in agreement.

Conference members claim that wasteful competition among members is avoided by regulating loadings. Conferences organize themselves so that they can combat outside competition through their collective strength. There is also the claimed added bonus that tariffs are maintained for long periods, and are not raised without due notice, and this gives shippers the chance to quote competitive prices in their market place.

Protectionist policies and their impact

There is no common definition of 'protectionism'. The term is applied to a wide variety of acts and pressures exerted by governments which are designed to increase the competitiveness of their national economies. In recent years protectionism has increased due mainly to the recession in the world economy and the growing international debt crisis.

This is particularly true in shipping. Most governments give some support to their national fleets through a range of measures both statutory and unofficial.

Subsidies occur where the losses by some business enterprise are borne by general taxation. Direct subsidies may be given to the shipping industry for ship construction, purchase or improvement or towards operating costs. Indirect subsidies may be given via loans made at low or zero interest, by making provisions for accelerated depreciation allowances against tax, via other tax privileges such as exemption from income or corporation tax or through the reimbursement of harbour dues, pilotage expenses or canal dues. Also, government contracts and cargoes may be offered at favourable rates.

Flag discrimination or flag preference has an advantage over subsidy in so much as it is not directly financed by the tax-payer. This may be more popular politically and is acceptable to very poor countries which do not have the finance available to give subsidies.

Flag discrimination takes the form of offering national flag vessels preferential treatment compared to the ships of other nations. One method is to offer own national flag ships preferential treatment in own ports. Foreign flag ships are made to pay higher port dues and charges as well as having to follow elaborate procedures with documentation which are not applied to own flag ships. There are some countries which impose extra fees and taxes on foreign vessels entering their ports or on cargo carried in foreign vessels. Others give priority in berth assignment or reserve certain berths for national vessels. Delays can also be imposed on foreign flag ships by rigorous health inspections.

These methods can be given some official standing by legislative positive discrimination regarding cargoes only to be carried in national flag vessels. This kind of legislation is often accompanied by bilateral trade agreements with other states. Bilateral trade treaties are agreements which limit the trade between two countries to the flag ship of those two countries, thus excluding other nations' ships from carrying a part of this trade. Tied in with this system is the tendency for some countries to legislate that all government owned or sponsored cargoes must be carried by that country's flag ships.

Preference may also be shown in respect of exchange controls or the granting of import/export licences. Cabotage, which is the reservation of coastal cargoes to national vessels, is common to almost all countries and French cabotage regulations extend this to French controlled territories which are thousands of miles apart. Lastly, a government may put pressure on conferences serving their trade to obtain entry for national flag vessels irrespective of the needs for trade or the possibility of overtonnaging on the route.

The major problem with protectionism by one country is that it prompts retaliation by other countries. The net result is overtonnaging, decreased competition and falling revenues. As earnings fall, subsidies or further protectionism have to be introduced and previously profitable competitors are driven from the market.

Protectionism is deplored by the established operators and the proponents of free trade but it is a growing factor in the world shipping industry.

World shipping

The state of world shipping can be understood by studying the Code of Conduct for Liner Conferences approved by the United Nations Conference on Trade and Development (UNCTAD). The code has six fundamental objectives:

1. To facilitate the orderly expansion of world shipping.
2. To stimulate the development of regular and efficient liner services adequate to the requirements of the trade concerned.
3. To ensure a balance of interests between suppliers and users of liner shipping.
4. That conference practices should not involve any discrimination against shipowners, shippers or the foreign trade of any nation.
5. That conferences hold meaningful consultation with shippers' organizations, shippers' representatives and shippers on matters of common interest, with the participation of the appropriate authorities.
6. That conferences should make available to interested parties pertinent information about their activities which are relevant to those parties, and should publish meaningful information on their activities.

The code is inherently restrictive and an aid to developing countries. Conferences are bound to accept as members liner companies from those countries whose trade the conference serves. The so called '40–40–20' principle is not actually set out specifically. The code does state that the national shipping lines of the two trading partners should have 'equal rights' to participate in the freight and volume of traffic generated and that third countries' lines should have the right to acquire 'a significant part, such as 20 per cent'.

From the foregoing, we learn that economic regulation is far more complicated when an international dimension is added. In the shipping industry there are not only inter-company agreements but also national regulations based more on a state's prestige than on any commercial criteria. Economic regulation of shipping is also part of international political tension and power play.

AIR TRANSPORT

The Paris convention of 1919 accepted that all states have sovereign rights over the air space above its territory. This agreement means that government interference in the operation of air transport became inevitable. Put simply, from that time onward, no aircraft could fly above the territory of a state without some form of official approval. Any airline wishing to establish an air service between two states had to gain prior agreement from both governments.

The Chicago Conference in 1944 which led to the establishment of ICAO was, in fact, called to debate the issue of some form of multi-national agreement on three aspects of scheduled air transport:

1. An agreed policy on the exchange of traffic rights.
2. The establishment of a mechanism for negotiating air fares and freight charges.
3. The control of international agreements on frequencies and capacities.

The conference failed to reach agreement on any of these three specific points. Many countries suffering from the effects of war favoured maximum control at least while they rebuilt their ravaged commercial air transport. Others, notably led by the USA, favoured maximum freedom of the air.

Although the Chicago Conference failed to reach agreement on these issues, it did formulate definitions of the international rights of civil aviation. These became known as the five freedoms of the air, with the evolution of several others since that meeting:[6]

First Freedom: The right to fly over another state's territory when en route to a third country. This freedom is often called the 'right of innocent passage' but the overflown territory has the right to be notified in advance and can refuse such overflight, although approval is usually automatic.
Second Freedom: The right to land in another state's territory for technical reasons such as refuelling or maintenance. This freedom is in the interest of air safety but confers no right to carry out commercial transactions like picking up passengers or freight.
Third Freedom: The right to establish a route to another country from the flag state and to carry passengers and freight.

Fourth Freedom: The right to carry passengers into the country of registry of the aircraft.

Fifth Freedom: The right to transport goods or passengers between two other countries other than the country of registry as long as the flight originates or terminates in the country of registry.

Sixth Freedom: The right to carry traffic that has neither origin or destination in the country of registry but which traffic stops for a limited period in the country of registry.

Seventh Freedom: The right to operate between two countries neither of which is the country of registry and with no connection to the country of registry.

Eighth Freedom: The right to cabotage traffic within a state which is not the country of registry of the airline.

How these principles are applied in specific cases is left to the bilateral negotiations regarding air traffic rights between states. The control of capacities and frequencies is in some cases left to the airlines and tariffs can be regulated by participation in the International Air Transport Association (IATA) traffic conferences.

Bilateral air service agreements

Bilateral air service agreements are negotiated by nation states regarding the establishment of air services between that state and other states. They are the rules that govern the operation of air services between the two countries. The fundamental principle of air service agreements being reciprocity that is the exchange of rights on the basis of equal opportunity for the two countries airlines. Bilateral air service agreements set out the rules for all economic aspects of the air services provided.

There are many types of bilateral air service agreements but three broad categories of agreement can be identified.

The restricted agreement specifies the routes, named airport to named airport that may be operated by the designated airlines of the two countries, the capacity to be provided including the capacity to be provided by each of the designated airlines and the prices that can be charged.

The liberal type agreement that controls entry by the designation of the airlines on any given route. There is no control of frequency or capacity on any route and no control of prices.

The open skies agreement in which the market is deregulated so that air carriers of the two nations are free to establish air services between the two countries. Fares are set by the airlines according to operational and commercial standards and not by government regulation.

The major stumbling block to further liberalization of air service agreements within the air transport industry is the ownership rules for airlines applied by most countries. Almost all air service agreements require that designated airlines be substantially owned and effectively controlled by the country or nationals of the country. Though there is no international agreement on a definition of 'substantially owned', most countries have included a definition in their air transport legislation.

Although the Chicago Convention gave a role to the ICAO for the economic regulation of international air transport, the ICAO has not been active in this area for many reasons. However, the ICAO administers the air service agreement system with copies of all air service agreements and other related documents registered with the ICAO.

The result of this system is that every country in the world with an air transport industry has a complex web of air service agreements with every other country to which they are connected by an air service. Most of the agreements specify the routes that can be served, the airports that can be used and the airlines designated to serve those routes. Governments often have to approve the fares and conditions though in most cases airlines submit fares to the governments for approval.

The economic regulation of air transport through the bilateral air service agreement system creates a significant degree of restriction on the market for air services and on the capacity offered on many routes. It is these restrictions, and the pressure from the USA, which has led to a questioning of the whole system since it was established by the Chicago Convention. One factor that is often forgotten in the heat of the debate about the future of air transport is that the bilateral air service agreement system allows countries to retain control over entry into their air transport markets. This is important to many countries in terms of prestige and retaining a presence in the air transport market. There is also the fear in many countries of a US domination of air transport if a more open system were to be applied. On the other hand, the bilateral air service agreement system does impede the development of global networks and imposes impediments to airlines planning route networks on a commercial basis.

To combat the restrictions of bilateral air service agreements, many airlines have entered into alliance agreements to extend the scope of their operations. At present there are five global alliances which enable airlines with strong regional networks to come together to form world-wide networks with their alliance partners. Some commentators believe that alliances are rather fluid structures with airlines switching between alliances as they see better commercial interests from a different grouping. That said, because of regulatory and national considerations it is through alliances that airlines continue to respond to the changing needs of customers and the forces of globalization elsewhere in the world economy. The pressure for change in the bilateral air service agreement system stems from a number of issues:

1. The strong growth in the demand for air services world wide has revealed the inefficiency and certain inflexibility in the provision of capacity through the traditional route system.
2. There is strong evidence from aviation sources that the consumer benefits from lower fares and more frequent services that result from air transport deregulation.
3. There has been a greater emphasis in recent years on open skies policies being included in bilateral air service agreements.
4. The users of air transport are demanding better and 'seamless' air travel.
5. There has been a greater use of code sharing, alliances and charters to get round the restrictions of the bilateral air service agreement system.
6. Many large national carriers have been earning inadequate returns on investment and there is reluctance on the part of governments to continue subsidizing their airlines.
7. The financial markets having supported moves towards privatization of airlines and airports are demanding improved performance for their investments.
8. The organizing of regional agreements especially within the European Union.

International Air Transport Association (IATA)

The International Air Transport Association (IATA) was created by a special Act of the Canadian Parliament in 1945. Unlike the ICAO which is an organization of governments, IATA is a trade association for airlines.

Membership of IATA is open to any airline licensed by an ICAO member government and a schedule carrier. Carriers operating international services are 'active' members, those providing domestic services are associate members. The organization is democratic in that each 'active' member has one vote at the annual general meeting which decides overall policy. An elected executive committee provides direction throughout the year between annual general meetings. There are our four standing committees, financial, legal, technical and traffic, which conduct most of the routine work of the association.

The main area of economic regulation affected by IATA is the traffic conference system of which the traffic committee is the steering body. All traffic conference sessions are closed to the public. These traffic conferences are geographically based and deal with the harmonization of operating costs, fares, rates, schedules and travel agencies. All actions must be covered by the unanimous vote of the members present. It is through these conferences that many fares and conditions are agreed and controlled.

In 1978, following problems stemming from the USA, IATA divided its membership into two categories. Airlines could elect to participate fully in all IATA activities, or become only trade association members without the right to take part in the tariff setting conferences. The trade association membership involves technical, financial and legal work, including the debt clearing house.

Deregulation

In 1978, the US Congress passed the Airline De-regulation Act[7] which is characterized by the following aspects:

1. The elimination of all route entry and exit regulations.
2. Replacement of the 'public convenience and necessity' requirements for entry into the industry as a carrier with a 'fit, willing and able' criteria.
3. Elimination of all regulation of prices and conditions of service.
4. A subsidy programme to maintain services to small communities for a period of 10 years.
5. A labour protection programme.

This has led to the US trying to get other countries to liberalize their international air transport by making open skies arrangements through bilateral air service agreements. In 1986, the member states of the European Union agreed to create a single European market for the exchange of goods, services (including air transport) and capital.[8] The date of the commencement of the single European market was 1 January 1993. The regulation of intra-European air services was changed by the Commission by introducing three packages between 1987 and 1993 to gradually harmonize existing regulation of European Union air services and to introduce greater competition for international air services between EU air lines. The measures included establishing common licensing standards, allowing airlines to set fares without government approval and removing restrictions on third, fourth and fifth freedom. Since April 1997, there have been no cabotage restrictions on any European Union airlines, thus giving all European airlines the right to operate domestic services in any EU member state. The Commission of the European Union is seeking to exercise authority to negotiate air service agreements as a single body on behalf of European Union member states and carriers.

RAILWAYS

The office of the Rail Regulator regulates the competition and monopoly issues arising from the British railway system. The Rail Regulator's functions are:

1. The regulation of Railtrack in respect of access charges, its financial framework and the public interest aspects of its operation.
2. The issue and enforcement of licences to operate trains, networks, stations and light maintenance depots.
3. Approval of agreements for access to the railway facilities like track, stations and light maintenance depots.
4. Under the Competition Act 1998 to make sure there are no anti-competitive behaviour on the railways.

In addition, the Rail Regulator must help the Strategic Rail Authority further strategy, protect users of railway services, promote the use of the railway network and provide competition in the provision of railway services.

Under the Transport Act 2000, the Strategic Rail Authority has the power to regulate fares through the franchise agreements with the train operating companies where it is deemed this is in the interests of the passenger. Put simply, the Strategic Rail Authority imposes a cap over the prices that were charged in June 1995.

TRANSPORT PRICING

Every trading organization depends for its revenue upon the prices charges for its products or services. In the context of economic regulation one of the main determinants in a competitive market of any company's share is, usually, the price charged. As seen in Chapter 5, this is not necessarily the case because other aspects of the marketing mix can have effects.

There are two methods commonly used by companies to plan a pricing policy:

1. The cost plus profit method involves calculating in advance the cost of producing the service and adding a margin on top of this to cover overheads and profit.
2. The marketing approach involves an analysis of the price the market is prepared to pay, taking into account the actions of competitors, and deducting from this the cost of providing the service to ascertain if a reasonable profit margin can be earned.

With both methods it is ultimately assumed that the costs of production are easy to estimate. The harder it is to allocate costs to specific units of production, the more likely a company is to use the marketing approach.

The railways have always found difficulty in competing with other modes by price because they maintain there is no accurate method of allocating costs to individual consignments or hauls. Therefore it is almost impossible to relate charges to costs.

The railways have two main problems with cost allocation, joint costs and overhead costs. To illustrate the problem, let us start with a simple example from road haulage. A lorry carries 100 cartons from Loughborough to Hull. It is easy to calculate the cost of running the lorry to Hull and back to Loughborough by adding all the individual costs, ie wages, fuel maintenance, depreciation, etc, dividing by 100 and arriving at a cost of carrying one carton. (We will ignore for the moment overhead costs.)

Now, suppose the lorry picks up a return load of timber from Hull to Loughborough. There are three ways of allocating the costs of the journey between the cartons and the timber:

1. Assume that the lorry has to return to Loughborough with or without a load and allocate all the costs to the cartons.
2. Split the costs up in proportion to the weight or the capacity of the timber or the cartons.
3. As costs tend to be the same for both legs of the journey, allocate the costs 50–50 between the timber and the cartons.

This example assumes that the timber was booked before the lorry left Loughborough. Although this is a very simple example, it does illustrate the absolute necessity to allocate costs logically. The profit or loss on carriage and the prices quoted in a competitive situation depend to a large extent on correct allocation of costs.

When looking at joint costs on the railway, the picture becomes much more complicated. Not only will the cartons be carried by road for part of the journey but they will be conveyed over track which is used by different types of services. To get at the true cost, the contribution that each carton must make towards the track costs must be calculated. Do we break the total track costs for the BR system into an average mileage charge? Would this be fair on the cartons when some of the track needs to be of a higher quality because it is used by fast passenger trains? The passenger trains should bear a higher proportion of track costs, but how much higher a proportion? The same circular argument can be followed when looking at management, terminal and staff costs. So we can clearly see that the problem of allocating joint costs, found in all branches of transport, is more difficult for the railways board.

Price competition

The pricing of services is one of the major factors in competing with other business open to most organizations. By fixing prices below those of competitors, a company will hope to get a greater share of the market, all other aspects of competition being equal.

There is nothing difficult in one company cutting prices but in a freely competitive market, other companies retaliate by reducing their prices in an attempt to retain their market share. During these so-called 'price wars', the market becomes very unstable, but stability usually returns at a lower level of prices. These lower prices result in lower revenue and many companies operating at rates which do not cover their operating costs. Companies in the market have a choice. Either they cut their costs to match their reduced revenues or they withdraw from the market. In shipping, for example, any period of low freight rates results in the number of ships laid up and not trading increasing rapidly. Price competition and the need to reduce costs can force companies to merge and form larger units. There is some evidence to suggest that this is what is happening in the US domestic air transport market since deregulation in 1978.

For the consumer, any period of intense price competition will mean reduced travel or freight costs. There is always a danger that as the less efficient companies are squeezed from the market, prices will rise. In the long term it has been found that the final price stability has been reached at a higher price level than that applying before the price war started.

Price changes and revenue

A major consideration for any transport business when initiating price changes must be the amount of business that will be affected by any price change. There are two factors which are most important:

1. The amount a given price change will affect a company's market share.
2. The effect the change will have on a company's revenue.

The first can only be ascertained by analysis of market conditions and consumer characteristics. This analysis should enable a company to estimate the elasticity of demand for its services. Account must be taken of the effect of all price movements in the market.

Once estimates of the change in market share caused by price changes are made, the likely effect on revenue can be calculated.

A simple example will serve to illustrate the necessity for any company to grasp these principles:

A flight from London to Gatwick is priced at £40. On average, 500 passengers are carried per day.
The revenue will be £20,000.
Analysis shows that a £2 rise in fare will cause a 5 per cent reduction in passengers.
Therefore at 475 passengers will be carried.
The total revenue will now be £19,950 per day.
The revenue will fall by £50 even though the price has risen from £40 to £42.

If the increase in price was planned to take account of increases in direct costs, the company would be running an even greater loss than if the price had remained the same. In these circumstances, it is a far better policy to institute cost reduction plans rather than increase prices.

As stated before, people rarely travel purely for pleasure, but rather to achieve other objectives. In general, the price of travel will represent varying proportions of the total cost of achieving those objectives but in many cases will only form a small proportion of the total cost. It is important for any transport company (this applies with equal force to freight transport) to know what proportion of total cost is represented by the transport cost.

For example, the total cost of a holiday might be £300 with the cost of travel £50. A 10 per cent increase in the cost of travel will only result in a 1½ per cent increase in the cost of the holiday. The majority of people will still travel, viewing the cost in total, ie £305, rather than only the travel element.

It is a different story with the journey to work. The cost of travel is viewed on its own and in this case any increase assumes a much greater significance.

References

1. Aldcroft, D.H. *British Transport Since 1914* David and Charles, Devon 1975
2. Wykoff, D.D. and Maister, D.H. *The Owner Operator: Independent Trucker* Lexington Books, England 1976
3. Lockhead, M. 'Weighing up the risk factor' *Transport Magazine* June 1986
4. Hibbs, J. *Bus and Coach Management* Chapman and Hall, London 1985
5. Gubbins, E.J. *The Shipping Industry* Gordon and Breach, New York 1986
6. Gidivity, B. *The Politics of International Air Transport* Lexington Books, Massachusetts 1980
7. Gillen, O. and Trethaway *Canadian Airline Deregulation and Privatisation Centre for Transport studies* University of British Columbia 1975
8. European Union www.europa.cu.int, 2002
9. SRA www.sca.gov.uk, 2002

8

Logistics and Transport

LOGISTICS

There are a number of definitions of what is understood by the word logistics and, in some senses, the use of the word is simple, while in others it is more complex. The following two definitions will help understand the term:

'Logistics is the art of maintaining control over worldwide supply chains by a combination of transport, warehousing skills, distribution management and information technology.'[1]

'Logistics is the process of strategically managing the movement and storage of raw materials, component parts and finished goods throughout the business from suppliers to final delivery to customers.'[2]

Logistics therefore is concerned with the total movement of materials through the enterprise, including the movements of documents and other facilitators to movement. It includes the management of the interruptions to movement, such as storage, if storage is necessary, to the efficiency of the production process. Logistics can only be successfully undertaken as an integrated activity in the business environment if it is allied to information systems that IT developments have provided. In addition, manufacturing and retail companies have been able to contract out parts of their logistics operation to third parties like distribution companies, while still retaining effective control by the use of accurate and timely information transfer. This information transfer involves the use of the latest developments, such as satellite technology, barcodes, hand-held terminals, EDI and EPOS. The use of open information systems providing clearer, more reliable information can be shared by different organizations using electronic data transfer and enabling the development of a leaner logistics chain. These developments can result in reduced lead times from ordering a product to delivery, lower inventory because of better production and distribution planning, reduced total logistics costs and better customer service.

Seen in the light of the definitions, logistics touches a wide range of activities within the business. If logistics as a system within the business is to play its part in making the business successful, all managers must understand the result of their decisions on the logistics function.

Like any other part of the business, the logistics function must have objectives. These can be summed up as follows:

1. Set the standards for, and control, customer service performance.
2. Keep inventory to a minimum and, whenever possible, set in motion a policy of inventory reduction.
3. Have a minimum of disruption to planned operations to eliminate inessential costs.
4. Strive for a minimum total cost of operations and in the procurement function.
5. Set standards for product and distribution quality control.

Like any other manager in the company, it is the function of the logistics manager to help achieve the objectives of the organization by planning and supervising the activities concerned with the supply chains into, within and out of, the business and keeping them free from holdups, breakdowns and documentation difficulties. It has to be remembered that production is rarely a one-site activity where all production functions are carried out. Manufacturing involves raw materials, components and partly finished goods moving from site to site and being processed until final assembly and distribution to the customer. In many cases, this movement is international, involving movement across national frontiers with all the logistical problems that this entails.

The costs of the logistics function can be split into three categories:

1. Materials handling and transport costs.
2. Inventory or storage costs.
3. Systems costs such as computer costs, order processing, planning and forecasting.

As has been stated before, the logistics function can either be carried out in-house, by a manufacturing company or a retailer, or contracted out to a third party or specialist logistics company. If the company decides on a policy of third party logistics, it is the logistics manager's job to make sure that the contractor can meet the requirements for logistics of the contracting company.

JUST-IN-TIME

Closely allied to the logistics concept is the strategy known as just-in-time. A just-in-time strategy is one which is used by manufacturing for the production process, but it is a strategy which impinges on every other aspect of the business, including logistics and transport. By careful planning and improved communications, the strategy makes sure that supplies of products, such as raw materials and components, reach the place on the production site where they are needed just in time to be included in the production process. In other words, supplies are fed straight into the production line. There are savings to the production company in both capital and running costs if the strategy is made to work properly. For example, if raw materials are processed immediately on arrival, there are savings from reduced storage, double handling in an out of storage, documentation and records. Just-in-time manufacturing programmes require substantial organizational commitments to improve quality, eliminate all inventory, increase manufacturing efficiency and respond effectively to market demand. They also require reliable and well planned transport networks. In other words, all the activities of the company have to be geared to the just-in-time concept.

Just-in-time manufacturers have sought to include their suppliers in their programmes to enhance effectiveness. These supplier-oriented programmes include technical support for statistical quality control, sharing production planning information and engaging in long-term contracts.

In logistics, just-in-time brings new relationships with both suppliers and carriers. In addition, the location of distribution centres and the management of inventory require new approaches. If suppliers are going to deliver just in time, they are going to have to use or design a distribution system which meets the just-in-time requirements. If the production is cleared from the line and packaged for immediate delivery to customers, this calls for a regular pattern of deliveries. There has to be a close communication link between the suppliers, the distribution function and the customers. The system must be considered in detail before implementation and solutions to the problems of distribution and transport are found. Just-in-time is an overall system and each element, supply, distribution and production, must be planned together. Just-in-time also means that great attention must be paid to quality, not only the quality of the products supplied, but of the transport provision as well. It is no good having a just-in-time production strategy with a minimum of stocks, if the transport or distribution company or own account company cannot supply the quality, both on reliability of transport or in caring for the goods.

One aspect of just-in-time which is often overlooked, is the way this concept enhances concentration on quality of service. A large proportion of just-in-time manufacturers have stated that just-in-time programmes have led to changes in the modes of carriage used for both inbound and outbound movements. The railways have great difficulty in matching just-in-time requirements because just-in-time requires more frequent, smaller shipments. Shipments by air are more frequent and can be incorporated into just-in-time systems. Contract carriers gain the most from just-in-time. There is a reduction in the number of carriers used by any one manufacturing company.

The major criteria for selecting carriers seems to be in rank order:[3]

1. On-time performance and responsiveness to short-term needs.
2. Vehicle tracing capability.
3. The extent of the route network covered by the transport company.
4. Terminal proximity to just-in-time company.
5. Availability of specialist equipment.
6. Price of the service.

As can be seen from this list, for the transport or distribution company wishing to become involved in just-in-time systems, of overwhelming importance to contracting companies is the reliability and performance of the contractor, coming way above price in importance. Quality has to be an integral part of the process and this applies to transport as much as to the production process. Hold-ups caused by unreliable transport, late deliveries and damaged cargo can cause more expense than just the extra price needed to pay for reliable and on-time guaranteed transport. Just-in-time contractors demand quality performance from their transport in the same way that they demand quality standards from their suppliers. To those involved in logistics, a company commitment to just-in-time manufacturing will mean major changes. These changes includes the criteria for selecting carriers and the mix of modes employed.

There is a need for increased communications between the just-in-time company and the transport company following the introduction of just-in-time process. Familiarity with newer forms of information technology will also be required. Just-in-time therefore demands the use of the latest information technology for electronic data transfer between the transport company and the just-in-time company. The extent of the communications between carrier and vendor increases dramatically, as does the quality of the information. The major problem found with the implementation of just-in-time transport is getting the transport company to be responsive to the just-in-time company's needs.

The type of training needed in transport companies contracting to a just-in-time manufacturer are problem solving skills, improving communications, planning techniques, managing information systems and analysing quality.

Benefits to a transport company of being involved in just-in-time are:

1. Service quality of transport improves and is more consistent.
2. Transport costs decrease.

Just-in-time manufacturing is an industrial process where material passes from supplier to buyer according to detailed fixed-time schedules, theoretically without warehousing on either side.[4]

It is sometimes concluded from the institution of just-in-time that the warehouse will become extinct. While in theory it is possible to get to this state, there are situations where this is not possible and some intermediate warehousing is needed. In cases where a professional logistics organization takes over the responsibility, that organization inserts the warehouses holding sufficient buffer stocks to effect the correct and timed supplies. Warehouses are not going to disappear but, in many instances, are transferred to other organizations who include in their charges a warehousing element.

Preparing the transport services for just-in-time calls for the purchasing of carrier services on a long-term, open basis rather than short term.

Some of the key areas to address are as follows:

1. Carrier performance evaluation in terms of on-time deliveries, co-operativeness, reliability and stability. A review should be carried out of the carrier's business plans and any just-in-time customer service strategies, so that this can be matched to the company's own system for a good operational fit.
2. The objective is to reduce the number of carriers employed by the contracting company for dedicated carrier services with few contractors.
3. A key function in the success or failure of just-in-time with any carrier is the ability to provide instant status of the cargo, both

inbound and outbound. This calls for the use of the latest IT technology in the carrier's offices.

Problems in transport and just-in-time include unreliability, poor communications and a general lack of quality control.

Warehousing

Warehousing costs can be divided into two distinct categories: operating costs and product storage.

The consequences of inadequate information in warehouses can include delay, stockcuts and shortages, inaccuracies in order fulfilment, incomplete orders, slow response to customers and inflexibility. These can lead to poor customer service, lost sales and lost customers. In the logistics sense all of these can reduce the efficiency of the logistics function and affect efficiency in other areas of the business process.

Warehouses need information systems which are fast, flexible, accurate, work in real time on-line, capable of sorting information and presenting it where and when needed and with rapid response times, especially if they are to fit into a just-in-time process.

Distribution

The role of distribution in supply chain management is demand management which is the process of anticipating and fulfilling orders against defined customer service goals. Information is the key to demand management. Information is needed from the market place, information from customers, information on production schedules and information on marketing plans.[5]

Logistics and transportation strategies must be planned uppermost with the three 'R's' defined by Christopher, ie reliability, responsiveness and relationships. The critical interfaces of physical distribution are with the customers and manufacturing. These interfaces can be conflicting, in that marketing is reluctant to deny a customer and manufacturing wants long, steady production runs. Distribution can account for a high proportion of total costs and has an impact on sales revenue through the provision of customer service.

The distribution element has the task of fulfilling the demand for products through the cost-effective provision of customer service. It must be remembered that the output of all distribution systems is the provision of customer service.

Customer service

Definitions of customer service include:

1. Elapsed time between the receipt of an order and the delivery of the order to the customer.
2. The proportion of the orders filled accurately and to time.
3. The proportion of orders which arrive at the customer's premises ready for sale or use, ie without damage and in good order.
4. Ease and flexibility with which a customer can place the order.

Customer service is normally defined as the service provided to the customer from the time the order is placed until the order is delivered. In fact it is much more than this. It encompasses every aspect of the relationship between the manufacturer, supplier and customer. Under this definition it includes price, sales representation, product range on offer, after-sales service, product availability, in other words the total activity of servicing the customer.

It is fundamental for suppliers to derive and make their concept of customer service from a study of their customers' real needs rather than the perception of these needs. This will almost certainly mean designing different customer service packages for different customer market groups. The approach should be as follows:

1. Define the important service elements.
2. Determine the customer's viewpoint on these elements.
3. Design a competitive service package based on these elements.
4. Develop a promotional package to sell the service package idea.
5. Pilot test a particular package and the promotional package being used.
6. Establish controls to monitor performance of the service package.

When all the other terms of business have been exhausted it will be the service package which in the end determines who gets the order. Customer service must be looked at from the customer's point of view.

Requirements of a customer service-oriented distribution system are a responsible information system and a flexible organizational format.

The evaluation of service performance can only come from:

1. Reliable information.
2. Continual review of standards and customer requirements.

3. Continual dialogue between sales, marketing and the materials management functions of planning, purchasing and stock allocation.

Four crucial measures of customer service:

1. Customer delivery lead time.
2. Reliability of delivery.
3. Stock availability and continuity of supply.
4. Notification of non-acceptability.

Contracting out logistics

The major advantage from contracting out logistics is that the contractor has a wide experience of logistical activities and will know many of the problems and their possible solutions. There is a need for good contractor/customer relations. Unless a company can handle in-company distribution cheaper, contracting out should be considered.

Contracting out enables companies to concentrate on their core business and make larger investments in the core business, leaving distribution to the experts. The motives for contracting out must be acknowledged and any service levels negotiated with the contractor so that each party knows what is involved. Contracting out must not be solely based on cost cutting, the strengths and weaknesses of the proposal must be fully understood and analysed. Operators of third party distribution must make sure that they can deliver what they have promised.

Six reasons for contracting out cost are:

1. The need to employ capital to the best advantage of the business.
2. Investment should be in those areas which produce the most profit for the business and these are usually the core elements.
3. The need to change the way the company is organized by breaking down entrenched positions.
4. The need to recruit or train employees which can be better done in an organization whose core business is logistics.
5. Flexibility in leaving problems of peaks and troughs to the contractor.
6. To take advantage of developments in distribution which a contractor will be closer to than a manufacturing business.

The decision to contract out must only be taken after a full supply chain analysis where the objectives are clear and the business has identified all the benefits it can produce for the company from contracting out. In order to make a success of contracting out distribution or logistics the whole of the management must be committed to the decision and to have made the choice for the right reasons.

There must be a clear specification given in the contract outlining the needs of the company and providing as much details about the company's activities to enable the contractor to judge the quality needed. The needs of the information flow should be fully set out. The contractor's systems capability and compatibility is a key to making sure the right contractor is engaged in the first place. Being clear about the targets and parameters within which the contractor can work, so that the contractor is then free to manage the business, is a must.

THROUGH FREIGHT TRANSPORT

The through freight transport concept is a very important factor in the distribution of goods both domestically and internationally. The concept in international transport envisages a direct flow of goods from the exporter to the importer with a minimum of interruption and delay. It involves the exporter taking a direct responsibility for the state of the goods on arrival at the importer's premises and for the reliability of delivery dates. This flow is most efficient when undertaken as unit transport loads, whether by containers, pallets or by roll on, roll off shipping. Conceptually it can be viewed as an extension of the home delivery system where the shipper has control of the load until delivery into the international arena involving many different forms of transport.

When unit load methods are used, the goods can be packed at the premises of the exporting company and not unloaded, ie the individual packages not handled, until the unit reaches the final destination. The result is a reduction in handling costs.

Figure 8.1 illustrates the handling stages for individual packages and unit cargoes. One can see from this illustration the significant reduction in the number of handling stages that unit loads make possible. The most efficient loading method must be fully loaded vehicles leaving the consignee's premises with no intermediate handling necessary. Not all shippers are able to make up a full unit load but freight forwarders and consolidation depots help to create full loads as early in the transport chain as possible.

Through transport is a system by which goods can flow smoothly from origin to destination with the minimum of transhipment and under uniform control. Smooth flow is the physical characteristic in the method by which the goods are packed, handled and transported.

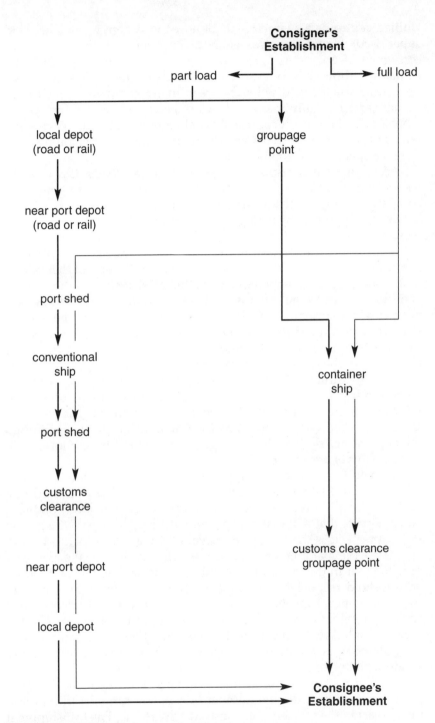

Figure 8.1 *Through transport system*

Unified control is a characteristic of how the system is managed and supervised. Unified control is more important to the shipper or consignee. If goods are transhipped many times between different vehicles or different modes, there is a tendency for the responsibility for safe transit to be divided between many companies. Each individual carrier is only interested in the goods while in their care or while under their direct control. It is only human nature for each separate carrier to attempt to blame other companies in the chain if something happens to the goods while in transit.

In conventional transport, as opposed to unit loads, this divided responsibility has always been the case where more than one company is involved in the transport. Responsibility is shared between shippers, forwarding agents, port/airport authorities, shipowners, airlines, hauliers or railway companies. The product of transport is the safe arrival but to each mode of transport involved in a multi-modal journey, this means the arrival at the end of that particular mode's journey; what happens to the cargo later on in the journey is of no concern to that operator. This is a producer-oriented system not a customer-oriented one. It is also, incidentally, one of the reasons why transport produces so much documentation. Each separate carrier attempts to protect his interests by having documents covering all aspects of the carriage and transfer of the cargo.

With the through transport concept, one organization assumes responsibility for the cargo from origin to destination, no matter which modes or companies are used during the transit. The attention of all those involved is focused on the unit of cargo as it goes through the system, not on the physical agent represented by the lorry, rail-wagon, ship or aeroplane.

The main factor that the shipper is interested in is when the goods will arrive at the final destination ready to be sold or delivered to a customer. In addition, he wants the goods to arrive in good condition and at a price that will make them competitive. As we have discussed in Chapter 1, it is the final safe arrival of the goods which is important. Also, the manufacturer wants one organization to take responsibility so that in the event of something going wrong, he can identify who to hold responsible without too much searching. The through transport concept meets these requirements because it is concerned with the total journey not each intermediate step. Once that point is accepted, it follows that the most efficient method to run multi-modal or multi-company transport journeys is to have the responsibility reside with one organization, not divided among many.

The physical aspect of through transport centres on the dual problem of minimizing the number of separate cargo handlings and on increasing the efficiency of those which are left. The transhipment of cargo between different size vehicles within a mode or the vehicles of different modes is time consuming and costly. The removing of cargo piece by piece from one vehicle in order that it may be transferred to another involves handling costs, storage costs, time losses and the chance of damage, pilferage and misdirection. The result is the customer receiving a more costly, less reliable service than he would with unit loads. Cargo handling charges have tended to rise at a faster rate than other costs, with extra costs incurred indirectly by the non-optimum use of the vehicles. Transport vehicles waiting to load/unload are not earning revenues, although they are still incurring costs.

All these factors point to the fact that there is no place in the transport chain for loose cargo unless this cannot be avoided. The solution is to package cargo into units that can be moved using mechanical handling equipment.

Unitization and unified responsibility have led to a rationalization of services, especially in international transport. Shipping services are being rationalized onto a few ports of call with extensive use of inland groupage points (inland container depots). For the shipper this means having to change traditional routes and distribution patterns.

The commercial implication of through transport is that the shipper/exporter is able to sell on a through transport basis. The traditional method is to sell on FOB (free on board) or CIF (carriage insurance and freight) terms but with through transport, the exporter can use the actual delivered price.

Where cargo is shipped by traditional methods, the division of responsibility creates a complex system of commercial procedures. Specialist companies have developed to advise shippers on the best method of shipping cargo. These are called freight forwarding agents. Given the complicated nature of exporting, freight forwarding agents provide a service that handles all aspects of transport, customers' procedures and documentation. Agents perform a legitimate function and fulfil an economic need.

There are inherent weaknesses in the system, no matter how necessary and efficient it may be. A complex system invites over-complication, while a divided system means parallel but separate procedures. Over time these procedures proliferate and there exists no ready-made focal point for rationalization. Even when a focal point is provided, the process of simplifying and harmonizing procedures can be time consuming, especially where there are a great many diverse interests involved.

A smoother, faster flow of goods physically through the system creates the need for the user to improve the procedures to enable the goods to keep flowing. Manufacturers quoting delivered prices require that the goods are monitored in their progress through the system. This physical movement is helped if the essential part played by the information flow is understood. Information must accompany the goods and, in many cases, arrive before the goods arrive. If one organization has control of the movement of cargo, the carriers have one source to which to provide information on the movement of the goods. This information control can be used to monitor the performance of the transport.

Unfortunately, commercial procedures only operate on the backs of a pile of documents. A smooth, speedy flow of goods needs a smooth flow of standard, easily understood documents if all the advantages of through transport are to be realized.

THROUGH TRANSPORT AND THE TRADER

There are several possible savings and advantages to the trader from the institution of a through transport system.

Speed

The speed of through transport is not only a function of the movement speed of the vehicles but of the speed of goods transfer and handling.

The total effect of increasing the efficiency of handling, sorting and storage (in the sense of holding the goods while waiting for transport rather than stockholding, for example in a transit shed in a seaport) will depend on the length of the journey. The shorter the actual journey, the greater the possible time savings to total transit time from more efficient handling.

The advantages of speed alone should not be over-emphasized, however. A UK government survey (*Movement of Exports to Europe*) found that although transit time may have been reduced, the average time between placing an order and despatch was more than 50 days and had not reduced noticeably for a number of years. To the customer, the most important factor was the time taken to fulfil orders, from ordering to delivery, not just the transport time. Incidentally, the same survey found that almost 60 per cent of exports went straight into stockholding warehouses rather than delivery to final user.

Reliability

Greater reliability from the through transport system arises from the fact that handling, storage and sorting are reduced, leading to a reduction in the risk of goods being damaged, stolen, misdirected or lost. As the system becomes more mechanized, the risks of human error are also reduced. If the management of the whole journey is under uniform control, the management task becomes more straightforward.

However, there are some dangers in the concept which can affect the reliability of services. Economies of scale in operation lead to a rationalization of services and fewer but larger depots. What will be the result of a mechanical failure or a labour dispute immobilizing one of these facilities? Reliability can be sacrificed to the interests of commercial enterprise building if the *flexibility* of a system is compromised in order to utilize the benefits of economies of scale.

Research into customer attitudes to freight transport shows that the reliability of a service is a far more important factor in the decision on whether to use a particular service than is transport speed. Indeed, with many products reliability is more important than price. It is vital for the freight transport operator to create an impression that the service is reliable. It is also important for the carrier to inform the customer as soon as possible when delays do occur and that measures are taken to minimize the effects on both the company and the customer of any delays.

Safety

The word 'safety' is used in the sense of reducing or eliminating the physical loss or damage to the cargo. As discussed in Chapter 1, safety allied to the arrival is the prime objectives of transport and its true product. One claim of the through transport system using containers or other unit loads is that the chance of loss or damage to the cargo is less than with conventional methods. This is because of the better organization and planning of the handling process. For the trader this can lead to greater goodwill from the customer because his deliveries arrive undamaged and ready for market.

Simplicity

There are three major factors to be considered when looking at simplicity in freight transport and how through transport enhances simplicity:

1. The through transport system lends itself to a simplification of documentation. Systems and procedures for documents are being standardized with greater use of electronic data processing and data transmission.

2. The container system in international trade is leading to freight of all kinds (FAK) rates where the payment is related to the weight or size of the container rather than the contents. This is a very logical system of charging because costs of handling are related to the size and weight and have no relationship to the contents. The only reasons for complex charging systems are tradition and applying the principle of 'what the traffic can bear' rather than relating charges to the actual costs of handling and movement.
3. The trader is able to quote a firm delivered price using a door-to-door rate rather than having to calculate the price from a series of tariffs for each stage of the journey.

Cheapness

The cheapness of any particular freight transport service must be relative to the average price charged for similar services. With any manufacturer the question of cheapness can only be answered with a study of the real costs of distribution. There must be cost savings from quicker service because fewer goods are held in transit. Gains are also made in customer goodwill from the greater reliability and any reduction in rates.

FREIGHT FORWARDING AGENTS

A combined transport operator is any company which forwards goods from one point to another and issues a through freight document. This was recognized in English Law with the case of *J. Evans and Sons (Portsmouth) Ltd* v. *Andrea Merjario Ltd*. As a result of damage which was incurred on the sea leg of the journey, the importers claimed against the freight forwarder since they had a contract of affreightment between Milan and Portsmouth. The judge made it quite clear that the function of the freight forwarder is to procure transport but he is not a carrier himself though he might perform part or all of the carriage.

The principal objectives of a freight forwarder are as follows:

1. To secure individually a sufficient volume of cargo to gain an adequate return on investment in cargo moving and handling equipment.
2. To secure cargo in balanced flows so that empty return journeys are eliminated or at least minimized.

3. To achieve this, freight forwarders must establish their own offices, groupage and storage facilities within the areas which they serve.
4. To set up a network of electronic communications and data processing equipment to control the movement of cargo and vehicles, with the accompanying documentation.
5. To establish delivery schedules and ensure that the cargo is delivered according to those schedules.
6. To keep shippers fully advised of the methods and concepts of cargo handling and carriage.

Economies of scale in the use of plant, equipment and facilities favour the larger companies. Consortia and pooling arrangements allied with co-loading help to provide increasing scope for groupage cargoes handled by forwarders, and give forwarders greater strength in their negotiations with carriers and shippers. The consortia exist mainly to pool equipment and cargo and normally serve specific trade routes. They do not as consortia own their own equipment or groupage facilities but use equipment owned by member companies. Consortia are formed to bring together a sufficient volume of traffic to take advantage of carriers' rebates or to aggregate enough cargo to make up full unit loads. Co-loading arrangements are mutually beneficial in so far as they increase the flexibility of the small forwarder, allowing him to offer a variety of services without the need for extensive capital. At the same time, the small forwarder gains a wider choice of cargo, is able to maintain a regular service schedule to a wider range of destinations and a greater chance of full unit loads.

The functions of a freight forwarder can be described as follows:

1. Documentation including bills of lading, certificates of origin, exchange control, customs papers, insurance certificates, shipping notes, calling forward notices, collection orders, port rate forms.
2. Planning and costing the route to give the desired combination of speed, economy, reliability, trading time and cost.
3. Booking and co-ordinating transport and freight space, both domestic and international.
4. Arranging any ancillary services such as warehousing and packing.
5. Consolidating and paying charges to transport operators, port authorities, customs, etc.
6. Presenting goods for customs clearance, both for imports and exports through offices in a number of countries.
7. Advising clients on special requirements, both trade and financial, of foreign countries and preparing the necessary documents.

8. Providing exporters with information to prepare quotations on export orders.
9. Advising importers of details of any changes in import procedures.

Forwarders can also supply a range of other services with the forwarder acting as a principal, rather than the traditional role of procuring services on behalf of the client:

1. Groupage or consolidation is the grouping of small consignments from several shippers into single large loads, which the forwarder sends in his own name taking advantage of discounts offered by shipping companies.
2. Road haulage, especially cargo collection and delivery to and from the consolidation/groupage point. Some freight forwarders have extensive road haulage fleets offering scheduled domestic and international services using their own equipment.
3. Warehousing is a natural extension of the forwarder's move into providing their own transport, groupage and consolidation. This type of forwarder is closer to providing an integrated through freight transport service.
4. Some forwarders provide export packing departments in addition to the advisory role.
5. Co-ordination of multiple consignments. An example of this is where an importer buying from a number of exporters in the same country engages a forwarder to take the responsibility of co-ordinating the loads and making the deliveries.
6. Forwarders offer insurance cover either through their own policy or by acting as insurance agents.
7. Some forwarders act on behalf of their clients in making arrangements with banks over letters of credit, purchase/sale of exchange.
8. Assisting exporters by providing market research, local market information and introduction to overseas buyers.

THE DELIVERED PRICE CONCEPT

Associated with the through transport concept is the system of selling on full-delivered terms, in contrast to sales ex-works, free on board (FOB), cost insurance and freight (CIF). In practice this means that all the arrangements for transport and insurance to the point of delivery are the responsibility of the seller.

All publications on through transport stress the significance of the delivered price system on the balance of payments and competitive position of exports. Only if the delivered price is charged can the exporter accurately assess the product's competitiveness in overseas markets. Techniques of distribution operating directly from the point of production and embracing a whole series of factors – packaging, stock control, documentation, transport, warehousing – provide inputs for calculating the delivered price. An awareness of the total cost is important because savings made by using modern methods are indirect rather than direct.

PHYSICAL DISTRIBUTION MANAGEMENT

Distribution is about making products available in their markets. Put simply, it is getting the right product to the right place at the right time.

There are two main facets to product availability. First, there is making the product available for sale to end users. This is the purpose of the trading side of distribution. Second, there is making the product available by enabling physical possession of the product to the end user. This is the job of physical distribution management.[6]

Physical distribution is the term applied to the broad range of activities concerned with the efficient movement of finished products from the end of the production line to the consumer. These activities include freight transport, warehousing, materials handling, protective packaging, inventory control, plant and warehouse location, order processing, market forecasting and customer service.

Physical distribution management is the overseeing of the responsibility of designing and administering the procedures that control these activities.

Distribution embraces the whole movement of the goods from production to consumer. It is the key link between production and demand creation. The efficiency of the distribution network and process has a profound effect on the profitability of any industrial company.

In simple terms, transport is the moving of goods from one place to another. Distribution embraces not only transport but other aspects of the movement as well, as illustrated in Fig. 8.2.

The total distribution concept[7] can be summarized by placing all the cost centres associated with distribution within the same boundary, as illustrated in Fig. 8.3.

Distribution is a service to the customer and that means delivering the goods required at the right time and in the right place. If the market is dispersed and demand fluctuates, stocks will have to be

	Transport	Protective Packaging	Warehousing	Inventory Control	Plant Warehouse Site Selection	Data Processing
Materials Handling	Ease and speed of loading and unloading	Unitization and handling systems	Design and operating costs			
Transport		Protection needed in movement and utilization	Loading and unloading facilities	Stock availability to complete orders	Trunking versus delivery costs	Paperwork systems routeing/ schedules
Protective Packaging			Unitization Storage systems and methods	Control of packaging materials		
Warehousing				Utilization of space	Availability of labour	Paperwork systems stock availability
Inventory Control					Stock levels for various stock holding points	Forecasting recording
Plant Warehouse Site Selection						Cost of communications and control

Figure 8.2 *Main areas of interaction*

```
Administration
Protective Packaging
Warehousing
Inventory
Transport
```

Figure 8.3 *Cost centres of distribution*

held somewhere in the transport chain against the risks of fluctuations in demand and production. Stockholdings for this purpose enable a predetermined level of service to the customer to be maintained. Both the location of warehouses, their size and the stock levels will depend on the size and speed of the transport system. Packaging of the goods, administration and handling are costs which are affected by other elements of the distribution cost formula. We cannot regard any of these cost factors in isolation; they must all be treated together – hence the boundary in the diagram. Treating them thus will help the manager arrive at a total distribution cost. It will soon become apparent, as we will see later, that any cost change in one element within the boundary will have effects on other cost elements.

COSTS OF DISTRIBUTION

The real costs of distribution must be identified when dealing with a company's cost structure. Distribution is an important aspect of a company's marketing and production effort and the costs of distribution bear on the final delivered cost of any product. In one sense, any major distribution decision can affect every cost centre in the business because all costs are related to other costs. Experience indicates that the following cost elements and interrelationships are the ones that are most likely to prove critical in evaluation of alternative distribution strategies and the effect on total costs and overall profits.

To provide customer service through the company's chosen channels of distribution, some warehousing is required. This requirement can range from one factory-based warehouse used to supply all customers, to a network of warehouses dispersed geographically for regional distribution. Service to the customer is usually higher as the number of warehouses increases. However, as the number of warehouses increases, the average size tends to decrease. Costs per item handled/stored tend to rise and customer service levels can be affected by space limitations. Any change in the number, type and location of storage points will have effects on customer service levels and distribution costs.

The keeping of stocks gives rise to costs which are not directly attributable to distribution but which must nevertheless be borne by that function. These costs include the capital tied up in stocks, insurance costs, warehousing costs, losses through pilferage or deterioration and in many cases stock taxes. Customer service levels improve when stocks are held close to the customer's premises but this usually increases the total of stocks held. This in turn increases the costs of stockholding. These costs are closely connected to warehouse location strategies and the desired level of customer service.

The greater the total level of stocks held by a company, the greater the risk of the products stored becoming obsolete. This will involve capital write-off. This is a particularly important factor in those industries whose products have a short shelf life, such as fashion goods and perishables.

Costs of production vary between locations, with the level of investment and with the volume of output. Production decisions must take account of distribution costs if the overall cost profile of the company is to be minimized. Changing the location and the number of warehouses changes transportation costs in unanticipated and complex ways. For example, an increase in the number of warehouses may initially reduce transport costs but, at some point, the transport costs rise as drop sizes decrease.

Communications and data processing costs vary with the complexity of the distribution function and operation. This includes the level of customer service provided, order processing, inventory control and transport documentation.

Stock-outs (the fact that orders are unfulfilled because there are no stocks of a product in a warehouse), excess delivery times or unreliability of delivery can all lead to lost sales. For the company this can be far more serious than the direct loss of that one sale. Stock-outs, excess delivery times or unreliability of delivery can lead to a loss of goodwill and affect repeat orders and brand loyalty. Any change in the distribution system which affects these factors, especially if it results in loss of goodwill, must be counted as a cost set against the distribution function.

Reducing distribution costs

Any moves to reduce distribution costs require an understanding of the following:

1. The nature of the individual cost elements which make up the total distribution cost package.
2. The way in which these cost elements vary when changes to the system occur.

A knowledge of the cost variations will provide a frame of reference within which a range of distribution plans may be evaluated.

As can be seen from Fig. 8.4, the cost of distribution to the customer decreases as the number of warehouses increases. This is because the average warehouse to customer distance falls. However, plant to warehouse transport costs increase and inventory costs increase as the number of warehouses served rises. The main reason for the plant to warehouse costs rising with the increase in the number of warehouses

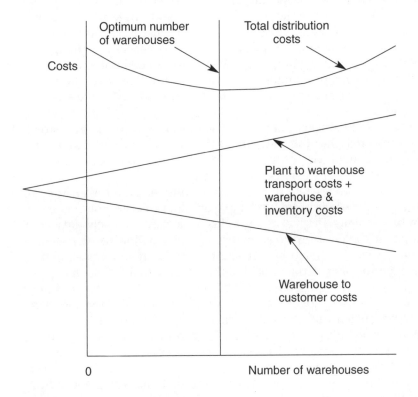

Figure 8.4 *Total distribution costs*

is because more shipments have to be made to a greater number of locations. Warehouse overheads will increase with more buildings and staff, while inventory carrying increases because each separate warehouse has to carry a wide range of products. The cumulative effect is a reduction in total costs until a point is reached at which costs start to rise. It can be said that this point marks the optimum number of warehouses.

Of course, this is only a simple illustration; in practice the picture is more complex, involving warehouse location studies, desired levels of customer service and any grants available from government for locating in different areas.

Once the individual cost elements have been identified, the whole system can be investigated to ascertain where improvements can be made. Savings in distribution costs can be made from a number of sources, the following factors being important:

1. Simplification of the system. Physical distribution combines the management of both the movement and the storage of goods. The more streamlined the system, the lower the cost and the easier the planning task. After the initial planning and implementation of a distribution system, additions can be made without careful consideration of their impact on the whole system. With careful planning as an on-going tool, the system can be kept as simple as possible with any changes being carefully implemented and monitored to make sure that the whole system is still effective after the changes.
2. Reduction of stocks. This can be achieved by rationalizing stockholding such that the shelf life of the products is determined and the stocks held for optimum periods. The consolidation of stocks in fewer locations serving more customers can drastically reduce the level of stocks held though this can only be undertaken after an analysis of the effect this will have on other distribution costs.
3. Improvements in packaging. This is a case of each area of a product's cycle from design through production to distribution being seen in isolation. Packaging serves two purposes. It is needed to enhance the appeal of the product to the consumer – the packaging designer, marketing people and product designer working closely together. Packaging is also protection, covering the product during transit to ensure that the product arrives in good order in the market place. Uniform and regular packaging sizes present greater efficiency in transport and storage but may be unattractive to marketing personnel. It is vital that each section understands the needs of the other and that packaging of products fulfils these needs.

4. A constant quest must be followed to find more efficient methods of transport, better equipped warehouses, the most cost-effective materials handling systems and documentation. Changes of methods are always occurring in these areas and efforts must be made to keep abreast of developments, implementing those that reduce costs and increase efficiency.
5. As technology changes, distribution systems must be adapted to these changes. Recently there has been a growth in the use of containers, the impact of desk-top computers and the greater use of electronic data transmission aids.

TRANSPORT AND DISTRIBUTION

The role of transport and distribution is so basic to the modern industrial economy that its efficiency is often taken for granted. This economic function has been carried out by firms since transport first came into being.[8]

Road transport and distribution

Road transport has a number of advantages over other modes of transport when used for distribution, the main two being:

1. Flexibility. Any place in the UK can be serviced by road without the need for transhipment from one vehicle to another. Allied to this comprehensive geographical coverage, road transport can economically provide a wide variety of capacities to suit the needs of individual customers. The truck is a very adaptable vehicle with the easy option of specialization in design and construction to cope with the special characteristics of different commodities and products.

   Because of the comprehensive nature of the road network giving a choice of routes between any two places, the chosen route can be changed at short notice, indeed even after the journey has begun. This can be accomplished with the minimum of extra expense. With modern lorries carrying their own handling equipment, there is no great need for expensive terminal facilities either for loading or discharge at a warehouse or a customer's premises.

   A road haulage company does not have to construct,maintain, plan or supervise the track: all these activities are provided for out of taxation. The sums of money involved are generally known in advance by the road haulage operator and can be easily accounted for in the price of the service.

2. Control. Each individual vehicle is under the full control of the driver who can make quick and on-the-spot decisions about changes of route, the safety of the load and informing the customer of any likely delays. Management time is spent controlling the operations of the fleet rather than supervising the planning, construction and maintenance of the infra-structure. It is easy in a road haulage company to monitor the progress of each consignment through the system. Finally, after careful analysis the manufacturer has a choice of whether to own and operate his own vehicles or contract his transport to some professional haulier.

There are some disadvantages of road haulage:

1. Load size. The size of the load that any lorry can carry is restricted by legislation concerning the overall weight of the lorry and the loadings allowed on individual axles. Within the confines of these restrictions in the UK the heaviest possible load is approximately 25 tonnes. For large bulk consignments even over very short distances, the lorry is far inferior to the train as a mode of transport. For example, to move 1,000 tonnes of coal would take 40 heavy lorries whereas the total load could be carried by one train. Some people would argue that this shows the intolerable pressure on the roads system imposed by heavy lorries because not enough money is invested in the railways.
2. Distance. The amount of mileage covered in a day by a lorry is restricted by drivers' hours limitations and road speed restrictions. If the lorry cannot get back to its base within the hours limits, the company faces additional expenses from overnight parking fees and accommodation for the driver. For a lorry to operate outside of one drivers' working hours, an additional driver can be carried but this also increases the costs. The company can achieve 24-hour operation by using some form of staging system where the trailers are passed from one driver to another along a route. This enables each driver to return to base within the hours limits but the trailers and loads can be continuously on the move. The management and organization of such a system is quite complex but achievable.
3. Road conditions. Road are not used exclusively by lorries and road congestion can lead to longer delivery times and unreliability. There are also restrictions on lorry parking and unloading in some urban areas with restrictions on through routes. These factors diminish the flexibility of the mode.

There are three main factors which have a bearing on the choice of road transport over other modes of transport:

1. The type of product to be carried is a major factor as the relationship between the product sales price and the cost of transport has an important bearing on the decision. Thus companies shipping low priced products generally have to use low cost forms of transport such as rail and water. Companies shipping higher priced goods where the transport cost is only a small proportion of the final delivered price generally consider other factors when deciding on the choice of mode. Fragile goods and perishable goods are largely carried by road because road haulage vehicles can be designed and utilized for special cargo.
2. The length of haul is a very important factor. The use of road haulage reduces the cost of cargo handling because the haulier can deliver door to door without any intermediate stages involving handling. This is absolutely vital in short hauls where the cost of transhipment can be a large proportion of total costs. As the length of the haul increases, the proportion of handling costs to total costs gets smaller and road haulage loses much of its competitive advantage. Where the end market outlets are highly dispersed, road haulage is often the only feasible mode of transport for distribution.
3. Service and reliability are important factors in choice of mode. The flexibility of road haulage enables the operator to adjust transport output in line with the needs of customers at short notice.

Choice of road carrier

The road haulage industry when used for distribution can be separated into two branches: those companies which operate their own fleets of vehicles as an addition to their main business (own account), and those companies which contract out their transport to professional hauliers (hire and reward). The choice for the manufacturer lies between these two options.

The reasons for a manufacturer deciding either to own and operate a company transport fleet or to contract the transport out are varied and complex. The decision is not always based on pure financial judgement after taking account of the financial position of the company, the nature and scope of the demand for transport from within the business, or the total costs associated with each alternative.

Many large companies argue that the transport they use should be under their own management control no matter what the costs to the company may be. These companies maintain that the average size of the commercial fleet is too small and their operations too localized to provide the level of service and reliability required.

They further argue that they prefer to have their transport requirements directly under their control and integrated with the rest of their business. In this way, they can ensure that the transport equipment and system is exactly tailored to their own requirements and not compromised by a professional haulier having to satisfy the demands of several different customers. Their argument is somewhat negated by the development of contract services where a hire and reward operator contracts to carry a company's goods in lorries designed and used exclusively for that company. With many of these contracts, the vehicles are painted in the hiring company's colours.

There is a certain amount of research evidence to suggest that many own account operators are not providing themselves with the most efficient service possible. Various surveys show that own account fleets are severely under-utilized, especially if the fleet is expected to meet all the company's transport requirements. One solution to this problem is for the company to use their own fleet to meet average demand and supplement their fleet with hired transport at times of peak loading.

One other reason for using own account transport is that the company wishes to employ driver/sales persons. Only by operating their own fleets of vehicles can the company control the driver, training and scheduling.

Obtaining a vehicle

Once the correct number and specification of vehicles to be purchased have been determined, the first financial problem is how to obtain the vehicles required. The vehicles can be bought outright, involving a cash outlay. Alternatively the company can borrow the cash and pay interest on the borrowing. Other alternatives lie in getting another company to buy the fleet and then leasing the vehicles back from them, or becoming a party to a contract for hiring vehicles. The competitiveness of these alternatives may be evaluated from quotations. The problem arises, however, when it is recognized that the right choice depends on the cash resources of the company, its capital structure and investment programme and the influence of taxation. Thus a reduction in tax liability, the conservation of capital/tax resources, or the priority of other investment opportunities may be the important factors which prompt a company to make what may otherwise appear to be an illogical choice. In the first instance, therefore, the details of each method of securing a fleet must be understood if these problems of finance are to be properly interpreted.[9]

Leasing

There are an infinite variety of leases available to the lorry operator but they are all variants of two basic types:

1. The fixed basic rate method, which can include an extra charge for servicing and maintenance. In some there is an extra charge if the leased vehicle is off the road for a set minimum period. The lease money is, therefore, paid as a set rate, usually monthly. At the end of the lease, the vehicle is sold and the money raised goes to the leasing company.
2. The fully amortized lease where the vehicle is depreciated over the life of the lease to some agreed residual figure. The payments are based on a sliding scale according to the depreciation rate. This is usually accompanied by a maintenance and servicing agreement.

Advantages of leasing

1. Reserves of capital which would otherwise be tied up in fixed assets can be used for other purposes.
2. Leasing assists in budgeting and forward planning such as cash flow forecasting. The payments are regular and known in advance.
3. Leasing can be a hedge against inflation because the lease payments are based on prices current when the lease is negotiated. In some cases, however, there can be clauses in the contract which vary the rate payable in line with inflation.
4. In certain cases, lease payments are an allowable expense against taxation.

Disadvantages of leasing

1. The lease can only be terminated at agreed dates without incurring large cancellation charges. This is particularly limiting during times of rapid development in vehicle technology when a company needs to have a flexible sale and purchase policy to keep abreast of competitors.
2. The equipment is never owned by the company and any capital allowances, either in the form of government grants or tax relief are only available to the leasing company.

Hire purchase

Hire purchase is the most common method of obtaining a vehicle by owner operators. This form of finance needs very careful consideration before any agreement is signed.

The major problem is with calculating the true rate of interest. This is because a flat rate of interest is charged on the whole sum involved over the whole life of the loan. This makes no allowance for any money paid off the capital as repayments take place.

The other main concern when entering into a hire purchase agreement is to get the greatest number of items included in the agreement. This can save scarce capital for other purposes.

Included in some hire purchase agreements are maintenance provisions. These include an agreement for routine inspections and servicing at predetermined intervals. Drivers are issued with report sheets to record defects arising *en route*. The operator is issued with service and inspection sheets to comply with the prescribed records for the licensing authority.

Contract hire

Contract hire usually involves contracting the whole service from a professional haulier. This can be with a driver or without.

Rail transport and distribution

The main advantages of rail in transporting freight stem from two operating characteristics:

1. It is more efficient to draw steel-wheeled vehicles along a steel track in terms of resistance to motion than other surface modes.
2. Potentially the railway should obtain greater productivity per man operating hour than road transport. (This ignores the man hours expended in signalling, track maintenance and freight handling. The road lobby conveniently ignores the man hours expended in these areas on the roads, the result being that productivity comparisons between road and rail are very difficult to make.)

Rail operating objectives can and do directly affect the use of rail in physical distribution. A balance has to be struck in the utilization of the track between passenger services and freight services. If the passenger side of the railway predominates, there is less opportunity for operating slower freight trains.

Where regular and substantial flows of heavy freight between rail connected points are concerned (coal, iron ore, semi-finished steel, heavy chemicals, oil, cement, and even grain) it is highly likely that rail will have advantages over road. It must be remembered that with heavy, even flows of liquid, pipelines are becoming a competitor.

In the case of light consumer goods, the lower costs of using trains for trunk hauls between principal centres are offset by higher road transfer costs and the need to use road for collection and delivery. In fact, the cost advantage of rail in trunking may be very small in comparison to road. This cost is very sensitive to journey distance, size of load, frequency and regularity of flow and the location of the origin and destination.

Markets and rail

In a country the size of the UK, there can be very little captive market for the railways, especially with consumer goods traffic.

The market outlets in the country are dispersed and require a complex system of distribution that is flexible enough to meet changing social and commercial patterns. It is the lack of flexibility in both route and origin/destination which is the main barrier to the railways expanding significantly into general merchandise distribution.

The railways need a pattern of industry that is rationalized into a small number of large plants distributing their products to an equally small number of large outlets. This would enable the railways to concentrate loads between rail-served depots.

The most suitable use for rail is the moving of large volumes of freight over long distances. Once the train load has been consolidated, it is an extremely efficient method of transport between two points.

The train is limited to its permanent way. It has the highest terminal route costs when expressed as a percentage of operating costs. Although trunking costs are low, operating problems often make the elapsed time of moving freight between two points unacceptably long.

The main disadvantages stem from its fixed track operations. Flexibility is almost non-existent and unit load systems can only have limited coverage of the country. Unit load systems can only be used on the railways if the customer and the consignee have facilities reasonably close to the rail terminal.

Air freight and distribution

When viewed in isolation from other distribution costs, air freight is more expensive than surface transport. Experience indicates that there are only four reasons why companies send freight by air:

1. Capital invested in products is tied up for a shorter period when using air freight by virtue of the fast transit times.
2. The cargo is at risk from damage, pilferage or deterioration for shorter period, which can cut the cost of insurance.
3. Air freight can be used in an emergency when the speed of delivery is paramount no matter what the expense, eg when a sale can be made which will enhance goodwill, or to overcome a

problem such as supplying spare parts for machinery which has broken down.
4. The use of air freight can lower the costs of storage and distribution in the country of sale.

Broadly speaking there are two advantages to be gained by using air freight: the marketing advantage and the technical advantage.

There are products which rely on the speed of delivery to gain market penetration. These are mainly perishable products and those which have a short selling season.

With perishable products, for example fresh cut flowers, markets which would normally be out of the question due to the distance from the producer and the time taken by surface transport to make deliveries, can be serviced with a high degree of reliability. As long as the product can stand the premium freight rate demanded by air transport companies, the use of air freight can be viable.

For products with a short selling season, the reasons for using air freight are more complex. The major advantage lies in being able to achieve shorter lead times between orders being placed and the product being delivered.

Air freight can give the manufacturer a certain flexibility when opening up new markets. Modern competition for most products demands that the organization establishes a complete selling operation in the form of distribution channels, after sales service and warehousing, before the product can be marketed. The risk of failure is high with new products, and failure can be very costly. Instead of committing capital to the venture, air freight can be used to supply the market until the likelihood or success or failure can be analysed. In this way, the risks inherent in penetrating any new market area can be reduced.

The technical advantages of faster transit times and better care of the goods are only important when it can be demonstrated that the total elapsed time between order placing and delivery is less for air freight than for surface freight. All air freight consignments have to be delivered to the airport by other forms of transport, sorted, and then loaded onto the plane. This takes time and for short distances, air freight is not competitive. For longer distances, the transfer time is not a problem but the processing of the order by the receiving company can take so long that even the greater speed of air freight will not make a significant difference to the total time from order placing to delivery.

The time taken from order placing to delivery is very important to the customer (although this is often overlooked by transport people) for the simple reason that he requires the product he has ordered. To him, the time in transit is only a part of the elapsed time which itself is vital.

Stock savings and air freight

Capital tied up in goods, whether in transit or storage, is money not earning any return. Any company has several uses for its scarce capital and economists reason that the real cost to a company of their money being tied up in stocks is the loss of possible earnings from alternative uses of that money. In other words, the true cost of money tied up in one aspect of the business is the return that could be obtained if the money was used in some other aspect of the business or invested somewhere else. (It is often stated that since 1945, all British liner shipping companies could have earned a far greater return on investment by selling their ships and investing in financial investments.) If a company has more capital in stocks than it needs to have, this is costing the company profits which could be earned by using the money elsewhere.

To calculate this cost, we have to know the value of goods in transit and storage over a period and the opportunity cost of money to the company. By multiplying the two figures, we can arrive at an estimate of the cost of stocks to the company in addition to the direct costs of storage and transport. Of course, some of this cost will have to be borne by the company if it wants to supply its markets but any reduction in the size of stocks or the number of goods in transit at any time will save the company money in addition to savings in direct costs.

Example

A company transports £3m of goods by surface transport each year.

The opportunity cost of money to the company is calculated at 10 per cent.

The opportunity cost of having £3m worth of goods in transit or storage is £300,000.

If the company calculated that they could save 30 days of stock by switching to a faster form of transport

$$£300,000 \times \frac{30}{365} = £24,658$$

£24,658 could in theory be earned by the company by using the money saved elsewhere.

Lead time and stock replacement

We have discussed briefly how the use of air freight can help the marketing effort and reduce the capital tied up in stocks.

The reasons for holding stocks are:

1. If the demand for a product is uneven or seasonal, it is economical to spread the production evenly over a period and keep stocks to satisfy customer demand during peak demand periods.
2. Stocks are kept against uncertain supply. A warehouse manager will hold stocks as a protection against delay in delivery or a manufacturer holds supplies of raw materials or components against the possibility of supplies being interrupted.
3. Stocks are kept as a buffer against the variability of customer demand.

The average stock level in any warehouse depends on:

1. The quantity of each delivered load.
2. The lead time from order placing to delivery.
3. The amount of safety stock calculated to satisfy variations in both supply and demand.

Let us now look at the basic function of stocks. As illustrated in Fig. 8.5, when demand is known and lead time is certain there is no need to keep safety stocks. The rate at which stocks are depleted (customer demand) and the replenishment cycle are constant. The replenishment quantity BA will be enough to maintain customer service represented by the line AC over the time period BC. Obviously, stocks will drop to zero at time C but replacement stocks will arrive to bring the quantity up to D. The replenishment/stock depletion cycle can be maintained without the danger of a stock-out.

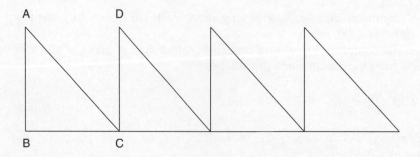

Figure 8.5 *Certain lead times*

In practice, the demand can never be as certain as the slope represented by AC, as illustrated in Fig. 8.6. If the demand fluctuates, the zero stock position could be reached as early as time E, leaving time EC with no stocks in the warehouse.

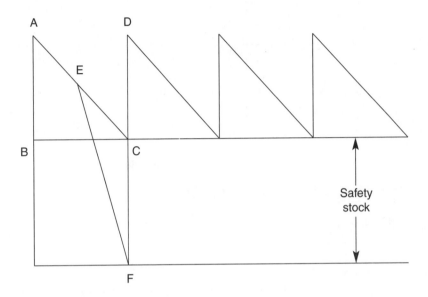

Figure 8.6 *Safety stocks*

To prevent this type of stock-out occurring, estimates of demand fluctuations are made and a quantity of safety stocks held. If the replenishment cycle has to remain the same, the quantity FD will have to be supplied. CF represents safety stocks held against the eventuality of greater demand than average.

Only rarely is it necessary to hold safety stocks to 100 per cent service levels but some safety margin must be built into the system.

It is also apparent that for any given level of demand, the stock held will not only be a function of the desired customer service levels but also the frequency of delivery.

Figure 8.7 illustrates how shortened delivery times can reduce safety stock levels. Stocks would now zero at E1, instead of C1. The safety stock level can be reduced to F1, by shortening the delivery time. Any savings in stock levels must be compared with the increased costs of faster forms of transport. Only if it is financially viable should the new form of transport be used.

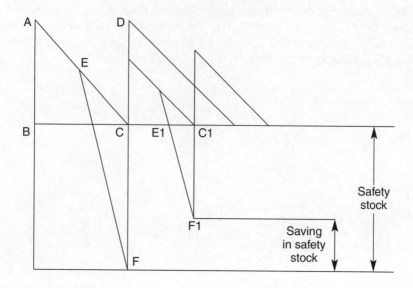

Figure 8.7 *Use of air freight*

Warehouse savings

Since the use of air freight for distribution can reduce the levels of stock held by a company, savings in warehousing can be achieved. However, care must be taken when looking at potential warehouse cost reductions. Savings can come from the reduced cost of moving the stock in the warehouse though this can only be achieved if operating economies are made in line with the reduced stock levels.

There will be space available in the warehouse, but this then becomes an under-utilized asset. There are a number of ways in which these assets can be more fully utilized.

1. The company can move to smaller premises, thus liberating some of the capital tied up in buildings. It must be remembered that moving entails a cost and this cost must be compared to the financial savings made by moving.
2. The company can lease the space created to some other company, which will bring in some revenue. Again, it must be remembered that leasing space involves some expenses and these expenses must be compared to the revenue earned to make sure that the leasing is financially viable.
3. The company may regard the under-utilization of storage space as giving flexibility for future expansion of the company's market or product range. While the space is under-utilized, the company's

current distribution system and products must bear the cost of that under-utilization.

Attitudes of air freight

In spite of the potential advantages and savings from the use of air freight, there is a reluctance on the part of many companies to fully use air freight. This mainly stems from the belief that air transport is more expensive to use than surface transport. Many companies have at some time used air freight in an emergency to supply customers at short notice but this is a case of customer service and goodwill being more important than any extra expenses involved. It must be emphasized that transport costs cannot be quoted in isolation from all other costs and all relevant costs must be considered when making distribution decisions.

Modal choice will depend to a great extent on the company's method of operation and the particular commodity involved. In general there are few commodities that are suitable for transportation by all modes and it is usually a choice between road and rail transport.[10]

CARGO UNITIZATION[11]

Unitization involves the packaging of small items of cargo into standard sized units that can be handled by specifically designed mechanical equipment. This has the effect of reducing the labour content and speeding up the handling of goods.

In international trade, the major method developed to fulfil these principles is containerization. This is the packing of individual pieces of cargo into standard sized boxes as early in the transport chain as possible. These standard sized boxes can be easily transferred between modes without disturbing the cargo inside.

Advantages of containerization

There are large gains in productivity in through transport when containers are used to transport goods rather than break bulk methods. However, efficient organization is required to reap the benefits of greater use of mechanical handling equipment. Any container system must utilize the equipment and facilities fully to be efficient. The most costly item of equipment in international through transport is the ship, but the productivity gains needed to earn adequate financial returns on the investment in container ships are to a large extent outside the control of the shipping company. This fact illustrates the inter-dependence of the various elements in the through transport system.

The major influence on productivity of international through transport services is the technical efficiency of the marine terminal. This link in the transport chain and its efficiency has a major bearing on whether the other links – shipping, trucks or rail freight – spend the majority of their working life in profitable employment. The design and management of port systems is a vital factor in the success or failure of the whole container system. No matter how efficient the ship or the inland transport, if the marine terminal causes delays through lack of investment, poor design and bad management, all gains in productivity in the other parts of the transport chain can easily be lost.

The most important advantage of containerization is the reduction in the total time taken to transport freight from producer to consumer. This reduction can save the producer other costs inherent in the order cycle of goods from the customer – the lead time from placing the order to the delivery of the goods. To make sure of delivery to customers, most manufacturers hold stocks close to the market. As we have seen, speed of transport has a direct bearing on stock levels in order to make guaranteed deliveries to customers. The shortening of delivery times is accomplished using containers by shorter transfer time between modes. The actual time saving is dependent on the installation and use of properly designed handling equipment throughout the transport chain. It follows that if less time is taken in handling the actual goods and proper packaging is used, minimal loss, damage or pilferage take place. Traditionally, it is during the handling process both in the port terminal and elsewhere in the chain that the greater losses occur. Although use of containers has minimized these risks, there is the added danger that all the contents may be stolen by the whole container being taken.

With conventional break bulk cargo handling methods, high costs are involved in packaging goods to prevent damage in transit, in large amounts of documentation and in high insurance premiums. Containerization has brought benefits by lowering these costs but the reductions are not as large as those first claimed by the pioneers of the system.

Handling containers in specifically designed terminals leads to lower labour costs per ton of cargo handled and higher labour morale. The lower costs are due to the reduction in manpower needed to handle the same throughput when compared to conventional methods. The labour morale is higher because of better working conditions.

Disadvantages of containerization

There are major disadvantages attached to the container system although from listening to people engaged in container operations, this fact is not too apparent.

The container system sets out to give a door-to-depot service which involves complex control mechanisms, especially in keeping records of where the individual containers have been despatched. To initiate a system, a great deal of very sophisticated handling equipment must be provided. This calls for a large input of finance for both the equipment and training of personnel.

To earn the required returns on such high levels of capital investment, intensive use is necessary. Intensive use implies strict organization of the whole system to ensure that the throughput of containers is sufficiently high to warrant the expenditure.

Containerization has reduced the number of workers involved in handling and carriage but has increased the industrial power of this reduced workforce. A small number of workers in strategic positions can halt the whole operation.

There is still a large amount of freight which cannot be containerized and on services where containers have taken a major share, this non-containerizable freight can be subjected to delays because the non-container service must of necessity be less frequent.

CONSOLIDATION

Consolidation is the joining of small parcels of cargo from different sources into larger units for onward transport. It aims to facilitate and optimize the number of links in the transport chain. In fact, consolidation is the organization of product flows and activities which occur in several links in the transport chain.

Keeping in mind that the movement of goods is not an isolated event but part of a product chain consisting of one or more production stages and a number of transport links, it will be understood that optimization of the transport element cannot be completely isolated from the production process. All activities within the boundary of a company's operations have to be analysed and organized as an integrated system in order to control the chain of activities of both production and movement.

Logistical co-ordination is concerned with the identification of internal requirements and the establishment of specifications that tie together a particular firm's physical distribution and material management. Co-ordination is required to establish operational continuity. For physical distribution and materials management substantially different operational requirements exist. The function of logistical co-ordination is to reconcile these differentials to the maximum benefit of the enterprise.[12]

Given the connection between production and movement, attention has to be paid by a company's management to the following:

1. The interrelationship between successive links in the product chain from raw materials to finished product.
2. The interrelationship between the different transport chains belonging to the same product chain.

The ultimate objective has to be the optimization of the overall process, both production and movement. Within the objectives of the company this means minimizing the costs of the finished products while maintaining the required quality. In the past, the links in each transport chain were approached in an isolated and technical way. Since then it has been realized that the transport vehicles and the handling equipment must be designed together, hence the development of unitized systems.

In order to minimize the costs of transport and to raise the quality of service, attention has to be paid to the following elements:

1. The adaptation of transport systems to products or the adaptation of product packaging to fit the transport system.
2. The integration of the flow of information with the physical flow of the goods.
3. The provision of inter-modal transfer systems within the transport chain to make use of the benefits of economies of scale.

Under continuously changing conditions, the optimization of transport systems requires a very flexible management which will form part of business logistics as a whole. A transport chain consists of a number of links formed by separate handling and movement phases. A major part of the handling phases take place between two movement phases. The choice of location for these handling phases is very important because the choice strongly influences the possibility for consolidation. This is a form of handling which is mainly for economic rather than technical reasons. Consolidation is an attempt to lower the costs of the movement phases in the transport chain. As long as the consignment is less than the legal maximum weight or dimensions of the carrying vehicle, combining several consignments in one vehicle reduces the cost per unit moved. The cost advantages are greater the longer the distance and the smaller the relative size of the consignments. The greater the number of product flows for which consolidation can be undertaken at the same place, the larger the obtainable cost saving.

The economies of scale affect not only the handlings related to consolidation but also the provision of facilities for transport activity. The number of fully loaded vehicles increases and the greater volume of throughput decreases the costs of handling. The geographical location of consolidation facilities gives opportunities to optimize the links in the transport chain on a broader scale. It is significant that the consolidation centre has a broader importance for the transport manager than consolidation itself. Besides the technical handling necessary for cutting the costs in the following or preceding movement link, mutual storage and other handling facilities related to transport of products can be optimized as well.

In optimizing all activities within the transport chain, the objectives are to raise the quality of service to the customer and to cut overall costs. These are often conflicting requirements calling for a compromise between alternative levels of service and the related difference in cost.

References

1. Benson, D., Bugg, R. and Whitehead, T.S. *Transport and Logistics* Woodhead-Faulkner, London 1994
2. Christopher, M. *Logistics: the Strategic Issues* Chapman and Hall, London 1992
3. Garreau, A., Lieb, R. and Milled, J. *IT and Corporate Transformation: An International Comparison* Northeastern University
4. Bendal, H. Unicom *Logistics in the 1990s: Logistics of the Supply Chain* Conference, London
5. Christopher, M. *Logistics and Distribution Planning* (ed James Cooper) Kogan Page, London 1994
6. Christopher, M. *Effective Distribution Management* Pan Books, London 1985
7. Christopher, M. *The Strategy of Distribution Management* Gower, England 1985
8. Murphy, G.J. *Transport and Distribution Business Books* London 1978
9. Garrorna, J. *Handbook of Physical Distribution Management* Gower, England 1983
10. Ratcliffe, B. *Economy and Efficiency in Transport and Distribution* Kogan Page, London 1987
11. Gubbins, E.J. *The Shipping Industry* Gordon and Breach, New York 1986
12. Bowersox, D.J. *Logistical Management* Macmillan, New York 1974

9

Urban Transport

Decisive changes in thinking about the nature of mobility, accessibility and transport, especially in urban areas, took place with the publication of Professor Buchanan's report in 1963 entitled *Traffic in Towns*. Although it was generally agreed at the time that the solutions proposed in the report were unacceptable to society as organized, the report drew people's attention to the consequences of allowing traffic pressure to grow haphazardly and to the decisive part of land use patterns in the generation of traffic. From that time, the astronomical cost and the environmental damage caused ruled out the building of roads as the only possible solution to urban traffic problems.

THE BACKGROUND TO THE PROBLEMS

The origins of the present-day transport problems in urban areas can be traced back to events in the last century. As outlined in Chapter 1, the industrial revolution changed the balance of population in Britain from predominantly rural to primarily urban as people flocked to the new towns to work in factories. The geographical structure of towns could be attributed to transport. As populations increased, towns had to be densely structured to enable people to walk to work, shopping or leisure.

With the development of the railways, urban structures followed the line of the railway enabling people to live further from the town centre but still largely within walking distance of the nearest railway station.

After the 1914–18 war, towns mushroomed in size but the lack of planning controls and the development of cheap, reliable bus services meant that people could now live outside walking distance to the nearest station. Towns still had a star-shaped appearance with major development along the main public transport corridors.

In the 1950s, car ownership levels and usage grew very rapidly and changed the characteristic of people's travel behaviour. The effect was most severe in urban areas. The development of British urban areas has been based primarily on the different forms of public transport as they were instituted. Even with the growing of the town away from the closely structured centre, these central areas are still the main traffic generators. Unfortunately, they are the part of any town least able to cope with increases in traffic.

The last 20 years have seen a continuous migration of people away from areas adjacent to city centres under slum clearance programmes and the building of housing on green field sites. Work places, leisure facilities and shopping areas have become dispersed around the urban area, creating new, very diverse travel patterns. Even so, commuting to and from the city centre is still a major flow, especially at peak times, but more people now use their car. The result is traffic congestion which now occurs even in relatively small towns.

During this period of high road traffic growth, all forms of public transport have suffered drastically. Falling traffic led to reductions in service levels and to the standard of service on offer. Fare increases higher than the prevailing inflation rate, except in some of the larger conurbations, were implemented in an attempt to help the bus operator at least keep subsidy levels stable. These factors of declining service levels and large fare increases discouraged people from using the bus and even more people turned to the use of the private car. In addition, as more cars used the roads at peak times, the resulting congestion caused bus services to be unreliable and costs to rise as bus operators struggled to operate services prone to delays in traffic jams. Figure 9.1 details this cycle of decline in public transport.

THE SOLUTIONS

The objective of any transportation solution to the problem of traffic in towns must be to regulate the use of scarce resources. These resources must be husbanded so that people can move into, out of and around the urban area for the purposes of work, recreation and entertainment. This must be accomplished safely and conveniently in a reasonably acceptable time scale. Congestion can be considered as an excess of demand for the scarce resource of road space within the urban area.

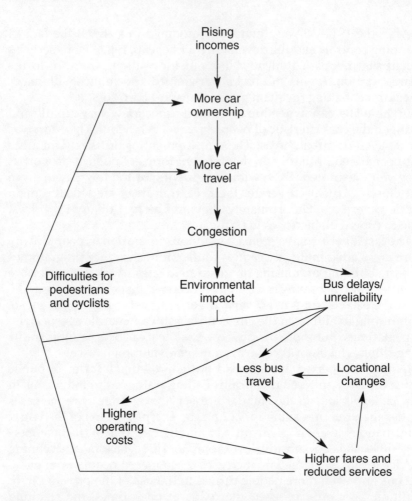

Figure 9.1 *Cycle of decline in public transport*

In his report, Professor Buchanan was far-sighted in seeing the motor car becoming essential for domestic purposes and, indeed, it has become almost indispensable for a great number of people. This demand by so many people to be given the opportunity to utilize their own personal transport causes considerable urban planning problems as well as changing the nature of social interaction of people living in the same area. Whereas previously people using public transport would see their neighbours every day, use of a car means that people can now live in an area without ever speaking to many of the other residents. Buchanan's solution, as seen in the United States, was to provide the road space to cope with ever increasing numbers of cars. The report started a trend in transportation studies which all predicted dire consequences for our towns and cities if new networks were not built quickly.

The reason why this scenario has not been fully followed is partly due to the work of transport planners and road traffic engineers in establishing techniques for dealing with traffic congestion. One of the many techniques that has been developed is that of traffic management.

The aims of traffic management are to provide higher road capacity on existing networks, to reduce the delays to traffic and to reduce accidents. There has been some concern about the effect of traffic management schemes on the environment in certain areas. This is especially the case when assessing the benefits/disbenefits of any scheme when applied to residents and pedestrians. Improving traffic flows by diverting traffic does not automatically allow greater safety or comfort for pedestrians, residents or public transports.

URBAN FREIGHT MOVEMENTS

It must not be forgotten that part of the urban transport problem concerns the movement of freight between and within towns and cities.

It is as well to remind ourselves just how important freight transport movements are in towns and cities.[1] Almost all deliveries to shops are made by road freight vehicles. Servicing premises which have no rear or exclusive access facilities is one of the major problems facing the vehicle operator and the traffic engineer. An over-riding factor in the choice of vehicle for delivery is not the location of the unloading space but the type of goods to be handled and the distance from the destination at which the goods are unloaded: for example, garages need to be serviced by large tankers; banks must have access close to the front of the building so that money can be quickly and safely transferred. In the eyes of many people, the delivery vehicle takes up valuable parking space and causes congestion by obstructing the free flow of traffic along urban roads.

Office blocks generate a high level of collection and delivery activity with the maintenance of the buildings calling for a great many vehicles. Offices also produce large volumes of outgoing parcels and mail which have to be collected. Similar needs occur in schools, hotels and hospitals. Even with exclusive unloading/loading bays the traffic generated has to use urban roads to gain access.

The transport requirements of industry are vast and cover the whole spectrum of vehicle types and sizes. Unless the factory has its own rail sidings, all inputs and outputs have to go by road. Where the factory is situated in an industrial estate with good access to the major trunk routes, the impact of the lorry on the urban population is minimal. However, much of industry is integrated into the community and the impact of road haulage vehicles is great.

The range of goods consumed in residential areas is to a large extent collected and delivered by the consumer but access is required for delivery of large items of furniture and other bulky appliances. Delivery of these items can cause congestion in narrow streets.

By their very nature, transport termini create problems in both rural and urban areas. A sea port may be well situated in an urban area but traffic converging on it will have to negotiate both urban and rural areas in order to arrive. Economies of scale and international standardization both dictate the use of large vehicles to and from the port. In terms of value of goods handled, the leading airports are among the country's largest freight handling termini. Goods shipped by air tend to be small packages of high value, calling for many small vehicles.

Even though the freight transport needs of urban areas have for simplicity been described in sectors, in reality the various sectors are totally inter-mixed. Residential areas are not compartmentalized away from shops, light industry is inter-mixed with both and all exist side by side with garages, railway stations and building sites. It is this mix of activities which compounds the already complex problem of how to control the lorry without depriving the community of the benefits which the lorry provides to society.

The issue is not one of cost, although cost is very important. Beyond a certain level of constraint on lorry movements there is a danger that the services will be discontinued. Large conurbations have very complex delivery patterns because of the enormous turnover of goods. However, the cumulative effect of congestion and restrictions on lorry movements in those areas can reduce the marginal utility of delivery to certain areas beyond an acceptable level.

Freight complexes

Communal transhipment centres or freight complexes on the outskirts of towns and cities are frequently regarded as a potential solution to environmental problems created by the lorry. In practice, several major problems can be identified with this concept.

How large is the physical scope for these complexes? Large quantities of goods are delivered into town centres through freight complexes operated by major suppliers or warehouses run by distribution specialists. Much of the remainder of freight is incapable of transhipment. Building materials comprise a proportion of goods movements in urban areas but are beyond the scope of transhipment. Similarly, vast quantities of foodstuffs are extremely perishable, easily contaminated or have a short shelf life. Many non-food items need specialist handling which make them incompatible with communal handling.

Extra handling, vehicles, storage, equipment and land increase the costs of delivery no matter how efficient the operation of the freight complex. Service levels to the customer tend to suffer. Manufacturers claim that they lose control over the key marketing weapon of the quality of the delivery service. Their ability to deal swiftly with urgent orders can be frustrated. Finally, the comprehensiveness of the system makes it very vulnerable to industrial disputes.

The end product of a system of freight complexes is claimed to be environmental improvement because orders and deliveries can be co-ordinated to reduce the number of vehicles making deliveries to any site. Large vehicles are utilized for the trunk haul, their scheduling enhanced by not having to make multiple drops.

Many people in the freight transport industry are sceptical about these claims. The number of heavy lorries actually making deliveries in an area tends to be very small compared with those passing through. In addition, reduction in the number of heavy lorries making deliveries would be offset by an increase in the number of smaller lorries which can add to congestion. There is the environmental disbenefit in the additional land needed for the complexes and the concentration of traffic flows to which transhipment centres would give rise.

Restrictions on movement

The solution lies in heavy lorry restrictions and routeing rather than in freight complexes. Local authorities have the power to restrict or manage the movement of heavy lorries within their areas under various pieces of legislation. The grounds on which the authority can control the movement of goods vehicles within their area fall into two categories:

1. Technical reasons such as bridges, narrow roads and public safety.
2. Abstract criteria such as the preservation, improvement of an area's amenity or the improving of an area's environment.

The tools available to the local authority are based on restrictions with regard to length, width, height, weight and the time of day.

The need for some control over the movement of heavy lorries is generally recognized by the road haulage industry but any restrictions make the task of collection and delivery very complex. All that the industry asks is that any controls are fair to all sections of the industry and easily understandable. Even the simplest scheme will increase costs while excessive restriction can make delivery almost impossible.

LOCAL GOVERNMENT

Local government in the UK is the creation of Parliament, which is often forgotten by many people. The structure and processes are created by Acts of Parliament and the same legislation decreases the power that can be exercised by any local authority.

Local government functions include responsibility for the following:

1. Education (except the universities).
2. Local health and welfare services.
3. Housing.
4. Public health.
5. Environmental planning.
6. Traffic management and transport.

All of these functions are subject to ministerial and Parliamentary control.

Since April 1974 there has been a two-tier local government structure in England and Wales with a different regional structure in Scotland. In England the structure comprises 47 county councils and 333 district councils. In addition, there were the Greater London Council (GLC) and six metropolitan county councils with 32 London boroughs and 36 metropolitan district councils.

The establishment of metropolitan counties under the Local Government Act followed the setting up of passenger transport authorities in these areas under the 1968 Transport Act. The local control of transport services passed to a body made up of representatives from the district councils in the major conurbations until uniform control was established by the formation of the metropolitan counties.

The metropolitan county authorities were given the task of operating and integrating all public transport within their area. The county councils were given the role of co-ordinating public transport within their areas.

In 1986 the Greater London Council and the metropolitan counties were abolished by the government. Transport is now under the control of passenger transport authorities as legislated under the 1968 Transport Act. In London much of the former powers of the Greater London Council has now been passed to the boroughs with the exception of London Regional Transport which is responsible directly to the Minister of Transport. All of this is complicated as far as co-ordination of services is concerned by the deregulation of bus services (see Chapter 7).

The case for abolishing the metropolitan counties, and for that matter the GLC, is based on the argument that they are a wasteful and unnecessary tier of local government. The counties argued very strongly that having their functions taken over by the districts will in itself cause duplication and that some functions can only be carried out at a higher level than the districts. The reverting to the system of passenger transport authorities seems to back up this point of view but there is no legislation to stop any local authority opting out of the system. If this happens to any great extent, road planning and traffic management schemes may become completely unco-ordinated in some of the major urban areas.

TRANSPORT PLANNING

There are three main planning processes through which local authorities present their policies towards transport in their areas and by which central government can monitor progress and influence the direction of transport policy locally:

1. *Structure plans*
   The Town and Country Planning Act of 1971 was a consolidation Act, combining all the previous legislation and some amendments. The main part of this act which concerns transport professionals is that dealing with structure plans.

   The structure plan when submitted to central government should provide a clear picture of whether and where development should take place, what any development should be, and the resources likely to be available from both the private and public sectors.
2. *Transport policies and programmes*
   These are concerned with transport matters rather than the land uses of the structure plans. County councils must submit each year a report outlining their transport policies for the following five years and making bids for funds through the Transport

Supplementary Grants system (TSG). Most items of transport were eligible for the grant including the construction and maintenance of highways, lighting, footpaths and cycleways, car and lorry parking, road safety and public transport.

As Beetham[2] pointed out at the time, the two main features of the grant system were:

1. The grant is not based on the actual costs of individual schemes as previous systems but on county programmes of estimated expenditure backed by a comprehensive statement of transport policies for the area.
2. Financial support for public transport would, as far as possible, be channelled through the county councils and not paid direct to the operators by central government.

These two aspects were of considerable consequence for the public transport operator. It meant that the operator had to work closely with the county council officials, divulging a great deal of information on costs of operation and being subjected to pressure on service levels from councillors.

The TPP process is essentially a submission made by a county to central government which sets out a five-year programme of capital and revenue expenditure for all forms of transport not financed by the owner or operator of the vehicle. It should contain the following points:

1. A summary of the main policies and proposals for the whole county.
2. A programme that is fully costed for a five-year period and set within realistic budget constraints.
3. A programme that can be clearly related to the stated policy objectives.
4. A programme that relates to the whole of the local authority's area that is presented but which treats each geographical area separately.

The TPP was both a statement of county objectives, policies and programmes and a bid for Transport Supplementary Grant.

From 1985, the Transport Supplementary Grant system has changed. TSG now only applies to capital projects covering highway schemes with a more than local value.

It has been stated by the government that the reduction in TSG was compensated for by a rise in the rate support grant but this grant is of a general nature. This means that local transport support has to compete with all other local authority areas for funds. The government argues that this is the proper way to deal with local issues, ie leaving local politicians to rank their priorities including transport.

The disadvantages are:

1. There is no central assessment in the light of the TPP proposals and the whole TPP process is undermined.
2. Most local transport schemes have to compete for funds which have often been deemed inadequate. Local road and rail support schemes can be very vulnerable in this situation because they are easily identified and the blame can be attached to central government.
3. The Department of Transport has become more involved by having to take the responsibility for inadequate services.

3. *Public transport plans*
These were established by the Transport Act 1978 and apply to the non-metropolitan county councils.

There is a great deal of overlap between public transport plans and TPPs but the PTPs have the following objectives:

1. They include a wide range of services in addition to conventional public transport such as school, hospital, welfare, community transport and social car schemes.
2. They reflect closer and extensive consultation with the operators.
3. They are formally published as the county council's considered policy for public transport.

As Bell *et al* [3] state: 'These three documents which local authorities are required to produce represent levels of Central Government supervision ranging from the strategic in the structure plans to the detailed operational in the public transport plans. Government is clearly very much involved in the transport sector. Conflicts between central and local government have occurred mainly because there has been a difference of views on the degree to which public transport should be controlled by financial means. Shortly after the TPP system was introduced, Central Government believed local authorities, particularly non-metropolitan counties, were not encouraging or subsidizing operators enough. Subsequently, though, and particularly with a Conservative Government, it has been more a question of Central Government demanding that the public transport sector be increasingly subjected to the vagaries of the market place.'

By freeing local transport from all but nominal local government control by deregulation and the arm's-length relationship of municipal operators, the Conservative government sought to bring innovation to the industry. By identifying those services that are commercial, how to support other services then becomes a political decision.

PUBLIC SERVICES

As discussed in Chapters 6 and 7, between 1930 and 1985, public road passenger transport in urban areas was controlled by the traffic commissioners. They awarded licences to bus companies wishing to provide services and tended to encourage companies who wished to build networks of services in an area and were willing to make extensive use of cross-subsidization.

The 1968 Act and the Local Government Act 1972 allowed councils to make grants for specific services to cover costs incurred by the operators in their area, including British Rail. County councils were given the responsibility for the promotion of a co-ordinated and efficient system of public transport to meet the needs of the county.

The sudden acceleration of the rate of inflation and the fall in bus operators' profits in the late 1970s enhanced the role of the local authorities in planning the local public transport network. County councils developed new techniques to test the justification put forward by operators in support of higher subsidies.

Since the Transport Act of 1985, the traffic commissioners no longer have such a high level of control. Local authorities can only support essential routes which are not provided commercially. Even these routes must be put out to tender, with the company offering to run the service at the lowest tender winning the contract. Local authorities now do not have the control in a planning sense of helping to build up networks of services in their areas. They are now primarily concerned with filling in the gaps between commercial services where there is a demonstrable need. New techniques, or old techniques re-learnt, will have to be employed in this situation.

Efficiency in public transport

Of central importance to the debate about the role of public transport is the issue of efficiency. Public transport is both a commercial activity and a social service. To some people it is a utility, like electricity, water, gas and sewerage that is supplied to customers day in and day out as long as they are connected to the supply. Public utilities charge a standard rate no matter where the customer resides.

From the passenger's point of view, public transport suffers from being a prescribed service, which although structured and timetabled to meet average customer needs, is inflexible and the passenger must fit the journey pattern to the service on offer. (The exceptions to this are the various demand responsive types of service which will be discussed later.)

From the passenger's point of view it is quite possible to identify two views of public transport efficiency. The first is that there is a service on offer when the individual passenger requires it. The second is that although the service supplied may not meet the exact needs of individual passengers, at least it is predictable and meets the major requirements of passenger journeys.

It is the second view that is most appropriate for most fixed route public transport services. This is the main area of passenger perceived inefficiency, especially during the rapid decline of the last 25 years. A great number of passengers or potential passengers perceive that public transport is inefficient because the service does not go where the passenger requires and it often does not go where and when timetabled. This is a sure recipe for making the potential passenger see the advantages of personal transport.

This type of reasoning highlights the nature of the action which must be undertaken by the public transport operator to increase the perceived efficiency of public transport in the minds of the general population. The first action is to find out the needs of people living in the area served and design a service which more closely matches those needs. The second action is to make sure that the service instituted is run reliably according to the scheduled timetable. The third action is to overcome any other negative aspects of public transport, such as lack of comfort and information. A great deal of research has been undertaken into passenger attitudes to public transport and the results show that above all other factors, public transport needs to be reliable.

From the government point of view efficiency of public transport is a complex mix of different factors. These include the utilization of resources including land, fuel and materials, the burden of finance and how the needs of any community for mobility and access are to be met.

In any commercial field, providers of goods and services have two important forces to cope with which tend to promote efficiency. The first of these is having to compete in the market place with companies providing similar goods or services. If one company becomes relatively inefficient when compared with other companies, its market position will suffer and, if it does not take correcting action, it will eventually go out of business. The second force is profit. Usually, greater efficiency in meeting the needs of customers means greater operating profits, which in turn meeting the needs of customers means greater operating profits, which in turn means greater rewards for all involved in the business. Commercial competition and the profit motive are strong inducements towards efficiency.

This is the main thrust of the 1985 Transport Act. Bus services are now virtually freed from restriction (except in London where some controls remain) and there are increasing opportunities for competition. According to the government, competition has led to a change in the industry with greater innovation in services, lower fares and much greater attention paid to the needs of passengers. Efficiency can now be measured in the same way as for any other commercial enterprise.

As David Bayliss concludes in his paper:[4] 'I think there is merit in viewing the notion of efficiency made up of productivity and effectiveness, put simply:

$$efficiency = productivity + effectiveness$$

However, productivity and effectiveness do not exist independently of each other and this must be recognized in considering what best to do about each. The different interests in public transport (passenger, operator, government) see efficiency in different ways and it is important for the providers to recognize and understand others' points of view of efficiency.' This government take the view that only commercial criteria can be used to measure efficiency, even for those services which are non-viable. The company placing the lowest tender, ie needing the least subsidy, wins the contract and is deemed most efficient.

Unconventional transport

For the last 15 years or so there has been a perceived rural transport problem. In areas where public transport provision has been poor for any length of time, people have adapted their way of living to manage without it. In rural areas a high proportion of the population own cars and those without cars gain mobility for essential journeys by getting lifts. Therefore there is little chance of reviving ordinary conventional bus services without the level of subsidy climbing steeply.

However, there are still a significant number of people who cannot arrange lifts and need some form of public transport if their needs for mobility and accessibility are to be met. Experiments have been carried out with unconventional transport alternatives involving village buses run by volunteers, shared taxis, car schemes and post buses.

Though it has been claimed that these schemes have been successful, these claims must be looked at critically. All the schemes are dependent on voluntary effort which is unpaid and not truly accounted for in the true costs of the scheme. When public money has been required to support a scheme, it has been found that the cost to the public purse per passenger was higher than that for other public transport.

Bus/rail co-ordination

The vital part played by the railways in public transport in the main conurbations seems to be subordinated to the inter-city aspect of rail operation. Railways provide greater passenger carrying capacity than any other mode, especially during peak periods. They also avoid the delays and unreliability associated with road congestion.

There are four main reasons why people in most situations, given a choice between private and public transport, opt for the private car:

1. Once a car has been purchased, taxed and insured there is a strong incentive to use it for as many journeys as possible. Individual journeys are marginally costed by the user because the capital, tax and insurance are sunk costs which have to be borne no matter how many journeys are made. Because of this view of sunk costs, the user accounts for the journey costs purely in terms of the fuel used. This may not seem fair when comparing costs of motoring with costs of using public transport but it is a fact of life which must be accepted.
2. Public transport is perceived by the average citizen as being very inferior to the car as a means of travel. In terms of flexibility and convenience, the car has the major advantage of direct control by the user. The journey can be planned without reference to a fixed route or a timetable. Given the constraints of road layouts and the availability of parking spaces, the car owner can choose the most convenient route, gains door-to-door travel and sets off at a time of the owner's choosing. Even when held up by congestion a certain flexibility is retained because it may be possible to switch to an alternative route. Where this is not possible, the comfort of the car makes waiting in a traffic jam more tolerable than on public transport.
3. As car interiors have become more refined, with better seating, ventilation and sound proofing, and more extras such as cassette players, the level of comfort throughout the journey is much higher in a car than on public transport.

4. The most important advantage is the undoubted shorter journey times offered by the car door to door. The exception to this rule is where the journey is very short, making walking quicker, or where origin and destination are very close to public transport links. In general car speeds can be as much as two and a half times faster than a bus. The bus has to stop and pick up/set down passengers and road improvements generally favour the car.

From the foregoing factors it is obvious that public transport has little to recommend it when compared with the car. It also explains why traffic restraint measures and restrictions on parking without improvements to public transport prove unacceptable to most of the population.

One method by which public transport can be improved is co-ordination of bus and rail services. Where rail routes link suburban areas to city centres, the train has advantages for trunk haul movement stemming from the reserved right of way. The problem with suburban rail services is the limited catchment area made up of the number of car parking spaces available for train passengers. Carefully planned co-ordination between suburban bus services and rail services from suburban stations can widen the catchment area and allow more people to benefit from congestion-free rail services. People who normally use the car or bus to travel to the city centre can benefit from reductions in journey time. Avoidance of congestion results in more consistent and reliable journey times. Passengers previously travelling by car can avoid parking difficulties and car parking charges.

There are problems with this approach. The attractiveness of the co-ordinated service depends on the complexity of the rail network and the location of the railway stations relative to city centre destinations. Inconvenient locations with long walking distances to shops or offices are a major disadvantage for people using the rail service. There is also the reluctance of passengers to change modes in the middle of a journey. Reducing the time taken for passengers to transfer from bus to rail and making this transfer as straightforward as possible are of great importance in making bus/rail co-ordinated services attractive to the travelling public.

It is hardly surprising that most bus/rail co-ordinating schemes have been implemented in metropolitan county areas such as Tyne and Wear. The concept of integated transport is emphasized in the 1968 Transport Act which set up the passenger transport executives. With the shire counties and other major towns, most passenger transport undertakings including local rail services remained outside the county councils' control. Against this background, most county councils have had difficulties in encouraging bus/rail co-ordination.

The concept of bus/rail co-ordination and planning of local services encourages the adoption of through ticketing. This is the issue of a single ticket valid for combinations of bus and rail journeys. Apart from the convenience for passengers in eliminating time required at the interchange to purchase a ticket, it also saves the operator money in fare collection and in having to publish separate fare scales for each mode.

Bus/rail co-ordination has been successful in widening the catchment area of suburban rail services and in attracting passengers from parallel bus services. Since the abolition of the metropolitan counties and the deregulation of the bus industry, there have been signs that this co-ordination is being challenged by other bus operators. Only time will tell about how this kind of competition will affect rail/bus co-ordinated schemes.

There is very little evidence to suggest that there has been any significant shift of passengers from private to public transport as a result of these schemes. The lack of such transfer is attributed to the lack of overall journey time savings. This is in direct contrast to the major theoretical studies which analysed these schemes before they were set up; all assumed that one of the major advantages would be the attraction of car users and resultant reductions in congestion.

Scheduled co-ordination between the road and rail modes is the single most important factor in success or failure. Interchanges must be designed in such a way that they facilitate quick and easy transfer which can only be achieved by careful planning, design and construction.

Park and ride

Park and ride as a concept aims to utilize the advantages of two modes of transport and combine them to give an optimum journey to the town centre for the traveller. By doing this, the overall objective of reducing congestion in the central area of the city is achieved.

The aim of the traveller is to minimize the time and money spent on the journey while maintaining an adequate level of comfort and convenience. Each traveller consciously or unconsciously undertakes a mini-cost benefit study before setting out, taking into account both purely financial costs and less quantifiable factors. The choice of mode or modes will be based on the analysis of the advantages and disadvantages involved. Thus any simple decision to increase public transport usage by lowering fares may have little effect on patronage unless the other factors in the package are equally attractive.

As stated in this chapter many times, the car has major advantages over public transport, the major one being its inherent flexibility.

Availability of the car to the user is virtually instantaneous and there is access to virtually every home or place in the land. This makes the car an ideal mode in the relatively uncongested outer areas of major towns and cities. Bus services are difficult to provide economically in low density housing estates, resulting in low frequencies and widely spaced routes. Bus travel is slower than the car due to poorer perfor-mance and stopping times.

Traffic congestion increases as the central area is approached and the car loses much of its speed advantage as both modes become caught in trafic jams. In the town centre, bus passengers can alight from the bus and walk directly to their destination. The car driver has to find a place to park the vehicle, often waiting in a queue for a parking space. This makes the car very inefficient as a means of travel in city centres and queues of cars waiting at parking areas can add to the congestion.

To make park and ride schemes attractive to potential customers, the scheme must offer a time or cost saving. The potential saving must be significant enough to outweigh the inconvenience of having to change mode. The aim of the traveller is to minimize the time and the cost of the journey to the city centre while maintaining an adequate level of comfort. The transit system for the public transport section of the journey must offer a high service level if it is to be compared favourably with the car.

The shorter the overall journey length, the less likely the traveller is to change modes: the time lost at the interchange will be a large proportion of the overall journey time which will mitigate against the traveller wishing to change modes. Any urban area has an identifiable threshold distance from the town centre nearer than which users will not be attracted to park and ride. In addition, if the public transport mode of travel is actually slower than the car, park and ride schemes are at a disadvantage. Ideally, the public transport mode should be an express service taking advantage of traffic management and bus priority schemes to avoid congestion and achieving very fast times from the car parking place to the town centre.

Central area penetration is very important to the user and is related to the other aspects of service quality. The greater the number of points served in the city centre, the shorter will be the average distance park and ride passengers have to walk to their destination.

The availability and cost of car parking in the town centre has a direct bearing on whether a park and ride system will be used by car users. If car parking is expensive and in short supply, park and ride systems will become attractive. It will attract more passengers if the car driver's search for a parking space can be shown to be much longer than the change-over time between modes at the interchange.

Obviously there is a drawback with successful park and ride after the introduction of the system: the average search time for a parking place in the town may fall, thus affecting people's attitudes to park and ride.

'Railheading' is a problem with rail-based park and ride schemes where the car driver selects the interchange with the highest level of advantage. Having started the journey by car, the driver is reluctant to leave the car until traffic congestion gets really bad. This means that a lot of drivers will drive as far as possible towards the town centre before changing modes.

The main advantage to the community of a successful park and ride system stems from the reduction of congestion on the road approaches to town centres. The number of places needed for car parking can also be reduced and any land put to more productive use.

Overall, an intelligently implemented and well-planned park and ride system should give a net benefit to the community by reducing congestion and environmental pollution, coupled with the chance of convenient and reliable bus service for both car users and non-car users. The aim for the community should be to maintain the most efficient transport system using the best combination of all available modes.

One problem with park and ride schemes, especially in the present climate of transport policy, is that they are unlikely to prove profitable, when measured by financial criteria rather than social welfare, to the bus operator. To be attractive to the potential customer, a high frequency service is required, yet the potential size of the ridership is limited by the number of parking spaces available at each interchange.

To maximize the usage of park and ride, whether bus or rail based, several factors are very important:

1. Measurement by the operator of the actual number of car passengers using the city centre coupled with a profile of actual congestion. This analysis must be undertaken before the service is developed.
2. The interchange should be located just outside the congested area so that cars entering the car park do not add to the congestion. Bus priority measures should also start as soon as these are needed to help the bus overcome the effects of congestion.
3. The frequency of the service must be such that the waiting time at the interchange is kept to a minimum. Nothing is more likely to put people off using park and ride than having to wait for what they consider to be a long time in a cold, damp interchange.

Park and ride is a method of utilizing the urban road space or capacity to a greater extent than would be the case without such schemes. To be successful financially, such schemes must be viewed in the broader context of savings in costs than just the pure financial accounting for the service. One large problem for many people using park and ride may be that they cannot return to the car at intervals to deposit packages in the car before continuing to shop.

Light rail

As an example of a light railway serving urban areas, the Tyne and Wear Metro can be used to illustrate the benefits. A report on the Tyne and Wear area in 1969 stated 'the only way to provide the level of service and accessibility required in the future, in the face of increasing road traffic, is by significant investment in a system with its own right of way. This system should be based on current railway facilities with the appropriate renewal and upgrading of lines and stations and the improvement of the central area accessibility by linking rail lines north and south of the river Tyne.'

The crux of the Metro system is the penetration into the heart of Newcastle and the integration with the rest of the transport system. The basic concept of integration between bus and Metro is that the bus services should not run parallel to the Metro routes but be used to serve local needs and feed into the Metro system at interchanges.

For integration and this interchange system to be accepted, the whole system must be publicized as one with a truly integrated fares system. This is the problem now confronting the Metro operator as buses have been freed from control and can now directly compete with the whole system.

Taxis

As stated in Chapter 2, the taxi is the closest mode of public transport to the private car. It requires no central long-stay parking facilities although it does use operational taxi ranks. Taxis are relatively expensive to use, often need prior booking and can cause their own city centre congestion. The number of passengers per vehicle is limited and from an urban transport planning view they are often treated like the private car.

Cycling

So far, when discussing planning for transport in urban areas, three main modes of transport have been considered – the car, the bus and the train. These three modes account for the majority of journeys, with the exception of short-journey walking, but they also account for the noise, pollution, visual intrusion and the other disbenefits of transport in urban areas. It must not be forgotten that a great many journeys are undertaken by cyclists.

Because of this, a number of local authorities have made provision for cyclists in their plans and as part of traffic management schemes. It is claimed that cycleways reduce accidents, reduce pollution, save energy – and can lead to a much healthier population.

ASSESSMENT OF TRANSPORT SERVICES

The major methods of assessing transport services are to measure their use of resources or their costs. It is often argued that the costs must be assessed in terms of their impact on society as a whole. This must include an assessment of any environmental costs or disadvantages from using different transport modes. True analysis takes into account the savings in other areas of activity from certain actions in the transport field.

The question is really one of the alternative uses to which the resources would be put if they were not used for transport. Recent studies suggest that aircraft have reached their design potential in the domestic market and improvement should be concentrated on making airports more accessible with less time taken up by airport processing. The greatest deterrent to using air for short domestic flights is the time taken for the passengers to pass through the airport.

Buses have also reached the limit of their potential on existing roads. Further improvement would require much better roads and technologically advanced buses with a number of driver assisting aids.

Rail has considerable potential for technical development but this requires a great deal of investment.

It is, in the transport planner's view, to the benefit of society to allow development in an evolutionary manner, ie in a series of small steps which make use of existing infrastructure and other developed resources. This is not the view of the engineer, who sees development as a series of revolutionary breakthroughs which can change the whole nature of transport provision. Ultimately, the transport planner has to plan systems which will take account of engineering breakthroughs but it is in this area that assessment is at its weakest.

SUBSIDY

The majority of transport systems developed as a result of what could be termed business enterprise. The developers started their services because they felt they had a product to sell which the public wanted to buy. By designing the routes to meet customer mobility and accessibility needs, the operator was able to earn profits and pay dividends to shareholders.

Always throughout history, new forms of transport have been developed which made the profitable operation of other forms of transport difficult. In our own age it has been the rise of motorized transport which has changed the shape of our access and mobility. The motor bus challenged the civic tramway and the railway but has itself been challenged by the car. Even though bus companies had been able to build substantial networks covering large areas with integrated services, the mass purchase and use of cars made the profitable operation of these networks almost impossible. Increasingly, public transport operators have merged and come under the control of some form of local or national government agency. This is not only a fact in the UK but is a world-wide trend. There is hardly an urban transport operation which is not controlled in some way by either the local council or the national government.

This change in ownership has frequently been accompanied by the operator suffering financial problems due to the intense competition from the car. To help maintain a comprehensive network of services, governments, both local and national, have had to step in with financial support.

The regulation changes under the previous Conservative government were an attempt to break out of the cycle of unprofitable services and higher subsidies. Where financial support began, the sums of money involved were small and seen to bring immense social benefits to the local community. As the use of the car grew, so the amount of subsidy needed increased until a point was reached where the very principle of subsidies was called into question.

Even though the discussion in this section concentrates on urban public transport, the principles of subsidy apply to all modes, just as do the disbenefits. Subsidies are found in shipping and air transport just as much as with bus and rail. Indeed, without subsidy, half the world's airlines would be bankrupt and unable to operate.

Definition of subsidy

Public transport operates, as do all businesses, in a situation where the company purchases inputs from various sources, 'processes' these inputs to produce a product, and sells that product, the revenue collected going to pay for the inputs and the costs of production. If the revenues do not cover these costs, the operator must be making a loss, ie paying out more than the company is getting in. This is a situation which cannot be sustained for very long.

There is no transport operator whether privately owned or publicly owned, which can operate at a loss. Of course, short-term losses can be sustained from any reserves built up while making profits, but losses in the long term are impossible. Where the government, whether national or local, pays some money to cover losses or support the business, this form of payment is usually referred to as a subsidy. If the money is paid to cover shortfalls in revenue, this is usually referred to as an operating subsidy. If it is paid to cover part of the purchase price of a vehicle or equipment, it is referred to as a capital or investment subsidy. No matter which form the subsidy takes, the government is making sure that at the end of the accounting year the company can balance the accounts because income will more than equal expenditure even though some of the income did not come from selling tickets.

The advantages of subsidy

The reasons put forward by those who support subsidy can be summarized as follows:

1. Declining demand for the services offered, which in the case of public transport is reflected in car ownership and usage figures. Although the number of passenger miles travelled has increased dramatically over the past 25 years a great proportion of the increased mileage has been accounted for by increased journeys by car rather than public transport. The use of cars for transport has led to changed land use patterns with much more dispersed settlements making the supply of a reasonable public transport service difficult.

2. With rising real incomes since the 1950s, industry in general has contained the rise in prices by increasing the productivity of the workers. Because of the nature of public transport employment, it is difficult to implement continuous increased productivity measures. Once the benefit of one-person operation of the vehicle has been utilized, there is not much else that can be undertaken within the limiting criteria of drivers' hours regulations and trade union negotiations. Bus companies are taking advantage of the de-regulation system to implement new types of service with new conditions of service which help to lower the wages bill.

3. As a result of the trends in costs and demand, fares have tended to rise at a faster rate than general inflation. Of course, this gives rise to the classic rising fares/failing demand cycle in turn leading to cutbacks in service levels.

Subsidies are given to public transport companies (and private companies under the 1985 Act) to overcome and mitigate the effects of the rising fares/falling demand cycle. By giving subsidies to transport, governments hope that fares will be kept lower than would be the case without subsidies, that service levels will be maintained at the highest level possible and that wages can be kept at a level sufficient to attract the right calibre of staff. There are in addition a number of objectives claimed to favour a subsidy policy, especially with regard to the provision of public transport:[5]

1. It is argued strongly by many organizations and pressure groups that the use of cars by large number of people in crowded city centres is environmentally irresponsible. Cars cause pollution of the atmosphere with emissions including lead, and are noisy. They cause congestion in narrow streets and account for a large proportion of serious road accident casualties. These organizations back their viewpoint by claiming that subsidies to public transport are worthwhile and economic. By keeping fares low, people are attracted to use public transport in preference to the car for journeys into the city. Any movement of people away from cars onto public transport will increase benefits to the community as a whole through the reduction of pollution and accidents.
2. Studies have indicated that there is a close connection between land use patterns and the need for transport. In the past, with transport networks feeding into the city centre, most businesses were located in the inner city area. With widespread car ownership, the patterns of land use have changed with housing, business and leisure locations reflecting the accessibility to car owners. It is hoped that by subsidizing services feeding into the town centre, the forms of land use will change and the central business district will again become the main part of any city. There is, however, a paradox in the idea of subsidies to passenger transport in urban areas. People tend to use the subsidized transport to live further from their work, creating expansionary pressures on villages surrounding the town. The transport is then used for the journey to work at peak times but the car for all other purposes. These subsidy prices must be closely tied in with car parking charges and planning.
3. An argument which is particularly relevant to the railways is that there are high infrastructure costs involved in creating and

maintaining the system. It is a misallocation of resources to have capital assets under-utilized. By subsiding the operation of the system, it is argued that services will be used to a greater extent than before, thus rectifying some of the misallocation. In the true commercial world, any under-utilized assets which were costing the company money would be liquidated so that the resources could be used elsewhere.

4. One of the major arguments used in support of a subsidy policy is that subsidies can achieve a much better modal split in favour of public transport to the advantage of the community. This should result in better public transport services for non-car owners as well as less congestion, pollution, visual intrusion, noise and accidents.

5. Public transport when fully utilized is more energy efficient than private transport. Because of worries about future energy supplies (see Chapter 10) the use of public transport should be encouraged by subsidy ensuring the fullest possible use of the public transport system.

6. As has been stated before, transport is a political subject. The issue of subsidy policies revolves around the social aims of a particular set of people. It is argued that the provision of transport services cannot be left solely to market forces because the market will never ensure that all members of a community have adequate access to the essential services within the community. There has always been an element in public transport management which has a strong sense of social obligation especially towards the young, old and other disadvantaged groups of citizens. Subsidies can be either direct or indirect. Concessionary fares for school children or old-aged pensioners are examples of direct subsidies. Operating subsidies or capital grants are examples of indirect subsidies. For all its emphasis on commercial viability and market disciplines, the 1985 Act makes provision for a local authority to provide subsidies to public transport. These subsidies are intended to cover services which cannot be provided commercially but which are politically deemed necessary for the community. By 'politically' is meant 'by decision of local authority committees' rather than bus companies. The criterion used is known as the tendering system. All such routes are put out to tender by the local authority and the company which requires the lowest subsidy wins the contract to provide the service.

Opposition to subsidies[6]

The greatest opposition to any subsidy policy arises from its cost to public funds. A subsidy involves greater taxation for the community, whether from local or central government. Opposition involves two aspects – the opportunity cost of money and whether the subsidy will be passed on to the passenger in the form of lower fares.

1. In situations where public funds are limited by the desired level of taxation and the government's borrowing ceiling, any public expenditure in one area of the economy must be financed by savings made in other areas. To put this simply, if there is a rise in the level of subsidy payments to public transport, decreases must be made in the amount spent on health, education or defence.
2. There is a widespread belief that a subsidy undermines the motivation of public employees to be efficient. At the end of the day, public transport managers do not have to rely on their management skill to sell the service so that revenue covers costs. Any shortfall in revenue will be covered by the government by means of a subsidy. This, it is argued, encourages public transport management to allow costs to rise unchecked because they employ too many staff, pay higher wage rates than necessary and invest in resources which are not really needed. All this results in substantially higher unit costs. (Public transport managers would defend themselves by pointing out that very often they have no control over some of these variables, decisions about staff and investment being made by politicians.)
3. The social service or equity argument in support of subsidies is invalid because public transport is not a social service. It can be argued that rich people benefit more from rail subsidies than poor people because rich people use the railways more. Pensioners' concessionary fares do benefit a specific sector of the community but those who are against these specific subsidies argue that it would be better to increase pensions and allow pensioners to spend the money how they wished rather than on travel.

As a past president of the Chartered Institute of Transport, Sir Robert Reid, in a paper to ITEC 83 Conference in South Africa, approached the subject of subsidies on public transport:[7] 'For a subsidy to be justifiable by economic criteria it must contribute to the achievement of some valid end and not be disguising operational or commercial inefficiency.'

When studying the UK, it does not take a great deal of insight to recognize that there was one factor above all others which heightened the conflict between central government and the politicians serving the major conurbations. This was the disagreement over the distribution of the metropolitan counties' income. A large proportion of that income came from central government funds. Transport was one of the few easily identified policy areas over which the metropolitan county had any effective control and influence. The way in which this control was used and the income spent became the major area of disagreement. On this subject there could never be any real meeting of minds. The metropolitan countries, especially South Yorkshire, had a policy of support for local public transport which involved large subsidies locally; these subsidies were defended by arguing that the benefits gained in extra mobility and business far outweighed the cost. It was not the only reason for their abolition but it played a major part in that process.

The issue of subsidies for transport operations cannot be isolated from that of the economy as a whole. While the social justification for subsidies is easy to identify, the measurement of the benefits is extremely difficult. The costs of any subsidy in pure financial terms are easy to calculate; the financial benefits are hidden in other areas.

TRANSPORT POLICY

The prime objective of any transport policy must be to create or support an efficient system which provides good transport facilities at the lowest cost in terms of the resources used.

The 1968 Transport Act created passenger transport authorities and passenger transport executives with the objective to co-ordinating local passenger transport. With local government reform there was a chance to jointly consider general urban planning and public transport at local level in the metropolitan counties. In addition there were financial reforms intended to eliminate the bias against public transport. Finally, increased planning powers were given to local authorities to use traffic management measures as part of a comprehensive local transport policy. The Local Government Act of 1972 aimed to create local government units of an appropriate size and competence for the functions assigned to them.

Taken together these measures were supposed to make local transport planning comprehensive, locally responsible and only slightly and flexibly monitored and controlled by central government.

Professor K. Gwilliam,[8] in a paper to the Chartered Institute of Transport Hull congress of 1977, expressed disappointment that these laudable aims had not been fulfilled. He felt there were five main reasons why expectations were not borne out by practice. It must be remembered that he was writing only a few years after the whole system was in place. His reasons, though, can be seen to underpin the present government's policies towards public transport:

1. The institutional flexibility has been more apparent than real. Partly this has been due to the unforeseen financial stringency in which [the system] was implemented. But partly it was due to a fundamental flaw in the arrangements, whereby local authorities are expected to compile their plans on the basis of local objectives and criteria. While central government allocates funds, ostensibly on the basis of these plans, according to its own analysis and criteria.
2. The dearth of really attractive urban public transport capital projects.
3. The apparent irrelevance of public transport subsidy to the congestion issue, given the combination of low demand cross-elasticities for public transport and the high marginal costs of public transport at the peak.
4. The weakness of parking restraint policy, given the large amount of uncontrolled or private non-residential parking in many areas.
5. The inadequate arrangements for administrative co-ordination between counties and PTEs, counties and bus companies, counties and districts, counties and British Railways.

References

1. FTA *Planning for Lorries* FTA, Croydon 1974
2. Beetham, A. 'TPPs: Review and prospects from a public transport viewpoint' *Transport*, 1976
3. Bell, G., Blackledge, D.A. and Bowen, P. *The Economics and Planning of Transport* Heinemann, London 1983
4. Bayliss, D. 'Efficiency in public transport' Conference Paper, University of Newcastle 1979
5. Goodwin, P. 'Public transport subsidy and economic efficiency' Conference Paper, University of Newcastle 1979
6. Pryke, R. 'Public transport subsidy and economic inefficiency' Conference Paper, University of Newcastle 1979
7. Reid, R.B. 'Subsidy in British transport' *Transport*, September 1983
8. Gwilliam, K. 'Urban road and rail policy' *Transport*, July 1977

10

The Future

To look into the future is like playing blind man's buff, but there are developments, trends and problems that can be extrapolated forward into the next century. These developments can be summed up in the electronic revolution sweeping the globe, the moves to privatize state owned transport organizations and to loosen the economic regulation which has guided transport operations for so long. The problems stem from the ideas concerning which direction transport policy will take.

Starting with transport policy, we are faced with a dichotomy. On the one hand there are moves to free transport from the shackles of regulation and state ownership, on the other there is the need to provide access and mobility for all peoples. It is often said that transport policy should be about providing people with the means of satisfying their needs for mobility and access. Transport policy should not be purely about making money, although if the people's needs for access and mobility can be satisfied while the businesses providing the service can make a profit, there is nothing intrinsically wrong with this approach.

The basic problem of transport in most of the developed world and in many fast developing countries, is to view transport as a series of rights rather than as a means of enhancing the quality of life for all.

If we look at transport in this light, a number of questions can be posed about the sustainability of transport in its present form. People in most developed countries have the freedom to move from one place to another by whatever means they choose, which in the vast majority of cases means using the private car. The net result of all this movement, especially by road, is that people are killed and injured, scarce earth resources are consumed and the environment is harmed by the choices of mode which people make every day.

The problem is how to get from this stage in transport development to one where people are not killed and injured, the consumption of resources is slowed and the environment is not harmed, without introducing draconian controls which the people might not accept in a political sense. We have to face the fact that people like, for any number of reasons, their own personal transport, ready to leave when they want to leave and controlled by themselves. People want to have the ability to choose where they will live and where they will work.

The issues which will have to be addressed in the future in the light of people's preference for personal transport can be summed up as follows:

1. Transport must be planned in a way which enhances the quality of life for all rather than a few. Those who, for one reason or another, cannot use personal forms of transport must be catered for in such a way that they have accessibility to the normal places which people wish to visit. This must involve a greater degree of integration of land use planning and transport, with the aim of reducing the need for travel.
2. One principle that must be established is to develop measures which help transport to enhance the environment, not merely to minimize the damage. This will involve setting quality standards and setting up the means to enforce those standards. This is dealt with later in the chapter.
3. There must be a system which encourages everybody to participate in the transport planning process so that the people affected can influence the decisions make in their name. If there is a move to make public mass transport the norm, this must be accomplished by an improvement in the choice of destinations and to allow people to travel on public transport without the perceived fear of personal injury, assault and harassment.
4. In addition, research effort must be put into developments of technologies which benefit all people, including those for whom personal transport is the ideal. Energy and efficiency must be considered by research into how to meet accessibility requirements at the lowest resource cost, especially in terms of energy usage and a reduction in congestion. This aspect will in turn be affected by developments in electronic communications which are discussed later in the chapter.

The world is going though an 'electronic revolution' leading to the growth of global communications and the development of more sophisticated but easier to use computers. It is now possible to tele-phone directly to the other side of the world, transmit television pictures from remote areas, transmit documents over facsimile or e-mail and transmit vast amounts of information over the Web. There is no doubt that these developments will have effects on transport, both in the types of service and methods of operation.

The telecommunications revolution could lead to a fall in demand for transport as business people use teleconferencing facilities rather than travel for face-to-face meetings. It could also lead to less traffic on urban roads when people use television and cable to order from shops rather than driving to the shop in person. Of course ultimately somebody will invent some form of teletransport and transport will then be redundant!

The other great problem facing transport is that of fuel and what happens when supplies of oil run out. In the 1970s research into this seemed vital, but since then there appears to have been a lull and oil supplies again seem plentiful. This can only be temporary. Oil is a finite resource and at some point in the not too distant future thought must be turned to the problem of when the oil becomes scarce.

Transport regulation and operating methods are changing. The bus industry in this country was effectively deregulated in 1985, the airline industry in the USA in 1978, and the road haulage industry in 1968. The world trend seems to be one of freeing transport from the shackles of regulation as much as possible. Even in the European Union there are moves to liberalize air transport. The aims of the programme are two fold:

1. To give the consumer, be it passenger or freight shipper, an increased measure of choice of price, convenience and service level.
2. To free the airline operator from the need for state support and the state from heavy involvement in financial obligations towards its principal airlines.

All of this points to changing methods of management necessary for tomorrow's transport leaders. They will have be to better educated, able to understand the use of computers and mathematical tech-niques, and keep up to date with current developments. In addition, some managers will have to drop their concern for social justice in transport and start to concentrate on the balance sheet. Opportunities to make profits will have to be grasped and loss-making services dropped. This in itself will change the political solution of blanket subsidization to specific subsidies for specific routes. In short, trans-port managers will have to become more professional, like all other managers in any successful business.

TELECOMMUNICATIONS AND TRANSPORT

As discussed in Chapter 1, people transport their goods and themselves to fulfil needs other than purely transportation. People have needs for business, work, shopping and leisure. Goods are transported so that they can arrive in the market place. People also need to communicate. Both the needs for communication and transport are the result of the basic interdependency of people within society. During the last century, travel and telecommunications have grown side by side, complementing each other rather than competing. The lack of competition resulted from the relatively similar rate of development in both areas. The submarine cable arrived as the sailing ship was replaced by steamship, the radio telegraph with the advent of scheduled shipping services and satellite communications with fast jet aircraft.

Presently, the need for both transportation and communications stems from the need to uncover latent demand in the market place, the increasing pace of technological change, competition on a world scale and the pursuit of economic growth. As economic growth continues, the interaction of communications and transport also increases. Transport development has resulted in the growth of suburban areas and the decentralization of business. These moves in themselves have called for more communication. Better communications bring more contact opportunities, both for business and pleasure. With business, the opportunity for better communications can generate more business, which can itself generate the need for more transport.

There are indications that developments in telecommunications and transport are now progressing at different rates. The union of computers, micro-electronics and telecommunications has speeded up the advance of electronic information services. There seems to be no near future development of supersonic flight, for example, to push forward the corresponding development of the technology of transport.

There has been considerable speculation and research about the impact that advanced telecommunications will have on travel patterns and transport. Khan[1] asks the question of whether substitution between telecommunications and transport can take place. Different kinds of travel are exposed to the risk of telecommunications substitution to different degrees. Most researchers generally believe that travel undertaken mainly for social contact or recreation is least at risk. In other words, holiday travel and family visits are not likely to be affected until it is technically possible to transmit electronic images which carefully simulate relatives or locations.

Business-related activities are viewed as more attractive with respect to the substitution between telecommunications and transport. From a practical viewpoint it can be argued that the degree of substitution will depend on tasks to be undertaken, the characteristics of the journey in terms of cost and duration, the travellers' attitude to any savings, the willingness to pay and, obviously, the service characteristics of each mode.

It is important to become aware of the possibilities for telecommunications and substitution for business transport. One result of any decrease in business travel demand could very well be a substantial rise in fares or rates. Sir Edward Fennissy, writing in *The Times* in 1977, predicted that advances in international communications links would make face-to-face conferences by television an economic attraction for 10 per cent of the 12,000 people who fly the Atlantic each day. Outside business hours the same equipment could be used to send letters across the Atlantic by facsimile transmission. An examination of the past trends would seem to suggest that, if anything, these predictions are fairly modest, especially in light of the development of the Web and e-mail.

Although there is little doubt that the functions of transport and telecommunications will, in the main, remain separate in the near future in most instances, the main competition will take place in two main areas, travel to work and travel to business meetings, conferences and conventions.

On the other hand, it cannot be assumed that if communications can be effectively substituted for certain trips, this substitution will reduce the absolute level of demand for transport. Harkness[2] writes: 'The absolute growth in the number of contacts may be enough to offset any trips lost by a shift in modal split share. For example, the growth in social and recreational travel could greatly exceed any loss of business travel. There is the possibility that communication may stimulate travel, and vice versa. Usually telephone calls precede meetings and a meeting itself provides topics for further communications. This argument has been used to disclaim the threat which telecommunications might pose to the transportation industry; however, its validity remains to be proved. Meetings do beget meetings but is it necessary that the meetings involve travel? Would not a teleconference be as effective as a face-to-face meeting in stimulating new contracts? And might not telephone calls lead to teleconferences rather than trips?'

It is often stated that advances in telecommunications have been so rapid in the last few years, so powerful in their utility and are becoming so widespread, that the impact on society is revolutionary. With CATV, picture phones, rapid facsimile transfer on documents and new data networks, this revolution is sweeping through all aspects of society. As a result, there is of course a broad spectrum of speculation about where the revolution will take us.

Day[3] sums up these speculations: 'At one end [of the spectrum] there are broad generalized scenarios optimistically postulating many forms of substitution of local and intercity travel through the use of a host of computer/communications services. The links between today and the future are not usually detailed and we are left with considerable uncertainty as to how this future communications based society evolved. At the other extreme there are very specific studies of how specific technologies may augment with substitution process for individuals working at certain institutions within defined travel patterns.'

There are a number of questions that must be answered before any accurate estimate of the impact of telecommunications on transport can be made.

1. To what extent can telecommunications replace travel on any scale?

This is a very difficult question to answer with today's state of the art. It is accepted that it will be a long time before telecommunications can have any appreciable change in leisure and social trip-making. Most research therefore concentrates on the business travel/telecommunications substitution. The size of substitution will depend on the tasks that have to be performed and on the individual company's attitude to the mode used for communication. Experience gained from studies shows that any assessment must include the total control, the individual, the task, the organization and the available nodes. As Murray Laver states in *Telecommuncations Magazine*: 'One reason for sending a man to the moon rather than more accurate and cheaper robot instruments was to observe the unexpected and to seize the passing opportunity.' With telecommunications being substituted for travel in the sense of teleconferences, there is little doubt that when the outcome depends on expert analysis and rational choice, this mode is effective. In situations of high risk, especially in commercial and political negotiations, getting to know other people is important. Face-to-face meetings provide the personal contacts and the clue which come from being in the presence of another person. It is suspected that things can be 'hidden' over video links. Personnel work is dominated by human factors, with no substitute for face-to-face dealings in recruitment and union negotiations.

2. What are the various telecommunications terminals and networks that would be required to support widespread substitution between transport and telecommunications?

Numerous terminal devises and transmission systems are not available.[4] The three basic services that need to be provided for teleconferences to compete with travel are multi-user link-ups on real time audio, real time video and real time facsimile transmission of documents. The networks are provided by telephone lines, fibre optic cables, microwave systems, satellite communications, etc.

3. How effective are the various types of telecommunications systems as substitutes for face-to-face contacts in terms of accurate and efficient transfer of information, emotions, impressions and feelings?

The extent to which advanced teleconference media could be substituted for face-to-face meetings has been well studied using laboratory experiments and large-scale surveys. It has been generally found that over 30 per cent of meetings involve tasks and discussions which could easily be carried out using audio medium only. Something like 10 per cent more meetings would be easily carried out with some form of video.[5]

As Goddard and Pye[6] state when writing about telecommunications and office location: 'If a widespread network of cheap teleconference equipment were available, considerable substitution of travel could be achieved. Moreover regions might become more locally self-sufficient in terms of contact sources or more dependent on neighbouring regions, instead of being very heavily dependent on London. For the latter to occur, supplementary travel facilities would, of course, need to be adequate; in addition, increased awareness and better information about local contact sources might be necessary. Information should be available concerning the types of office services, clients and customers that are available locally and in adjacent regions.'

From what I have written about telecommunications, there is now little doubt that technically telecommunications could quite easily be a substitute for a great deal of travel, especially travel which does not involve the movement of freight. People could use teleconferences and video phones for contact, facsimile machines to transmit and receive documents and could shop using video and computer links from home. All of this is now feasible. Unfortunately, for the physical transfer of goods there is no substitute.

The factors which influence any choice between telecommunication and travel are both financial and psychological. The costs can be ascertained and compared with each other. The psychological factors include the personal motives of individual people. These motives vary between people and circumstances. Some managers welcome travel as a break from routine, with some forms of travel being visible signs of status in the company and society.

The greatest congestion occurs as a result of journeys to and from work, as the experience of most people every morning and evening will testify. Although little can at present be done to change the travel patterns of those people engaged in manufacturing, retailing or other jobs involved with physical products, it is quite possible to allow a large percentage of white collar workers to stay at home using data transfer techniques to connect their activities. There are two problems with this scenario. The first is that companies are very wary about transmitting classified or highly sensitive information through multi-user transmission systems. The second is that man is a social animal. He needs his group, the companionship of work acquaintances and his feeling of belonging. Many people feel that job satisfaction would fall without the personal contact associated with most jobs.

Then there is the promise that the travel involved in shopping can be reduced by people using television to examine products, ordering by some remote means and using credit cards to pay for purchases. All the shopping needs of most people could be satisfied without having to leave their home. Shoppers create that travel, though, partly because they like the idea of the physical bargain hunting involved in going from shop to shop, and partly because of the enjoyment of human contact involved in shopping.

One of the problems in this area is that many information technologists believe that the management of life and especially of a business can be modelled as an information/decision system, based on making rational choices. This assumption underlies their design of information networks, and colours their view of what is possible. If their assumption is true, then much of human activity could be replaced by electronic communications media and the appropriate computer programs. It is essential to recognize, however, that management is primarily a social and political system in which personalities and competition for power and resources play a very large part.

As Laver states when writing about travel and telecommunications:[7]

> The demand for travel is not an undifferentiated lump. Travel takes place between specific locations and the decision whether to travel or telecommunicate will depend on the actual facilities that exist in each case. Some under-developed countries now served by indifferent travel could switch to teleconferencing as satellite links liberate communications from reliance on obsolete and primitive telephone networks.
>
> Travel and telecommunications are not in the end mutually exclusive. Preliminary communications often stimulate a demand for subsequent

travel – as negotiations enter a critical phase, or to see what he or she is really like. Is he as effective as he appears to be? Can he hold his liquor? Satellite will make mobile communications immeasurably better, and the top status symbol could become not a platinum credit card but a personal in-flight terminal connected directly into the corporate teleconferencing network and responding to the users' voiceprint for the release of reserved information from a headquarters data bank. In the near future, it is unlikely that developments in teleconferencing will make any serious inroad into demand for travel.

Despite the conclusion that in the near future telecommunications will not make any appreciable impact on travel demand, it is important that the transport industry is aware of the possibilities of substitution. Without a doubt, the advances in telecommunications systems discussed will make these systems more and more widely available. The choice of how to undertake decision-making will be placed on the user. The growth of freight traffic alone will support a vast infrastructure to facilitate the movement of goods.

POLICY IMPLICATIONS OF TELECOMMUNICATIONS

Another important consideration is that the substitution of electronic communications for transport would change the nature of our towns and cities. At present, most major businesses are located in cities served by comprehensive transport links with other major cities. The availability of excellent transport links is a major factor in site selection, especially for the company headquarters. If transport links become less of a factor, the company would have few incentives to locate in large cities, speeding the decay of metropolitan areas while increasing the number and dispersion of smaller towns.

There are important policy issues that must be considered in the light of these possible changes:

1. The decision to substitute electronic communications for travel will be made by individuals and companies. Governments can encourage or discourage such substitution because it is governments which regulate both telecommunications and transport. Government priorities such as energy conservation, environmental protection and enhancement and the question of safety in transport can lead governments in the direction of encouraging substitution. Governments can either sit back and leave the question of how much substitution will take place to the workings of a

competitive market, or they can intervene to force people to use telecommunications. Regulatory measures that are available include rate setting, standards setting, route licensing and subsidies.

2. It is in most governments' interests to integrate planning in both the electronic communications and the transport areas. Long-range planning of both the transport and electronic communications systems is essential if a meaningful transport policy is to be developed. At present there appears to be no co-ordination in this area.

3. The magnitude of the impact on future transport demand cannot be predicted with any confidence at this time since it depends on actions in both the private and public sectors, the pace of techno-logical change in both areas, and the costs of energy, electronic communications and transport relative to one another. The government should undertake research before any policy deci-sions are taken.

Environmental issues

There are a great many environmental fears associated with devel-oping transport systems. These issues have become more prominent in policy discussions at both national and local levels. One rather simplistic solution to the problem of the adverse environmental impact of transport is for governments to promote electronic commu-nications as a substitute for travel.

Any comprehensive analysis of the environmental costs associated with transport and electronic communications must not only account for the operational costs but, in addition, the costs of constructing the infrastructure and of maintaining the infrastructure in environmental impact terms.

An indication of the environmental costs associated with travel and communications systems is given from L.H. Day's paper:

1. Energy consumption of transportation and communication systems.
2. Energy consumption required to construct, operate and maintain plant and industry infrastructures for both sectors.
3. Resource consumption for construction, operation and mainte-nance of the required infrastructures.
4. Pollution factors associated with the two industries, eg air, water, radiation, noise, thermal and visual pollution.
5. Damage to ecological systems.

Energy and telecommunications[8]

The subject of energy policy and transport is covered in detail later in the chapter but, as we have seen already, telecommunications developments can induce changes in business practice, travel patterns, urban development and environmental quality of life. Telecommunications can also play a part in any energy conservation policy.

There are several factors which may lead to energy savings by the greater use of telecommunications:

1. The substitution of face-to-face meetings by teleconferences, leading to less travel, thus savings in total fuel used in transport.
2. Total or partial avoidance of the journey to work by means of workplace dispersal either to the home or close to the home.
3. Substitution of telecommunications for some personal travel for non-work purposes like remote shopping.
4. Substitution for goods transportation in the area of information transfer, especially small packages of documents.
5. Improvements in the energy efficiency of transportation due to the use of telecommunications-based information and control systems, as in the case of radio controlled fleets of delivery vehicles, or dial-a-ride buses.

INFORMATION TECHNOLOGY AND TRANSPORT

Up until now, we have discussed the future impact of the electronic revolution in terms of its substitutability for transport services. There seems no great rush to produce the dispersed offices or work stations in the home. Signs that it is coming can be glimpsed by the transformation that has taken place in the City of London. Even so, there will be some impact over the next 15 years as teleconferencing techniques and new developments in facsimile transmission and computer networking come on stream.

Attention is focused, however, on the way in which the electronic revolution is having an impact on the industry itself in terms of efficiency and productivity. A number of airlines are installing computer controlled automatic facilities on passenger handling services, the production of tickets and boarding cards. Computerization is making transport costings far more accurate, with information of fuel consumption, maintenance costs, depreciation and vehicle downtime instantly available. Several computer software houses have produced computerized databases of the UK road network and the software to route and schedule vehicles using the database. Engine management systems and tachographs are being linked to improve engine efficiency, control fuel usage and limit driver error.

IT and the bus industry

Within public transport, information technology can be used in many functions including management, engineering, fare collection and service planning. Electronic ticketing is the most successful application of information technology in the public transport industry. Almost all large bus operators have converted to electronic ticket machines. The electronic machine has the ability to store information on every passenger transaction that takes place on the bus. This provides the company with a great deal of information which would previously have to be collected using surveys. The electronic machine reduces the need for hand-written way bills and has a reducing effect on fraud. For the first time it is possible to monitor continuously the changing patterns of traffic; to measure the changes in passenger carryings in response to fare alterations or marketing initiatives, resulting in the chance of better management, more responsive to the needs of their customers. Machine readable tickets are the latest development.

Passenger information systems are benefiting from the application of IT with the use of dot matrix indicators at bus stations and on the vehicle. Unlike the railways or the airports, where VDUs, electronic flip boards and dot matrix indicators are extensively employed to give continuous updates on arrival/departure times, services and facilities, the majority of passengers board buses a few at a time along the entire length of the route. A large proportion seeking information cannot yet be catered for by electronic means and rely on the telephone to obtain information about unfamiliar journeys. Even here, computer technology is helping by monitoring and switching incoming calls to minimize delays.

It is hoped by many bus operators that, in the future, they will be able to inform intending passengers waiting at bus stops when the next bus will actually arrive. Market research by LRT has shown that people would like a display which showed the destination of the next two buses due at that stop and a continuous prediction of the arrival time. To achieve this amount of detail it is necessary to detect, identify and track many buses simultaneously, in other words install a full vehicle location system. Technically this is quite feasible but would require massive capital outlay, which in view of the likely returns would be uneconomic.

Coach operators have a finite number of seats for each journey, and the option of overloading by standing passengers is not available as it is to the railways. For services which pick up and put down passengers at a number of places along the route, there is a need to chart the number of seats sold to avoid overcrowding. This has been done manually involving large volumes of paper and difficulties for late-booking passengers. Passengers were sometimes so inconvenienced that they resorted to another mode. Now, viewdata services allow the travel agent or operator to input boarding and alighting points, date of travel and number of passengers, display the possible departure times and seat availability on that service. If no space is available on the chosen day, alternatives can be offered. Once the booking is made an instant confirmation is provided with a unique code number fed into the central computer for security.

In the field of engineering computer aided design is becoming increasingly important to engineers in design work. These techniques are of more relevance to vehicle manufacturers rather than the operators.

Since the late 1960s a number of bus operators have used computers to help in deciding which routes should be run, the number of buses required to meet the proposed schedule, and the allocation of crews to those schedules. Advances in computer technology are making this practice more widespread. Many packages have been developed for use with interactive computer facilities which allow the route planner to input the proposed route, getting a display of the route length, running time and expected loadings. By altering the various parameters of the service – timings and labour agreements on wages and timings – the variation in cost and likely profit/loss can instantly be assessed.

Since deregulation of the bus industry, management is greatly concerned with profitability. As we have seen, many factors influence profitability but good management and precise information are two of the most important. The two are complementary because the best decisions are made upon the interpretation of the most up-to-date information.

Given existing routes and schedules, any change represents a risk.[9] Because of deregulation, each bus depot manager should be looking at changes to schedules and service levels in an effort to make sure that the best course of action is being followed. The application of information techniques can transform depot management's focus from that of fulfilling financial targets laid down by head office to the profitability of the services. There are four basic requirements for a big move to employing information technology techniques at depot level:

1. A database must be collected to provide the comparison of revenue and costs at route, journey and depot level. This data can now be collected by electronic ticket machines, the information being automatically fed into the computer.
2. Using a spreadsheet, the figures are consolidated, subjected to sensitivity testing, and questioned.
3. Operations research techniques are available as a program package in which the operator only has to input data. These can be used to optimize manpower and vehicle schedules.
4. Adjusted schedules, timetables and vehicle allocations can be printed taking account of any engineering requirements.

All of these schedules can be undertaken on a desk-top microcomputer at relatively small cost.

Deregulation and privatization have led to dramatic changes in the way in which managers manage bus companies but the application of information technology techniques at all levels can ensure that bus company managers have all the data and techniques needed to cope with the changes that have been thrust upon them.

IT and the railways

The railway, like the air transport industry, has a real advantage over other forms of transport. The railway signaller knows exactly where each train is on the network to within a mile or so. This facility, through computers called 'train describers', is not only useful to the railway signal operator: the information can be used by announcers and supervisors to check the actual arrival times of trains and be linked automatically to platform indicators. This is a powerful tool for the dissemination of passenger information.

The computerized master timetable provides information on what each train should be doing, its route, stopping pattern and classification. An experimental automatic route setting (ARS) facility can show information from the train describer which will tell it what is actually happening on the track. The ARS computer then sets the routes in the signal box to optimize traffic flow through the area under its control.

It is now possible for a desk-top ticket issuing machine to store fares information between one station and every other station in Britain. This information can be accessed by a ticket clerk keying in a code and the correct ticket can be allocated. The accounting data collected can be transmitted to a central computer over existing telephone lines for central processing. In the reverse direction, a completely new fares table can be transmitted, updating the desk-top machine.

As Ford[10] states: 'For railways, information technology is all about running the system more efficiently and making it easier for customers to use the better system. The time needed to get new technology into service with the reliability demanded by the railways has not decreased in the same way as changes in that technology. If, say, development takes five years and step changes in technology occur with the same frequency, manufacturers could be locked in a cycle of developing equipment which is obsolete before it can enter service.

'In the case of information technology and railways, this permanent obsolescence syndrome is compounded by the longevity of railway equipment and installations. While investment may be authorized on a 15-year book life, actual service life for both rolling stock and fixed installations will be a minimum of 20 years. With mid-life re-engineering, a 40-year life is feasible. This upgrading of facilities may be restricted because of the need to maintain compatibility with older equipment.'

In reality, what this means is that as developments of computer systems including software increases at an ever faster rate, the railway will always be using non-optimal techniques. Unless the railways can find some easy way of updating IT equipment as developments materialize, they will always have this problem with electronic and computer technology.

IT and road freight

One of the greatest drawbacks against the rapid embrace of information techniques by road haulage operators is that the development has been producer-led rather than customer-led. In many cases, producers have tried to adapt packages designed for other applications for use in freight transport. Added to this, a very aggressive marketing campaign by the producers which subsequently proved rather ambitious when the packages were applied to road haulage problems, has reduced the application of IT techniques in the eyes of many road hauliers. Road haulage companies often did not appreciate that a problem even existed let alone whether the solutions offered by the suppliers of computer software were correct.

As Cross et al[11] point out, rapid developments in computer technology and software have occurred which increase any individual's ability to handle, collect and analyse data. The problem for the road haulage industry is to accurately specify the problem that needs solving rather than the type of data collected.

Basically there are three levels of information needed at the group, depot and vehicle levels of organization:

1. **Group level**:   Fleet costs – fleet reliability – fleet utilization – fleet replacement.
   Defect records – workshop performance – workshop communications.
2. **Depot level**:   Cost – manpower cost – inventory cost planning – planned repair time – actual repair time.
   Mechanic performance – skill records – diagnostic times – parts availability – inventory requirements – warranty records – department performance.
3. **Vehicle**:   Legality – defects record – availability – estimated reliability – vehicle cost – estimated repair cost – warranty history.

On of the drawbacks of the development of computer systems capable of analysing data is that someone at some time on some other equipment has to input data. It can be the case that the person inputting the data has no knowledge of its use and may not take too much care. If this is the case, it is better to use automatic data input.

One of the great dangers of computing systems when used by small or even large road haulage companies can be the large volume of data that is required by the personnel to undertake their various tasks. Collecting too much information and then trying to make use of it is almost as bad as collecting too little.

IT and shipping

The operational effects of the electronic revolution are now being felt in the industry. The world is straddled by advanced communications using satellites and optic cables which can now give instant information about the passage of freight through the international transport chain. These communications links are changing the nature of the relationship between carriers, forwarders, shippers and consignees.

The introduction of computers onto ships means that a wide range of tasks can now be undertaken including a daily analysis of vehicle performance. Such developments and the use of advance automation has allowed the cutting of crew numbers and has changed the image of the ship's officer. The obvious development is to link the ship's computer with that ashore so that shore-based personnel can monitor ship's performance and order changes. With sensors on board automatically transmitting operational data direct to head office, it is not too far fetched to see a time when the engine performance could be controlled by the shore in line with company fleet policy. (What this would mean for the remaining ship's personnel, I shudder to think!)

IT and public transport

Automation of public transport operations is technically feasible with urban mass transit systems operating on exclusive guideways. There are obvious advantages from this automation:

1. The cost of staff can be reduced though there is a certain amount of substitution of driver and control staff by more highly qualified and higher paid engineers to undertake maintenance of equipment and vehicles.
2. There should be an increase in operating safety because the element of human error can be removed from the system. Electronic control elements can be made fail-safe.
3. There is improved energy usage because the system can maintain an optimum energy profile over the whole network without having to take account of individual driver competence.

In air transport, shipping and railways, automatic vehicle location (AVL) is widespread but there seems to be no desire for truck operators to use such systems. The idea behind using AVL for international truck operation is that the company can keep track of where the vehicles are without the driver having to report his position. The growing demand for more efficient traffic control and management is being helped by advances in information technology. It comes in a number of forms including route guidance systems on vehicles, navigation aids on vehicles, traffic information readouts and the use of radio.

Radios used in road vehicles have the following advantages:

1. They help to save time, reduce mileage and thus help cut fuel bills.
2. They improve traffic management by providing a constant update on traffic conditions from drivers out on the road.
3. They help to improve crew and passenger safety because they act as a deterrent against vandalism and crime.
4. They improve accident and emergency report procedures by providing instant contact with the control base.
5. They simplify supervision of services during bad weather and road works.

TRANSPORT AND ENERGY POLICY

Over the past 15 years there has been a great debate about the future availability of energy supplies. One strand sees everybody on foot early in the next century, another with unlimited supplies as new discoveries are made. The truth must obviously lie somewhere between these projections.

The question of energy supplies is very import to both transport managers and regulators. The transport sector of the economy is a major consumer of energy accounting for about 18 per cent of the total with road transport, private and commercial, being by far the major user. Over 40 per cent of oil-based energy is used in transport which means that fluctuations in the price of crude oil have a significant effect on the cost profile. This is especially true when considering road and air transport which rely entirely on oil-based products. Railways can operate using electricity generated from a number of base sources such as coal and nuclear power. Ships can use coal, nuclear power or wind power. One had only to look back to the oil crisis of 1973 to appreciate the reliance on oil as an energy source. Prices rose dramatically increasing operating costs, fuelling inflation and even leading to fears of rationing. The cost of fuel is a major element in vehicle operating costs and rapid increases have to be recovered by raising rates and fares.

Energy planning

Most experts predict two things for the future, although they tend to be at odds over the time-scale:

1. That energy prices will continue to rise gradually until a balance is reached between supply and demand, and then price rises will accelerate.
2. The demand for energy will grow steadily and unless there are new discoveries and alternative sources, demand will outstrip supply.

The size and the time-scale of energy problems can only be ascertained when considering a number of factors:

1. Oil is a finite resource and it will run out eventually, though no expert can predict precisely when this will happen.
2. Because of economic laws, as supplies of oil become scarce, the price will rise. It must be remembered that this may be accelerated by oil being programmed for use in the petrochemical industries rather than transport.
3. Eventually new sources of energy will have to be found to replace reliance on fossil fuels. More resources put into research in this area could mean the development of new sources of energy before the oil becomes scarce. This would alter the size and time-scale of the problem.

4. All branches of industry, and especially transport, are very wasteful of their energy.
5. For the foreseeable future, liquid oil-based fuel will continue as the main source of fuel for most transport.
6. Conservation techniques can prolong the life of the oil energy system.
7. Again, in the foreseeable future there is little likelihood of road transport relinquishing its large share of the total transport market because of its flexibility and convenience. Road transport dominates because of the low density settlement patterns and the massive sum investment in roads.

Energy policy

Even though there is no short-term crisis with regard to energy supply, the government has a number of policy options in responding to energy planning:

1. Leave everything to the market place in the belief that economic pressure will force people and businesses to find alternative sources before oil runs out.
2. Encourage by means of fiscal policy the development of more energy efficient transport vehicles.
3. Directly manage the transport system to promote energy efficiency.
4. Promote higher load factors in existing vehicles by some form of road pricing or zonal control system where only fully loaded vehicles are allowed to travel.
5. Direct traffic onto more energy efficient modes.
6. Use planning systems to re-organize society so that the need for transport is reduced.

For a government which is against interference, the options open to it if oil becomes scarce are not very inviting. It must be borne in mind when addressing this question that crude oil is not only the source for petroleum-based energy products but is used to feed the petrochemical industries. It could become government policy in the future that as a scarce resource, oil is worth far more when used to produce products like plastics than as a substance to burn in engines. A government decision on these lines could dramatically alter the finite lifespan of our oil resources. This would, however, cause great difficulties for transport operators and society in general.

Many studies have found that to most people overall journey times and convenience are more important in travel decisions than cost. As a part of the overall cost, fuel cost would have to rise significantly before there is any significant change of mode.

Fuel economy in operations

If fuel costs rise as a percentage of other costs, it is imperative that operators develop ways to promote fuel economy. For any fuel economy programme to be successful, all staff involved, management, operating personnel, maintenance engineers and schedulers, must conform to the aims of the programme. The overall criterion that motivates everybody is that the rewards are worth the effort. Every person taking part in the programme must be convinced that the programme is worthwhile, will bring the company benefits, and that their jobs will be secure. Management will want to make sure that any system costs will be matched by savings in fuel costs (or covered by government grants if available). The operating personnel and maintenance engineers will reflect the importance placed on fuel economy in the company and how savings can partly be turned into some form of productivity bonus for them.

It is only at times of fuel price rises that fuel economy is ranked with factors such as vehicle and labour productivity, customer satisfaction, and late running, when looking at the efficiency of the company. In most forms of transport, fuel consumption per vehicle is recorded daily but the records are not used effectively to measure changes in vehicle performance. There is no real effort to ascertain whether different operating configurations will reduce fuel usage.

A planned system of fuel recording is only useful if it is analysed properly and is backed by positive action by managers, operating personnel and engineers to change the amount of fuel used.

The stages in developing such a programme are:[12]

1. Examination of previous years' fuel consumption records and fuel costs for particular vehicles.
2. Estimation of present fuel costs for each vehicle operated.
3. Estimation of the cost of fuel economy devices and methods.
4. Examination of present operational characteristics, such as route scheduling, loading methods and operating personnel. (It has been found that in all branches of transport the operating practices and skills vary enormously between individuals even though they may have the same qualifications and have undergone the same training. When studying fuel usage and performance this factor must be isolated.)
5. Investigation of the most suitable fuel saving techniques and estimation of the range of possible savings, cost of devices, etc.
6. Calculation of the percentage savings required to cover the cost of fuel saving devices and any other long-term benefits. (It must always be borne in mind that these savings depend on the price projections of the fuel used and any change in the price will have effects on the likely level of benefits.)

7. Investigations of possibilities of discounts in the purchase of fuel. In road transport this may mean buying bulk fuel tanks; in international transport, scheduling stops to take account of cheap sources of fuel.
8. Investigating ways of educating and training operating personnel in fuel saving techniques.
9. Display of general and company information on fuel economy measures and progress, for example with posters, pamphlets and graphs of fuel savings.

Since the oil price shocks in the 1970s, considerably more attention has been paid to energy conservation than before. There are signs that this attention is slackening due to the seeming abundance of energy. As the world economy pulls out of recession and energy requirements increase rapidly, the world could very well quickly be back in the same situation it faced in 1979. Energy planning and fuel efficiency will then again be top of the agendas of international agencies, governments and transport companies.

Two points must be emphasized:

1. Fuel economy cannot be considered in isolation and before a policy is developed, due regard must be paid to other important aspects of vehicle operations, eg additional journey times created by changing to a more fuel efficient route or methods.
2. Apparent savings in energy cost should be closely examined to ensure that they have not resulted in increased costs in other areas. Cost savings should be actual savings for the company, not just in one area of operation.

ENVIRONMENTAL IMPACT OF TRANSPORT

As we have discussed elsewhere, transport as presently constituted and for the forseeable future is essential to the life of mankind in our presently organized society. In the future, there may be substitution of some transport services by telecommunications but the majority of journeys will still take place.

There are projections that as society becomes more inter-dependent, the need for transport grows. Thus modern society is entirely dependent on the provision of services for transporting goods or people. The major problem is that along with this essential output of transport, there are certain disbenefits in the form of noise, pollution of the sea and air, visual intrusion of the infrastructure, and accidents.

Noise is a subjective disbenefit. The measurement of noise nuisance is very difficult since individual reactions to noise differ considerably.

There is evidence to suggest that the degree of reaction to noise may be related to occupation. Transport noise is produced by road traffic, railways and aircraft. Road traffic noise on busy roads tends to be continuous and more widely considered than either aircraft or railway noise which is intermittent. Improvements in noise levels come from advances in vehicle design, sound barriers along routes or insulating dwelling places. All of these methods of overcoming noise are costly.

The benefits of reducing air pollution, especially emissions from vehicles, are difficult to estimate quantitively. They are easy to list qualitatively, with the petrol engined car being the most offensive. The *costs* of reducing air pollution are easier to estimate quantitatively. They include higher capital and operating costs, higher fuel consumption and shorter engine life.

Considerable care must be exercised when trying to interpret accident statistics. Accident involvement does not imply responsibility and some vehicles have high involvement rates because they operate in high risk situations. Methods of estimating the cost of accidents to society are very imperfect as it becomes very subjective when deciding to place monetary values of aspects of losses due to accidents.

There is a growing awareness among the general public of the 'environmental' issues associated with transport. This pressure will undoubtedly grow in the future. The actions of 'pressure groups' such as Friends of the Earth and Transport 2000 have helped to heighten public awareness of environmental issues and led campaigns against environmental abuse. Transport professionals must become familiar with the arguments of these groups and be ready to answer their criticisms or change their practices to conform to the changing attitude of the public. This is an issue which will become more relevant in the future.

Pressure groups

Transport policy is made by governments after consulting the community but to an increasing extent there are now interests represented by 'pressure groups'. The British Road Federation openly campaigns for more roads, Transport 2000 for more railways. As transport decisions become more remote from the locality in which they have effect, these pressure groups will multiply and gain a bigger say.

Pressure groups are set up to protect and advance their particular interests. By means of campaigns, promotions, lobbying and increasing their membership, they seek to influence decision-making without being the actual decision-makers. They try to ensure that their issue is kept in the forefront of public consciousness.

Three examples of pressure groups in transport are:

■ *Transport 2000*, which was set up in 1973 after it was planned by British Rail to close a large proportion of the railway. Its aims are to improve bus and rail services and encourage greater use, to highlight the needs of cyclists, pedestrians and public transport users and to seek the maximum use of water and rail transport for bulk and long-distance freight transport.
■ *The Inland Shipping Group*, whose chief aim is to encourage the development of transport policy which gives greater preference to inland waterways than at present exists. The reasons given for this aim are that with an increase in water-borne traffic there will be an improvements in both the economic and environmental well-being of the UK.
■ *International Transport Workers Federation* has the following aims: to promote respect for trade union and human rights world wide; to work for peace based on social justice and economic progress; to help all affiliated unions defend the interests of their members; to provide research and information services to affiliated unions, to provide general assistance to transport workers in difficulty.

Trade associations

Trade associations are organizations which are formed by firms in the same area of business to discuss and if possible act on matters of common interest. These interests include terms of trade, fixing of prices, exercising influence collectively on issues affecting members and keeping members informed of current events. Much of their work is advice on legal, technical and financial matters including the likely cost of service. Trade associations are more likely to form where competition exists but this not always the reason. Many trade associations have regulations regarding competition in their agreements. Examples of trade associations will illustrate their role:

■ *Road Haulage Association* is an independent non-political organization set up to look after the interests of the 'hire and reward' sector of the road freight industry. Its aims are to improve standards in the industry and put forward a collective view on current policy in the interests of road haulage. It offers services to its members to help them become more professional, for example:
  1. Operational counselling to help road hauliers overcome problems.

2. Legal advice about contracts, licensing and employment law.
3. Education, training services and advice on using computers. These areas give some idea of the scope of the RHA and with the addition of a standard rates service show the comprehensive nature of the organization.

■ *International Union of Railways* is an example of a trade association of members who do not compete. Its aims are to standardize equipment and operating procedures for international traffic in order to achieve a more efficient and safe service. It also aims to develop mechanisms for international co-operation between railways and improve the image of the rail mode with governments and other decision-making bodies. It offers its members technical and financial advice, operating a clearing house for railway accounts in much the same way as IATA in air transport. It represents railways on international organizations and publishes a great deal of information.

Trade associations, especially in those aspects of their work which deal with information gathering, representation and publicity, will play a vital part in the future development of transport. As transport becomes fragmented by deregulation, very competitive and attacked by environmental pressure groups, collective action will be needed in many policy areas if the voice of that industry is to be heard.

Consumer interests

One area of future concern is the issue of consumer protection in transport. It is often stated that the more competition there is, the better the consumer's interest will be protected. In a competitive market, the consumers can go 'elsewhere' and find an operator who provides the service that they require. This may be true for freight transport but, even in competitive situations, there has been a need for organization independent of the operators to represent the consumer.

In air transport, for example, the CAA set up the *Air Transport Users' Committee* in 1973 to act as a 'watch dog' for airline users. It investigates complaints against the suppliers of air transport services, co-operates with airport consultative committees at airports and advises on the provision of facilities at airports, especially for handicapped persons. It also comments on and makes known the views of travellers to fare policies. The *International Airline Passenger Association* is designed to help anyone with problems who travels anywhere by whatever mode. The aim of the IAPA is not only to help passengers with problems but to make travelling life in general easier and more convenient. The *Transport Users' Consultative* committees are bodies primarily concerned with the services offered by the railway industries. They were set up following the 1947 Act which nationalized the railways to protect the public from abuse from the monopoly power of the state-run system. Their main objective is to investigate and report on complaints from users about the facilities and services provided by the railways.

Consumer protection, like concern for the environment, will play a leading role in shaping future regulation and policy on transport. It is likely that organizations representing consumer interests will assume a vital role and that they will become more outspoken.

PROFESSIONALISM IN TRANSPORT

As has already be discussed in this chapter and other parts of this book, the work of a transport manager is becoming more complex. Like the old-time airline pilot who flew by the seat of the pants but eventually had to learn to fly by instruments, the transport manager can no longer rely on his/her inborn experience or feel but has to be able to use the methods and technologies currently available. Even many owner drivers are using cheap microcomputers for accounting.

There are two aspects which must be considered:

1. The need for a thorough basic education, at least to degree level, and a training period after qualification.
2. The need for periodic re-training so that the manager will thoroughly update his or her knowledge as methods and technologies change.

The first need is already answered by universities and colleges offering degree courses in transport and distribution subjects, or by professional institutions like the Chartered Institute of Transport or the Institute of Logistics and Transport offering examinations.

Professional institutions have a number of objectives:

1. To ensure that educational and general standards are maintained in the profession.
2. To ensure that all qualified people are kept up to date for the whole of their working lives.
3. To play an active part in shaping future thinking within the profession.

In order to do this they:

1. Lay down standards which must be reached before people can be professionally qualified in their area.
2. Hold branch meetings, conferences, courses and seminars to allow members to keep their knowledge up to date and to exchange views on different aspects of their work.
3. Publish journals, papers, etc, on different aspects of transport.
4. Try to represent professional opinion to outside bodies like the government.

It is the second need which is somewhat lacking at the moment but, with greater use of computers and operations research techniques to solve problems, it is a need that will have to be satisfied. Whether the industry will have the foresight to give its people the opportunity to update their knowledge by giving time off is a question which will have to be seriously considered in the future.

References

1. Khan, A.M. 'Travel vs telecommunications: current understanding' *High Speed Transportation* Journal 1976
2. Harkness, R.C. 'Communication innovations, urban form and travel demand' *Transportation* 1973
3. Day, L.H. 'An assessment of travel/communications substitutability' *Futures* December 1973
4. Martin, J. *Future Developments in Telecommunications* Prentice-Hall, New Jersey 1971
5. Short, J. *et al The Social Psychology of Telecommunications* John Wiley, London 1976
6. Goddard, J.B. and Pye, R. 'Telecommunications and office location' *Regional Studies* 1977
7. Laver, M. 'How far will electronics intrude?' *Management Today* March 1983
8. Tyler, M. *et al* 'Telecommunications and energy policy' *Telecommunications Policy* 1976
9. Slater, A. 'In pursuit of profitability' *Transport* October 1987
10. Ford, R. 'Making the most of micro-processors' *Transport* October 1987
11. Cross, A.K. *et al* 'Hauliers reluctant to take IT opportunities on board' *Transport* August 1986
12. Ratcliffe, B. *Economy and Efficiency in Transport and Distribution* Kogan Page, London 1987

Index

Other transport titles from Kogan Page

Applied Transport Economics, 2nd edition
Stuart Cole (0 7494 2303 X)

The Certificate of Professional Competence, 3rd edition
David Lowe (0 7494 3475 9)

The Dictionary of Transport and Logistics
David Lowe (0 7494 3571 2)

A Practical Guide to Planning and Operation
Brian Marchant (0 7494 1897 4)

Global Logistics and Distribution Planning, 3rd edition
Edited by Donald Waters (0 7494 2779 5)

A Guide to the Large Goods Vehicle Driving Licence, Driving Test and Theory Test, 10th
    edition
David Lowe (0 7494 2870 8)

The Handbook of Logistics and Distribution Management, 2nd edition
Alan Rushton, John Oxley and Phil Croucher (0 7494 3365 5)

International Transport, 5th edition
Rex Faulks (0 7494 2832 5)

An Introduction to Transport Studies, 3rd edition
John Hibbs (0 7494 2946 1)

Logistics and Retail Management
Edited by John Fernie and Leigh Sparks (0 7494 2834 1)

Management of Dangerous Goods
David Lowe (0 7494 3021 4)

Managing Passenger Logistics
Paul Fawcett (0 7494 3214 4)

The Pocket Guide to LGV Drivers' Hours and Tachograph Law
David Lowe (0 7494 3572 0)

A Study Manual of Professional Competence in Road Haulage, 10th edition
David Lowe (0 7494 3417 1)

The Transport Manager's and Operator's Handbook 2002, 32nd edition
David Lowe (0 7494 3709 X)

All titles are available from good bookshops. To obtain further information,
please contact the publisher at the following address:

Kogan Page Ltd
120 Pentonville Road
London N1 9JN
Tel: 020 7278 0433
Fax: 020 7837 6348
www.kogan-page.co.uk